C000142131

ISBN 978-1-397-32548-8
PIBN 11374417

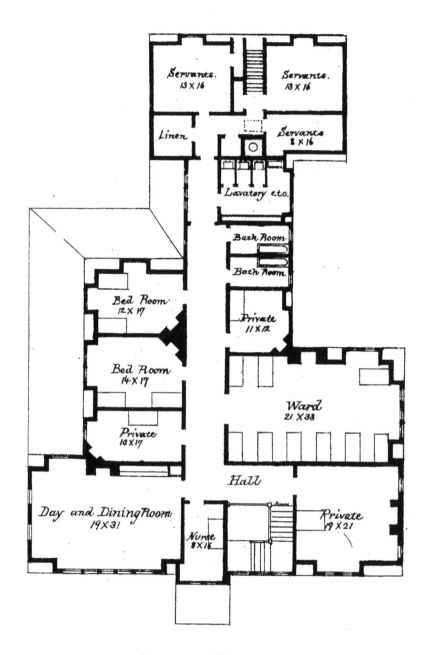

Servants.
13 × 16

Servants.
13 × 16

Linen

Servants.
8 × 16

Lavatory etc.

Bath Room

Bath Room

Bed Room
12 × 17

Private
11 × 12

Bed Room
14 × 17

Ward
21 × 33

Private
10 × 17

Hall

Day and Dining Room
19 × 31

Nurse
8 × 15

Private
19 × 21

SECOND FLOOR.
For Women, 17 Beds.

F.N. HOSPITAL: COTTAGE, BELMONT.

SIXTY-SEVENTH

ANNUAL REPORT

OF THE

TRUSTEES

OF THE

MASSACHUSETTS

ENERAL HOSPITAL,

1880.

Printed at the expense of the Bowditch History Fund.

BOSTON:
1881.
JAMES F. COTTER & CO., PRINTERS,
14 STATE STREET.

REPORT OF THE TRUSTEES

OF THE

MASSACHUSETTS GENERAL HOSPITAL,

For the Year 1880.

THE Committee of the Trustees appointed to prepare the Annual Report of the Board to the Corporation, to whom the Accounts of the Treasurer and the Reports of the other officials have been referred, respectfully submit the

SIXTY-SEVENTH ANNUAL REPORT.

The average number of patients in the Hospital during the past year was one hundred and seventy, against one hundred and sixty-three the year before. In the Asylum one hundred and fifty-two, against one hundred and fifty-seven in 1879.

The Treasurer's account shows an excess of expenses over income of $9,348.12, charged to the General Fund. In 1879 there was an excess of income of $12,382.17.

4

In the latter part of the year Dr. W. B. Bancroft, Second Assistant Physician at the Asylum resigned, and Dr. F. M. Turnbull was appointed in his place.

In November last Mr. Robert H. Stevenson resigned, after seven years of valuable service on the Board of Trustees. Mr. Roger Wolcott was chosen in his place.

The Trustees gratefully acknowledge the following

DONATIONS AND LEGACIES:

From Mrs. F. W. Lincoln, part of bequest of
$200,000, ... $10,000.00
From subscribers to Convalescent Home
Fund,. 2,513.00
From subscribers to Convalescent Build-
ing Fund, ... 17,938.83
From ninety-six subscribers to Free Beds, 11,300.00

In January 1880 the Trustees sold to the Fitch-burg Railroad two tracts of land on the outskirts of the Asylum estate at Somerville containing about twenty-three acres for about $70,000.

This, added to the damages received from the Lowell Railroad for running their track through the Asylum Grounds to their wharf on Mystic River, has been placed in a fund for future use to pay for new

Asylum buildings. The fund with its income added now amounts to $122,976.30.

Early in the year the Trustees decided to begin the building of a convalescent cottage on their estate in Belmont. A site was selected on the western part, one hundred and thirty-six feet above mean high tide, and plans were prepared by Mr. Carl Fehmer, Architect, a copy of which accompanies this Report. The situation has a fine southern aspect, sheltered on the north by rising ground, with an extensive and cheerful landscape to the south and west.

The grounds are sufficiently wooded by a varied natural growth, and there is an ample supply of pure spring water on the premises.

The site is distant but a few minutes walk from the Waverly station of the Fitchburg Railroad. The foundations and walls of the basement have been built, and it is the expectation of the Trustees that the cottage will be ready for occupancy during the current year. The resources of the Hospital were not sufficient for the building and maintenance of the cottage, and the public were therefore invited to contribute the sum of $100,000 for these purposes, one-third for the cottage, and two-thirds for a fund, the income only to be used for current expenses. With their customary generosity, the friends of the Hospital have already subscribed $87,947.85, and it is believed that the remainder will soon be supplied.

The Trustees desire to express their acknowledgments for the liberal manner in which the men and women of Boston have shown their sympathy with, and approval of, this proposed enlargement of the work of the Hospital. It not unfrequently occurs that patients who no longer require hospital treatment, and should no longer remain within the wards, either for their own advantage or that of the institution, are still unfit to return to their homes and renew at once their cares and work. Such cases are especially frequent in the female wards. It is the intention of the Trustees to transfer such patients, under the advice of the professional staff, to this cottage in the country, where their convalescence may be hastened and confirmed.

The Trustees are of the opinion that it will prove to be no unimportant department of the Hospital, and that its results will justify the humane generosity of those who have built and endowed it.

The attention of the Trustees has for some years past been attracted to the rapid increase in the number of out patients, which last year was twenty thousand five hundred and sixty-six. The whole subject has been so well treated by the Resident Physician, Dr. Whittemore, that we append to this Report a paper read by him before the Boston Society for Medical Improvement.

Briefly it appears, that while the population of Boston, including annexed territory, has doubled in twenty years from 1860 to 1880, the out patients treated at the Massachusetts General Hospital have doubled every ten years. Latterly the increase is more rapid. If the same ratio of increase, which occurred in 1880 over 1879 should continue, we should have about forty thousand patients in 1888.

There is no reason to believe that the class of needy poor, for whom this charity is intended, was neglected in 1860, or that it has increased during the last twenty years faster than the population. If this is true, we last year treated ten thousand patients who were not needy.

They come to us from motives of economy, convenience and safety, and of such patients the supply may be considered as practically unlimited. The evils of such a policy to the patients and the medical profession are clearly stated by Dr. Whittemore. The Trustees believe that the funds in their charge should be used for the poor, and not for the frugal, and that some measures should be taken to confine the treatment of out patients to those who cannot afford to pay physician's fees. The practice of taking a small fee from those who can afford it has been found to work badly, and has been stopped.

To many of the medical and surgical staff it appears that there can hardly be too large a number of patients for the exercise of their skill and the enlargement of their experience. The Trustees can never undervalue the zeal and devotion of gentlemen whose qualities they have the opportunity of admiring in the daily service of the Hospital. They will care-

8

fully guard the rights, and observe the wishes, of the medical and surgical staff who give their time and skill to the Hospital, and are its greatest and most constant benefactors. But they believe that a way may be found by which the evils of the present state of things may be diminished, while at the same time the proper objects of the profession are secured.

EDMUND DWIGHT,
S. D. WARREN, *Committee.*

REPORT OF THE TREASURER

OF THE

MASSACHUSETTS GENERAL HOSPITAL,

For the Year 1880.

To the Board of Trustees :

GENTLEMEN : —

I have the honor of submitting the following report of the finances for the year 1880. The Income from Investments has been : —

From Annuities Receivable	$11,263.17
" City of Boston Bonds	1,750.00
" Mass. Hospital Life Ins. Co. Stock	5,000.00
" Railroad Bonds	11,722.06
" Railroad Stocks	1,170.00
" United States 4 per cent. Bonds	10.00
" Manufacturing Stocks	4,644.00
" Bank Stocks	1,641.82
" Real Estate, Productive	18,090.55
" Notes Receivable	23,214.38
" Interest on Del. Mutual Ins. Co. Scrip	21.90
	$78,527.88

Less Interest paid	$1,840.27	
Expended on Land at Belmont	352.75	
Expended on Land at Waltham	91.20	
		2,284.22
		$76,243.66

Which has been distributed as follows : —

(See Inc. & Exp acc't)	To Redman Fund	$24,887.00
	" Warren Prize Fund	125.75
(See Table 8.)	" Bowditch History Fund	109.37
(See Table 5.)	" Wooden Leg Fund	273.42
	" Redman Annuities	936 00
	Amount carried forward	$26,331.54

Amount brought forward.............................:.. $26,331.54

	To Clara Barton Annuity.:.................	194.46
	" Surgical Instrument Fund.............	68.35
(See Table 7.)	" Amusement Fund.....................	546.83
(See Table 2.)	" Free Bed Funds, for use......... $24,612.40 for Joy Annuities 700.00	
		25,312.40
(See Table 7.)	" Beneficiaries at Asylum Funds..........	4,086.61
	" Warren Library Fund..................	54.68
(See Table 4.)	" Treadwell Library Fund..............	273.42
(See Table 7.)	" ½ Lincoln Fund......................	4,374.65
(See Inc. & Exp. acc't.)	" Funds with Income Unrestricted........	2,187.33
(See Inc. & Exp. acc't.)	" General Fund.........................	8,733.48
	" Convalescent Fund, Building...........	353.12
	" Convalescent Home Fund..............	297.80
	" Asylum Building Fund.................	3,428 99
		$76,243.66

The Income for 1879, was........................ $66,590.94
The Income for 1880, was........................ 76,243.66

THE INCOME AND EXPENSE ACCOUNT is as follows:

(See Table 1.)	Expenses Hospital Department..................	$92,077.90
(See Table 6.)	Expenses Asylum Department....................	131,172.69
	Publishing the Trustees' Report for 1879 at the expense of the Bowditch History Fund..........	260.96
	Insurance.....................................	217.20
		$223,728.75

INCOME.—FOR HOSPITAL DEPARTMENT.

(See Table 2.)	Income of Free Bed Funds... $24,612.40	
(See Table 4.)	Income of Treadwell Library Fund.................... 298.86	
(See Table 3.)	Donations from 96 Free Bed Subscribers.............. 11,300.00	
(See Table 5.)	Income of Wooden Leg Fund. 100.00	
	Net amount charged to patients. 12,797.29	
		49,108.55

Amounts carried forward...................... $49,108.55 $223,728.75

Amounts brought forward........................$49,108.55 $223,728.75

For Asylum Department.

(See Table 7.)	Income of Funds for Benefi-ciaries...................	$4,086.61
(See Table 7.)	Income of Funds for Female Beneficiaries..............	4,374.65
(See Table 7.)	Income of Amusement Fund..	546.83
	Net amount charged patients..120,195.22	
		————————129,203.31

For Sundry Purposes.

Income of Bowditch History Fund........... $	260.96
Income of Redman Fund...................	24,887.00
Income of Funds applicable without restrictions.	2,187.33
Income of General Fund...................	8,733.48
	————— 36,068.77
	———— 214,380.63

Deficit charged to General Fund .... $ 9,348.12

TABLE 1.

Expenses of the Hospital Department.

For Stores	$33,694.70
Gas and Oil...	1,938.45
Water...	1,524.64
Wages	21,421.53
Medicine	2,922 29
Furniture...	7,172.41
Surgical Instruments	1,312 15
Stationery..	522.26
Wines and Liquors..	1,325.85
Repairs...	8,105.25
Library	362.82
Salaries..	4,720.00
½ General Expenses..	1,155.84
Fuel..	5,220.89
Wooden Legs...	100.00
Contingencies...	578.82
	$92,077.90

These expenditures have been for account of : —

Library ....$ 362.82
Wooden Legs..   100.00
1,730 Free Patients, for 7,852 weeks.......................   81,085.73
393 Paying Patients, for 1,014 weeks 10,529.35
                                                              ─────────
                                                             $92,077.90
                                                              ═════════

The average number of patients has been in 1879, 163
  "   "   "   "   " 1880, 170½
The average cost per week has been, in 1879,
  8,476 weeks $10.54
The average cost per week has been, in 1880,
  8,866 weeks 10.39
The total expenses have been, in 1879 . . $89,295.57
  "   "   "   " 1880 . . .   92,077.90

TABLE 2

SUMMARY OF HOSPITAL DEPARTMENT.

The amount paid for account of free patients has
been $81,085.73

The amount received for them has been :

From Income Free Bed Funds, $24,612.40
(See Table 3.)   From 96 Sub-
    scribers for this object . .   11,300.00
                                  ─────────   35,912.40
                                              ─────────
                                             $45,173.33
                                              ═════════

The deficiency has been drawn from the General Fund.

TABLE 3.

SUBSCRIBERS FOR FREE BEDS.

Theodore Lyman	$100	*Amount brought up*	$5,700
Wm. Amory	100	Henry S. Shaw	100
Fitchburg Railroad Co	100	Amory A. Lawrence	100
J. C. Gray	100	J. Amory Lowell	100
Miss Mary Wigglesworth	200	W. O. Grover	100
Miss Anne Wigglesworth	200	Eastern Railroad Co	100
Union Railway Co	100	R. C. Winthrop	100
Boston and Providence Railroad Co	100	Mrs. Gardner Brewer	100
Miss Mary Pratt	100	Chas. Merriam	100
Geo. Higginson	100	Martin Brimmer	100
T. Jefferson Coolidge	100	W. D. Pickman	100
Miss Jane Wells	200	John R. Hall	100
H. P. Kidder	200	C. H. Dalton	100
F. H. Peabody	100	Mrs. L. G. Wadsworth	100
Boston and Maine Railroad Co	100	Nathaniel Thayer	500
S. D. Warren	100	Henry Saltonstall	100
Mrs. Gorham Brooks	100	H. H. Fay	100
James L. Little	100	Otis E. Weld	100
Shepherd Brooks	100	F. Gordon Dexter	100
Miss C. A. Brewer	100	W. Powell Mason	100
W. W. Tucker	100	Thomas D. Quincy	100
J. G. Cushing	100	Greely S. Curtis	100
Mrs. Anna C. Lodge	100	Chas. A. Welch	100
Moses Williams	100	R. C. Greenleaf	100
J. B. Glover	100	Henry Woods	100
P. C. Brooks, Jr	100	J. F. Anderson	100
J. L. Gardner, Jr	100	Sarah S. Fay	200
Peter C. Brooks	100	J. R. Coolidge	100
Miss Eunice Hooper	100	R. W. Hooper	100
Massachusetts Humane Society	200	Miss Josephine May	100
Mrs. N. I. Bowditch	200	J. G. Kidder	100
Samuel Johnson	100	Jos. Sawyer	100
Wm. Endicott, Jr	100	H. L. Higginson	100
Mrs. Charlotte A. Johnson	100	Ozias Goodwin	200
George A. Gardner	100	Miss Eliza Goodwin	200
Miss A. W. Davis	100	Mrs. Chas. Merriam	100
Geo. W. Wales	100	Mrs. Mary P. Cary	100
J. L. Bremer	100	Miss Madeleine C. Mixter / Miss Helen K. Mixter	100
Mrs. G. H. Shaw	100	J. M. Sears	100
Dr. C. E. Ware	100	J. T. Coolidge Jr	100
Geo. Dexter	200	J. Putnam Bradlee	100
F. R. Sears	100	F. L. Higginson	100
Mrs. Samuel Cabot	100	Pacific Mills Board of Relief	100
S. R. Payson	100	Webster & Co	100
Henry B. Rogers	100	C. P. Curtis	100
Mrs. Edward Wigglesworth	100	J. P. Squire & Co	100
Samuel Eliot	100	Jas. Davis	400
C. J. Morrill	100		$11,300
Geo. D. Howe	100		
J. Huntington Wolcott	100		
Amount carried up	$5,700		

Total Free Bed Subscriptions (87) in 1879, $10,350.00
" " " (96) " 1880, 11,300.00

TABLE 4.

LIBRARY ACCOUNT.

Paid for Books, ...		$362.82
Income Treadwell Library Fund, .	$273.42	
Balance Income Treadwell Library Fund for 1879, ...	25.44	
		298.86
Deficiency from General Fund, . .		$63.96

TABLE 5.

WOODEN LEG ACCOUNT.

The amount received for this purpose has been :

Income of the Wooden Leg Fund,	$273.42
The amount expended for Artificial Limbs has been, ...	100.00
The surplus is credited the fund, .	$173.42

TABLE 6.

EXPENSES OF THE ASYLUM DEPARTMENT.

For Stores....................................	$38,693.26
Laundry.......................................	6,782.16
Fuel..	6,485.23
Stationery....................................	322.08
Medicines and Liquors.........................	2,702.08
Contingencies.................................	855.76
Furniture.....................................	8,435.54
Repairs.......................................	14,644.07
Diversions....................................	1,292.04
Water and Ice.................................	2,949.31
Lights.	2,515.78
Amount carried forward.................	$ 85,677.31

Amount brought forward	$85,677.31
Wages	27,088.95
Salaries	6,165.32
¼ General Expenses	1,155.85
Library	300.00
Stables	7,256.72
Garden	3,528.54
	$131,172.69

These expenditures have been for account of :

Patients paying cost and more	$36,072.97
" " less than cost	95,099.72
	$131,172.69

The average No. of patients has been in 1879, $157\frac{102}{365}$

"   "   "   "   "   " 1880, $152\frac{97}{366}$

The average cost per week has been in 1879, $14.30

"   "   "   "   "   " 1880,   16.48

The total expenses have been in 1879, $117,250.02

"   "   "   "   " 1880,   131,172.69

The increase was in the items of Repairs and Furniture.

TABLE 7.

BENEFICIARIES AT THE ASYLUM.

The amount expended at the Asylum for patients who have paid less than cost has been:

$95,099.72

The amount received has been:

From patients 5,732 1-7 weeks' board	$46,095.13
" Income of Funds for Beneficiaries	4,086.61
" " " " " Female Beneficiaries	4,374.65
" " " Amusement Fund	546.83
	55,103.22

The deficiency has been drawn from the General Fund $39,996.50

Property on hand belonging to the Corporation.

Balance on hand December 31st, 1879.

Belonging to the General Fund	$1,101,071.88	
" " " Restricted Funds	1,159,725.11	
To pay Floating Debt	39,210.64	
Sundries in suspense	8.00	
		$2,300,015.63

Deduct from this amount :

(See Table 9.) Balance of entries to General Fund............ 134,497.11

$2,165,518.52

Add :

(See Table 10.) Balance of entries to Restricted Funds,	$26,074.04	
Increase of Debt	27,950.63	
(See Table 11.) Asylum Building Fund	122,976.30	
		177,000.97

Balance December 31st, 1880, being the exact footing of the trial balance sheet.... $2,342,519.49

Invested as follows :—

Investments producing no Income.

Asylum.—Land and Buildings occupied for Asylum..	$320,446.67		
Land in Belmont	45,000.00		
Steward's balance, consisting of uncollected board bills	$30,710 68		
Cash	2,279.72		
		32,990.40	
			$398,437.07
Hospital.—Land and Buildings occupied for Hospital.	$485,472.73		
Steward's balance	877.20		
		486,349.93	
Sundries.—Land in Waltham	$11,200.00		
Memorandum of expectancies	8.00		
Cash	1,377.03		
Land in Chicago	1,007.18		
		13,592.21	

Amount carried forward $898,379.21

Amount brought forward.......................... $898,379 21

INVESTMENTS PRODUCING INCOME.

Policies Mass. Hospital Life Insurance Co..........	$243,000.00
500 Shares Mass. Hospital Life Insurance Co.......	50,000.00
$35,000 City of Boston Bonds	35,000.00
$21,000 Eastern Railroad Bonds @ 70.............	14,700.00
$1,000 Kansas City and Cameron Railroad Bonds...	1,000.00
$5,000 Boston and Lowell Railroad 7 ℗ cent. Bonds.	5,000.00
$5,000 Boston and Albany Railroad 7 ℗ cent. Bonds.	5,000 00
$100,000 Chicago, Bur. & Quincy R.R. 7 ℗ c. Bonds.	100,000.00
$11,000 " " " " 5 " "@ 90,	9,900.00
$100,000 Atch., Top. & St. Fe R.R. 1st Mort. 7s	100,000.00
$25,000 Bur. & Mo. River R.R. in Neb. Non-Ex. 6s..	25,000.00
$10,000 Atchison Land Land Grant 7s.............	10,000 00
$10,000 Kan. City, Top. and Western R.R. 1st M. 7s,	10,000.00
$3,000 Old Colony Railroad 6s...................	3,000,00
14 Shares Merrimack Manufacturing Co..........	14,000 00
1 " Appleton " "	1,000.00
9 " Amoskeag " "	9,000.00
9 " Amory " "	900.00
9 " Stark Mills.......................	9,000.00
25 " Great Falls Manufacturing Co..........	2,500.00
5 " Boston " "	5,000.00
100 " National Union Bank..................	10,000.00
66 " Tremont National Bank...............	6,600.00
50 " Old Boston " "	2,500.00
25 " Suffolk " "	2,500.00
Land and Store 17 Blackstone Street.............	19,600.00
" " " 168 Washington Street............	45,000.00
" " House 61 Dartmouth Street............	10,000.00
Hospital Wharf................................	62,000.00
Redman Mansion Estate, Washington Street.......	106,000.00
Land and Houses on Warrenton Street...........	17,700.00
" " Store 496 Washington Street............	55,500.00
" " Houses, Chambers Street...............	23,900.00
" " " 42-50 Cross Street..............	10,872.50
Notes secured by Mortgage......................	390,600.00
$20,000 Note of Phila. Wilmington and Balt. R.R..	20,000.00
$365 Scrip Delaware Mutual Insurance Co.........	365,00
$8,000 Union League Club Bonds................	8,002.78
	$1,444,140.28

Total of Investments............................ $2,342,519.49

TABLE 8.

THE BOWDITCH HISTORY FUND.

Balance, December 31st, 1879.......... {	Principal,	$2,000.00	
	Income..	2,046 01	
			$4,046.01
Amount of Income expended...................		$260.96	
Amount of Income received...................		109.37	
			151.59
Balance, December 31st, 1880.......... {	Principal,	$2,000.00	
	Income..	1,894.42	
			$3,894.42

TABLE 9.

THE GENERAL FUND.

Balance, December 31st, 1879................................		$1,101,071.88
Add ¼ profits Mass. Hospital Life Insurance Co.......	$10,000.00	
Amount received of Francis James..............	846.07	
		10,846.07
		$1,111,917.95
Less amounts premiums paid on Raiload Bonds.......	$19,723.75	
" " " " Manufacturing Stocks,	144.00	
	$19,867.75	
" rec'd from U.S.Bonds, $ 42.50		
" R.R.Stocks, 3,377.50		
	3,420.00	
	$16,447.75	
(See Table 11.) Amount credited to Asylum Building Fund	119,547.31	
Balance of Expenses over Income...................	9,348.12	
		145,343.18
Balance, December 31st, 1880................................		$966,574.77

TABLE 10.

THE RESTRICTED FUNDS.

Balance, December 31st, 1879.......... {	Principal, $1,155,943.75		
	Income..	3,781.36	
			$1,159,725.11
Amount carried forward...........................			$1,159,725.11

<table>
<tr><td>Amount brought forward ....</td><td></td><td>$1,159,725.11</td></tr>
</table>

Add amounts received :

For the Convalescent Home Fund...............	$2,513.00	
" " " Building	17,938.85	
From Mrs. F. W. Lincoln (in part)..............	10,000.00	
" Edward Woodman—Permanent Free Bed..	1,000.00	
	$31,451.85	
Less amount expended on Buildings at Belmont for Convalescent Home...........................	6,273.90	
	$25,177.95	
Increase of unexpended Income, 1880, over 1879.....	896.09	
		26,074.04

Balance, December 31st, 1880................................$1,185,799.15

of which is Principal........................	$1,181,121.70
Income........	4,677.45

The Restricted Funds now consist of:

INCOME DEVOTED TO FREE BEDS.

The Joy Fund, being a bequest from Miss Nabby Joy...........	$20,000.00
Belknap Fund, being a bequest from Jeremiah Belknap.....	10,000.00
Wm. Phillips Fund, being a bequest from Wm. Phillips......	5,000.00
Williams Fund, being a bequest from John D. Williams, of estate No. 17 Blackstone Street.....................	19,600.00
Bromfield Fund, being half of a bequest from John Bromfield,	20,000.00
Miss Townsend Fund, being a donation from the Executors of the will of Miss Mary P. Townsend..................	11,486.50
Brimmer Fund, being a bequest from Miss Mary Ann Brimmer,	5,000.00
Wilder Fund, being a bequest from Chas. W. Wilder........	12,000 00
Sever Fund, being a bequest from Miss Martha Sever.......	500.00
Thompson Fund, being a bequest from S. B. Thompson.....	500 00
Tucker Fund, being a bequest from Miss Margaret Tucker...	3,312.37
Davis Fund, being a bequest from Mrs. Eleanor Davis.......	900.00
Loring Fund, being a bequest from Abigail Loring.........	5,000 00
Nichols Fund, being a bequest from B. R. Nichols..........	6,000.00
Amount carried forward	$119,298.87

Amount brought forward .... , $119,298.87

The Gray Fund, being a donation from John C. Gray............ 1,000.00
Dowse Fund, being a bequest from Thomas Dowse.......... 5,000.00
Todd Fund, being a bequest from Henry Todd.............. 5,000.00
J. Phillips Fund, being a bequest from Jonathan Phillips 10,000.00
Greene Fund, being a bequest from Benj. D. Greene........ 5,000.00
Percival Fund, being a bequest from John Percival...... .... 950.00
Pickens Fund, being a bequest from John Pickens.......... 1,676.75
Treadwell Fund, being part of a bequest from J. G. Treadwell, 38,703.91
Raymond Fund, being a bequest from E. A. Raymond.. .... 2,820.00
Harris Fund, being part of a bequest from Chas. Harris..... 1,000.00
Mason Fund, being a bequest from Wm. P. Mason.......... 9,400.00
Sawyer Fund, being part of a bequest from M. P. Sawyer... . 7,000 00
J. L. Gardner Fund, being a donation from J. L. Gardner... 20,000.00
B. T. Reed Fund, being a donation from Benj. T. Reed...... 1,000.00
Wm. Reed Fund, being a bequest from Wm. Reed.......... 5,233.92
McGregor Fund, being half of a donation and bequest from
    James McGregor................................. 7,500 00
Miss Rice Fund, being a bequest from Miss Arabella Rice... 5,000.00
Templeton Fund, being half of a bequest from John Templeton, 5,000.00
Mrs. J. H. Rogers Fund, being a donation from J. H. Rogers, 1,177.50
Beebe Fund, being a bequest from J. M. Beebe............ 50,000.00
Lincoln Fund, being half of a bequest from Mrs. F. W. Lincoln, 85,000.00
Blanchard Fund, being a bequest from Mrs. M. B. Blanchard, 4,000 00
Geo. Gardner Fund, being a donation from Geo. Gardner.... 1,000.00
Hemenway Fund, being a donation from the Executors of the
    will of Augustus Hemenway....................... 20,000.00
Jessup Fund, being part of a bequest from Dr. Chas. A. Jessup, 1,000.00
Tufts Fund, being a bequest from Quincy Tufts............. 10,000.00
Read Fund, being half of a bequest from Jas. Read........ 1,000.00
Parker Fund, being a bequest from John Parker, Jr......... 10,000 00
Miss Shaw Fund, being a donation and bequest from Miss M.
    Louisa Shaw.................................... 5,500.00
Eliza Perkins Fund, being a donation from Mrs. H. B. Rogers, 1,000.00
Dwight Fund, being a donation from Mrs. T. Bradford Dwight, 1,000.00
Hunnewell Fund, being a donation from H. H. Hunnewell... 10,000.00
R. M. Mason Fund, being a bequest from R. M. Mason...... 5,000.00
Anna Lowell Cabot Fund, being a donation from Dr. Samuel
    Cabot... 1,000.00

Amount carried forward $457,260.95

Amount brought forward........................ $457,260.95

Income devoted to Beneficiaries at Asylum

The Bromfield Fund, being half of a bequest from
    John Bromfield........................ $20,000.00
Read Fund, being half of a bequest from Jas. Read,   1,000.00
Appleton Fund,
    $10,010 being a bequest from Sam'l Appleton,
    20,000 being a donation from Wm. Appleton,   30,010.00
McGregor Fund, being half of a donation and
    bequest from Jas. McGregor..............   7,500.00
Austin Fund, being part of a bequest from Mrs.
    Agnes Austin.........................   5,000 00
Kittredge Fund, being a bequest from Rufus
    Kittredge............................   5,500.00
Templeton Fund, being half of a bequest from
    John Templeton.... ....   5,000 00
Cabot Fund, being a donation from Dr. Samuel
    Cabot........ ....   722.85
                                                     $74,732.85

Income devoted to Female Beneficiaries at Asylum :

The Lincoln Fund, being half of a bequest from Mrs. F. W. Lincoln,   85,000.00

Income unrestricted:

The Waldo Fund, being a bequest from Daniel Waldo..........   40,000.00

Income devoted to any purpose except buildings:

The Redman Fund, being a bequest from John Redman.........   455,113.34

Income devoted to a Triennial Prize

The Warren Prize Fund, being a bequest from Dr. J. M. Warren,   2,299.61

Income devoted to the Library :

The Treadwell Library Fund, being part of a bequest from
    J. G. Treadwell..................................   5,000.00

Income devoted to Books for Patients :

The Warren Library Fund, being a donation from Dr. J. C. Warren,   1,000.00

Amount carried forward........................ $1,120,406.75

Amount brought forward....................... $1,120,406.75

Income and Principal devoted to the publication of a History of the Hospital:

The Bowditch History Fund, being a bequest from N. I. Bowditch,   2,000.00

Income devoted to Amusements at the Asylum:

The Amusement Fund, $5,000 being a bequest from Miss Mary
Louisa Shaw,

5,000 being a donation from Mrs. Quincy
A. Shaw and other Ladies......   10,000,00

Income devoted to Special Surgical Instruments:

The Surgical Instrument Fund, being a donation from Dr. H. J.
Bigelow...   1,250.00

The Wooden Leg Fund:

Being a bequest from N. I. Bowditch.........................   5,000.00

The Convalescent Home Fund..................   7,959.00
"   "   " Building..............   11,664.95

Permanent Free Beds:

Miss Marian Hovey............................	$1,000 00	
Mrs. Fanny H. Morse............................	1,000.00	
Henry S. Hovey................................	1,000.00	
Edward Woodman.............	1,000.00	
		4,000.00

Redman Annuities.................................   15,600.00

Clara Barton Annuity 3,241.00

Add unused Income at credit of:

The Warren Prize Fund............................	$511.81	
Warren Library Fund........................	216.53	
Bowditch History Fund........................	1,894.42	
Surgical Instrument Fund.....................	865.96	
Wooden Leg Fund.............................	537.81	
Convalescent Home Fund.......................	297.80	
" " " Building...............	353.12	
		4,677.45

Total of Restricted Funds....................... $1,185,799.15

TABLE 11.

ASYLUM BUILDING FUND.

It has been decided by the Trustees to hold the proceeds of sales of the Somerville Estate, with a view of using the money for the future construction of Asylum buildings on the Belmont Estate.

This fund now amounts to :

Principal	$119,547.31
Income	3,428 99
	$122,976.30

CONVALESCENT HOME.

This enterprise has met with generous support, subscriptions now amounting to . . . . $83,797.85, of which has been paid in 25,897.85

leaving . . . .$57,900.00 yet to be paid.

It is very desirable to complete the one hundred thousand dollars needed for this purpose.

Respectfully Submitted,

F. H. PEABODY,

Treasurer.

BOSTON, December 31st, 1880.

Table of the Expenses of the Hospital and Asylum for Nineteen years—1862 to 1880.

ORDINARY EXPENSES.

Year.	Cost of Paying Patients. Hospital.	Cost of Free Patients. Hospital.	Other Charities. Hospital.	Total Expenses of Hospital.	Total Expenses of Asylum.
1862	$6,628.65	$35,072.01	$414.15	$42,114.81	$71,823.46
1863	6,151.27	40,575.14	695.30	47,421.71	69,300.63
1864	10,224.81	49,286.53	648.21	60,159.55	101,484.38
1865	23,119.62	34,131.83	717.35	57,968.80	120,885.84
1866	30.086 08	37,538 12	1,162 60	68,786.80	126,015.83
1867	26,086.67	33,758.02	1,164.53	61,009.22	133,844.14
1868	23,663.50	42,481.71	1,419.26	67,564.47	142,535.36
1869	20,128.86	40,736.44	1,373 50	62,238.60	138,132.02
1870	15,844 35	46,087.42	883 05	62,814.82	134,339.63
1871	15,266.51	47,126 12	1,133.74	63,526 37	146,191.23
1872	12,664.70	56,537.74	1,497.86	70,700 30	153,327.60
1873	16,681.66	69,109.97	2,135.29	87,926.92	165,023.79
1874	14,198.41	64,266.27	2,634.60	81,099.28	161,934.11
1875	10,677.72	71,447.23	1,761.59	83,886.54	165,660.47
1876	11,344.58	82,033.60	1,312.94	94,691.12	164,973.80
1877	10,833.10	72,678.63	279.16	83,790.89	143,148.94
1878	11,252.42	85,102.61	588.98	96,944.01	136,394.36
1879	11,564.44	77,216.88	514.25	89,295.57	117,250 02
1880	10,529 35	81,085.73	462.82	92,077.90	131,172.69

Year.	Average cost per week per patient. Hospital.	Average cost per week per patient. Asylum.	Cost over Board. Hospital.	Cost over Board. Asylum.
1862	$6.04	$7.27	$36,260.92	$6,640.81
1863	6.66	6.98	41,109 46	2,170.56
1864	8 38	9.76	52,445.01	4,523.85
1865	9.86	12.49	43,121.53	9,507.86
1866	13.88	12 30	53,809.36	558.19
1867	11.28	13.84	44,291.54	....
1868	12.74	16.51	52,893.02	14,642.07
1869	10.14	14.21	48,811.90	....
1870	10 05	13.83	50,811.01	....
7871	9.96	15.80	52,447.68	9,996.88
1872	10.10	16.93	59,547.91	14,917.57
1873	10 29	19.23	72,435.94	26,404.27
1874	10.13	19.59	67,548.81	2,750 66
1875	9 72	21.07	71,989.93	11,872.47
1876	9 41	19.72	82,027.86	13,019.51
1877	9.47	15.66	72,957.79	....
1878	9 87	15.55	83,516.61	....
1879	10 54	14 30	73,440.58	....
1880	10.39	16 48	79,280.61	10,078.33
19 years....................			$1,138,747.47	127,033.03

ANNUAL REPORT OF THE RESIDENT PHYSICIAN

OF THE

MASSACHUSETTS GENERAL HOSPITAL,

For the Year 1880.

-- -- -

Number of Patients in the Hospital, January 1st, 1880.

Paying, 17. : : : : Free, 140. : : : : Total, 157.

Admitted from January 1st, 1880, to January 1st, 1881.

	Males.	Females.	Total.
Patients paying board................	225	129	354
" " " part of the time...	34	` 11	45
" entirely free................	1100	624	1724
	1359	764	2123

	Medical.	Surgical.
Male.........................(Boys 134)	434	926
Female......................(Girls 63)	380	383
	814	1309

Of these 1 paid $42.00 per week; 22 paid $35.00; 2 paid $28.00; 1 paid $25.00; 74 paid $21.00; 6 paid $14.00; 2 paid $12.00; 63 paid $10.50; 2 paid 10.00; 161 paid $7.00; 2 paid $6.00; 1 paid $5.50; 35 paid $5.00; 3 paid $4.50; 12 paid $4.00; 2 paid $3.50; 6 paid $3.00; 1 paid $2.50; 1 paid $2.00.

Whole number of patients treated during the year: paying, 371; paying a part of the time, 45; free, 1,864;—total, 2,284.

Discharged during the Year.

	Medical.	Surgical.	Males.	Females.	Total.
Well	375	811	752	434	1186
Much relieved	153	132	186	99	285
Relieved	130	130	147	113	260
Not relieved	53	21	48	26	74
Not treated	31	93	74	50	124
Dead	71	80	122	29	151
Insane and eloped	2	24	23	3	26
	815	1291	1352	754	2106

Number of Patients remaining December 31st, 1880.

Males......106	Females....... 68	Total......174
Paying..... 17	Free..........157	Total...... .174
Medical 64	Surgical........110	Total......174

Proportion of deaths to whole number of results, 7.16 per cent.

Number of patients received on account of accidents, 351.

The greatest number of paying patients at any one time, was 35; in private rooms, 9; the greatest number of free patients, 165; the greatest total, 188. The least number of paying patients at any one time, 12; in private rooms, 1; the least free, 132; the least total, 156. The proportion of ward beds occupied by free patients, was 85 per cent.; by paying patients, 15 per cent.; about 2.45 per cent. of the paying patients occupied private rooms.

The average number of patients was 170; males, 64; females, 36.

The average number of paying patients was 19; Americans, 12 2-3; foreigners, 6 1-3.

The average number in private rooms was 5 1-2.

The average number of free patients was 151; Americans, 75; foreigners, 76.

. The average time of paying patients was 2.58 weeks, and that of free patients 4.53.

Residences.

Boston	993	Rhode Island and Connecticut	11
Massachusetts, (excepting Boston)	988	Other States	26
Maine	33	British Provinces	26
New Hampshire and Vermont	46		

Birthplaces.

Boston	175	British Provinces	244
Massachusetts, (excepting Boston)	525	Great Britain	121
Maine	167	Ireland	511
New Hampshire	84	Germany	34
Vermont	29	Norway and Sweden	35
Rhode Island and Connecticut	37	France	17
New York	41	Western Islands	8
Southern and Western States	59	Belgium and Holland	4
		Italy	5
		Switzerland	6
		Other places	21
Total Americans	1117	Total Foreigners	1006

Occupation.

Males.	Paying.	Free.	Partial Payment.
Mechanics	34	177	8
Laborers	36	534	10
Farmers	16	45	4
Miners	9	126	2
Seamen	18	49	1
Clerks	17	34	2
Teamsters	2	23	1
Traders	16	18	2
Servants	3	28	..
Lawyers	4	1	1
Clergymen	1	1	
Physicians	6	3	..
Merchants	23	8	2
Students	11	6	2
Other Professions	30	49	..
	226	1102	35

Total Males 1363. Of these 65 were in private rooms.

Females.	Paying.	Free.	Partial Payment.
Domestics	12	244	1
Minors	10	62	..
Wives	69	195	6
Widows	13	25	1
Seamstresses	3	35	
Spinsters	16	15	..
Operatives	1	11	1
Teachers	2	5	
Clerks	1	4	..
Nurses	1	26	1
	128	622	10

Total Females 760. Of these 33 were in private rooms.

Twenty per cent. of the free patients were female domestics; thirty-one per cent. were laborers; ten per cent. were mechanics; and nine per cent. were minors.

Admissions Refused.

Phthisis, (Consumption).	68	Paralysis..............	21
Syphilis..............	24	Epilepsy........... ...	8
Chronic Ulcers........	38	Cancer................	21
Scrofula and Abscesses..	5	Uterine............	19
Insanity and Delirium		Injuries..............	13
Tremens........	11	Of Skin..............	13
Hip and Spine........	38	Contagious............	28
Debility and Senility....	20	Other Diseases........	220
Chronic Rheumatism....	31		
Total...578			

Males................328		Americans 368	
Females 250		Foreigners.............210	

Residents of Boston.....................242
"   " Massachusetts..............282
"   " Other places................ 54

Out-Patients.

Number of new patients..............20,566

Men.........7,809	Women....8,568	Children 4,189
Americans.......... 12,328	Residents of Boston...13,516	
Foreigners.......... ...8,138	Of other places........7,056	

Medical Department for Women..................... 3,971
       "   " Men and Children.'.......... 4,181
Surgical Department............................. 4,750
Ophthalmic   "   464
Dental   4,217
Department for Diseases of the Skin................ 1,330
    "   "   " Nervous System....... 463
    "   "   " Throat.............. 1,190
Total attendance 37,245
Average daily attendance........................ 120

Of the Surgical cases, there were :

Fractures and Dislocations.290	Genito Urinary.........400
Wounds...............410	Club-Foot.............. 24
Sprains and Injuries.....716	Specific................212
Abscesses..............393	Hernia................114
Ulcers 153	Necrosis.............. 52
Felons 117	Fistula in Ano.......... 22
Tumors...............492	Diseases of Joints.......141
Diseases of Hip......... 48	Referred 145
Diseases of Spine 86	Miscellaneous..........1033

Of the Dental patients, 755 had 1,027 teeth filled; 3,341 had 5,069 teeth extracted.

By referring to the tables for "Admissions, Discharges and Results," in this report, it will be seen that the number of patients admitted this year exceeds that of last year by three hundred and ten, and exceeds the number admitted in 1876 by two hundred and seventeen, the number admitted that year being the largest ever admitted in any one year until the present.

The number of acute cases admitted has been very much larger. The average time of residence shorter, and for paying patients two-thirds of a week less than in 1876; for free patients one and one-fifth's weeks less.

We most gratefully acknowledge the gifts of the many kind friends who have remembered us through the year, and especially those who gave so abundantly of their time and means on Thanksgiving, Christmas and New Year's Day. Messrs. Lockwood, Brooks & Co., and the Forbes Lithograph Co. made us ample and most acceptable gifts of Christmas and Lithograph cards for which we are very thankful.

The Young Men's Christian Union has furnished seventy-five "Patients' Rides," taking out three hundred and twenty-four patients.

Respectfully submitted,

JAMES H. WHITTEMORE,
Resident Physician.

To the Board of Trustees, }
Boston, January 1st, 1881. }

THE AMBULANCE

OF THE

MASSACHUSETTS GENERAL HOSPITAL,

Accompanied by a Medical Officer, will be despatched to any point north of Dover and Berkeley Streets, for the conveyance of cases of *accident* or *urgent sudden sickness, not contagious,* to this Hospital, or elsewhere, upon notice from a Physician, the Police, or other responsible source, subject to the approval of the undersigned.

In cases requiring gratuitous treatment, no charge will be made.

By order of the Board of Trustees.

JAMES H. WHITTEMORE, M. D.,
Resident Physician,
Mass. Gen. Hospital, Blossom St.

APPENDIX.

ARE FREE DISPENSARIES ABUSED?

READ BEFORE THE BOSTON SOCIETY FOR MEDICAL IMPROVEMENT AND
BEFORE THE SUFFOLK DISTRICT MEDICAL SOCIETY.

BY J. H. WHITTEMORE, M. D.
Resident Physician Massachusetts General Hospital.

The subject of free dispensaries and the question of their abuse, both in this and foreign countries, had attracted so much attention and consequent discussion, that in 1877 the Trustees of the Massachusetts General Hospital requested me to investigate the out-patient department of said hospital, and ascertain, if possible, if a large class of people did not come there for free treatment, who, by reason of their ability to pay for medical services ought not to be allowed this privilege. Sufficient was learned to show that the charity was abused. Since that time the number of patients has steadily and rapidly increased. Inquiry at the Boston Dispensary, and at the Boston City Hospital Dispensary, shows that the same feeling of abuse of their dispensaries exists in the minds of their respective superintendents. With this general feeling existing in the minds of the trustees and superintending officers of the three principal dispensaries of the city, I feel that the subject ought to come before the profession to be discussed, and plans for correction made, if abuses are really believed to exist worthy of notice. To this end I wish to lay before the society certain statistics and facts, perhaps not new, but to refresh your memories, if need be, so that discussion of the subject may be had, and the feeling of the society on this subject may be learned ; also, to see if any action to correct abuses seems advisable, and if so, what the course to be pursued shall be.

The Boston Dispensary was opened in 1796 " for the purpose of affording medical advice and relief to the sick poor of said town." To July, 1856, there had been treated in this dispensary 118,802 patients. The population of the City of Boston when the dispensary was opened was about 21,000, and had increased in 1856 to about 162,000. In 1860 the number of patients treated in the Boston Dispensary was 16,000. In the Massachusetts General Hospital Out-Patient Department, which had been open fourteen years, the number for 1860 was 4,433, making 20,433 the total number treated in the Boston and Massachusetts General Hospital Dispensaries. The population of the city at this time, 1860, was 177,840, so that there was one free patient to every eight and eight-tenths of the population. During the next ten years, to 1870, the number of patients had more than doubled, being in 1870, at the Boston Dispensary, 25,928; at the Massachusetts General Hospital Dispensary, 8,767 ; at the Boston City Hospital Dispensary,— which had been open six years,—8,899; total during the year 1870, 43,594; population of the city, 250,256,—one patient to every five and seven-tenths of the population. The last reports of the three above-mentioned dispensaries give the Boston Dispensary 34,648; Massachusetts General Hospital Dispensary 20,566; Boston City Hospital Dispensary 10,309, and in addition to these, I find that during the last year, or in their last reports, the following dispensaries treated patients as follows : Homœopathic Hospital Dispensary 11,826 ; New England Hospital Dispensary 5,212; Charlestown Dispensary 1,103; making a total in the six dispensaries of 83,664. Population of the city about 360,000, and one patient to every four and three-tenths of the population. In addition to the above dispensaries, Dr. Charles W. Williams, in a report to the Common Council in March last, showed that there were fourteen other free dispensaries and hospitals in the City of Boston.

It has been impossible to get full reports from all of these hospitals and dispensaries. Is it unreasonable to estimate, with above facts, that more than one-fourth of all the inhabitants of Boston receive free medical treatment?

The Boston Dispensary, previous to three years ago, admitted all who applied from the city, and furnished them with medicines, the only care taken being to prevent, if possible, non-residents from being treated. Three years since a man was employed to see every person who came for treatment, and an attempt was made to exclude non-residents and undeserving people, especially those, who, on inquiry, did not seem worthy or needing charity; this plan is still kept up with satisfactory results, as the number has fallen from 48,000, in 1877, to 34,648 at their last annual meeting. The superintendent believes that there is still a decided per cent. of those now treated who are unworthy, from their ability to pay for medical services. In June last the dispensary stopped giving medicines and charged ten cents for all prescriptions, except in cases of extreme poverty. Dr. Hastings says the result has been most satisfactory to the financial interests of the dispensary.

In the Massachusetts General Hospital Out-Patient Department, prior to 1877, there were placed in conspicuous places in each room of the department, a box with a card over it, inviting all those liberally inclined, who came there for treatment, to deposit in these boxes what little money they felt disposed to. The amount was never burdensome to the hospital, and never exceeded one hundred dollars a year. In 1877 a person was employed by the hospital to see every person who came for treatment, and asked them if they could afford to pay for medical treatment or not? If not, they were at once admitted after giving their name and address. Those who said they could pay, were asked to give according to their means, but less than twenty-five cents was not desired. Those who could pay a dollar and over were told not to come again after their first visit, as they were not of the class for whom the department was opened, but that they must seek advice outside, at the physicians' offices. This did not result in any diminution of patients, and in a short time but very few could afford to pay over twenty-five cents. This system is not satisfactory, and seems to act as a premium on deceiving. In November, 1877, a competent and experienced man was employed to investigate the condition of all who came to the department from Boston (old city) and South Boston. The result was as follows: number of visits, 386; number of deserving poor, 254; number giving wrong addresses, 79; number amply able to pay, 53. Of the fifty-three able to pay, nineteen owned their houses and other property in the city. The number giving wrong addresses were classed as undeserving, as is the custom in other cities and countries; with these and those able to pay we have one-third of the whole number considered as undeserving applicants. The Massachusetts General Hospital Dispensary gives no medicines, only in extreme and recommended cases.

The Boston City Hospital Dispensary, when first opened in 1864, furnished medicines and advice free to all residents of the city who applied. In 1869 (?) they stopped giving medicines except in the most extreme cases. They continue the same plan at present, and strive to exclude non-residents.

The classes of people who come for advice and treatment are nearly the same in the three mentioned dispensaries, and are as follows: (1) The needy and deserving poor; (2) those who come because they can be treated free, or nearly so; (3) those who come for free examination and opinion, to see if they are being treated correctly by their own physician; (4) those sent by their physician for free examination, to find out what really is the matter; (5) and last, patients brought by their physicians to get a free consultation. All of these classes visit the different dispensaries, but the last three classes are found more in abundance at the City Hospital and Massachusetts General Hospital Dispensaries, and particularly so at the Massachusetts General Hospital, as *one-third* of the patients there come from outside of the city, some even as far as forty miles away.

Let us, for a short time, see what has been done in similar conditions in England. The subject had received much attention prior to 1870; in that year, at a meeting presided over by Sir William Fergusson, at which one hundred and fifty-six members of the medical profession were present, the following resolution was passed:—

"That this meeting is of opinion that there exists a great and increasing abuse of out-door relief at the various hospitals and dispensaries of the metropolis which urgently requires a remedy; and that, in the opinion of this meeting, the evils inseparable from the system of gratuitous medical relief administered at the out-door department of hospitals and in free dispensaries, can be in great measure met by the establishment on a large scale of provident dispensaries throughout the kingdom, and by improved administration of poor-law medical relief." Following this were meetings of various societies, and in April,

1875, the following memorial, of which I quote only a part, was made to the president and committee of council of the British Medical Association: "We, the undersigned, members of the British Medical Association, and others, beg most respectfully to request the committee of council to take into consideration the relation of the medical profession to the hospitals and free dispensaries throughout the kingdom. Your memorialists are convinced that the manner in which these institutions, with some few exceptions, are at present conducted, inflicts a serious injury upon many most deserving members of our profession; while the indiscriminate (or almost indiscriminate) bestowal of gratuitous medical relief upon all applicants lowers the whole scale of our professional remuneration, it is far from being a real boon to the working classes themselves, and cannot fail, in the long run, to have a prejudicial influence upon the nation at large." At this time investigation was made as to the number receiving medical aid in London, and it was found that one-fourth of all the inhabitants were receiving free medical care. In a report of the Medical Committee of the Charity Organization Society I find the following: " It is the out-patient departments of hospitals that are most abused, and it is in these departments that your committee desire to see the indiscriminate relief at present given largely curtailed." They believed that this could be done without seriously affecting the supply of cases which are needful for clinical instruction at those hospitals which have medical schools attached to them, and without limiting the true province of Christian charity."

"Under the present circumstances, when there are in the metropolis about one hundred and five hospitals and dispensaries to which the artisan or laborer can turn at any moment, and which may almost be said to be bidding against one another for his patronage, it is obvious that the inducements to providence and self-reliance are entirely taken away. This state of things your committee regard as a very great evil, and they believe that there is no one class of charities which is doing so much to pauperize the population, to undermine their independence and self-respect, and to discourage habits of providence, as the medical charities. The committee are well aware of the great benefit that these institutions, if properly used, are capable of conferring upon the humbler ranks of our population. These benefits it would be difficult to exaggerate, but the committee deplore the almost indiscriminate relief which is given."

The outgrowth of this movement in England was the establishment of provident dispensaries, which, I presume, are more or less familiar to all of the society, and I will only briefly describe them. They do not care for those provided for by the poor-laws, or what we call paupers, but receive those of the lower middle class who, under the ordinary circumstances of life, can care for themselves, but are unable to obtain medical care when sickness comes. This class pay a small amount each month, say a shilling or twenty-five cents, and then when sick are cared for by the provident dispensary, who, on being notified of the case, send some of their physicians, who, in turn, are paid a small fee by the dispensary. Thus the patient has proper medical care, and the physician is not deprived of his entire fee. The result of these provident dispensaries has been most satisfactory, according to recent reports.

Should any change from the present course be deemed advisable, to my mind the first and most important step to be taken is the earnest, hearty, and complete coöperation of all the hospitals and dispensaries in some one distinct plan of work.

When the associated charities were first started I hoped we could find aid in this work from them, but further thought and examination induces me to believe that such aid, as now organized, would entail so much delay that suffering would follow.

The provident dispensaries are quite satisfactory in England, but from my imperfect knowledge of them my impression is that the detail and machinery connected with their working would render them impracticable here at present.

My last suggestion—and the one in which I have at present the most faith—is that of a competent and experienced paid inspector at each of the large dispensaries.

Such an officer should examine each and every person who applies for treatment, and should have power to exclude *all* except the deserving poor. He should personally examine each case, and after the hours of admission to the dispensary, should devote the remainder of the time to visiting and examining into the condition of those who have been treated, in order to ascertain if they are as represented—poor and deserving people.

SIXTY–THIRD ANNUAL REPORT

OF THE

SUPERINTENDENT OF THE M^CLEAN ASYLUM FOR THE INSANE,

TO THE

TRUSTEES OF THE MASS. GENERAL HOSPITAL.

JANUARY I, 1881.

To the Trustees of the Massachusetts General Hospital,

GENTLEMEN,—

In preparing the following report relating to the number and condition of the patients treated in the Asylum during the past year, I have used the new tables recommended by the Board of Health, Lunacy and Charity, for the use of the Massachusetts hospitals and asylums for the insane. Such of the tables are omitted as do not relate to such an institution as this, or, for which the data is not available.

TABLE No. 1.

General Statistics of the year.

	Males.	Females	Total.
Patients in the Asylum, January 1st, 1880........	66	85	151
Admissions within the year....................	17	34	51
Whole number of *cases* within the year..........	83	119	202
Discharged within the year....................	16	32	48
Viz:—as Recovered......................	6	6	12
Much improved	2	8	10
Improved......................	4	6	10
Unimproved....................	1	9	10
Deaths..	3	3	6
Patients remaining December 31st, 1880, } supported as private patients, }	67	87	154
Number of different *persons* within the year......	81	118	199
" " " " admitted............	17	34	51
" " " " recovered..........	6	6	12
Daily average number of patients..............	67.593	84.672	152.265

Of the admissions, two men and one woman were discharged and admitted again during the year, but no one was twice admitted during that period. There were two hundred and two cases treated during the year, representing one hundred and ninety-nine different persons. Of the fifty-one persons admitted, twenty-eight were regarded as recent cases, and twenty-three as chronic, or as incurable, at the time of admission.

Thirty persons—six men and twenty-four women— had never before been in any hospital. Of the remaining twenty-one persons, ten—seven men and three women—were admitted for the *second* time; seven—two men and five women—for the *third* time; one man for the *fourth* time; one woman for the *fifth* time; one woman for the *sixth* time; and one man for the *sixteenth* time. Of these twenty-one persons, fifteen—seven men and eight women—had formerly been inmates of this Asylum.

There were twenty-five less admissions, thirty-one less discharges, and twenty-eight less cases under treatment than during the year 1879; and the number present was three more at the end than at the beginning of the year.

Of those discharged, six—one man and five women —were transferred to other hospitals; four women to Danvers; one woman to Butler Hospital; and one man to an asylum in Germany

Of the eleven persons discharged recovered, nine had never before been inmates of any hospital; one had been at Taunton, and one had been an inmate of this Asylum. Three persons were admitted and discharged recovered within the year.

The expenses of the year were considerably increased over those of the immediately preceding one, chiefly because of large expenditures which had become very necessary in general repairs and plumbing, and in furnishings. This work has been going on during the whole of the year, and all the plumbing of the Appleton Buildings, and about two-thirds of that of the other buildings, has been taken out and replaced with new and well ventilated apparatus. Considerable outlay has been made in renovating rooms and wards, particularly in the Appleton Buildings, in improving ventilation, in new carpetings and furnishings in general.

The new gas-house, which has been in operation nearly a year, has effected a saving of more than one-half in the cost of lights.

Much attention has been given during the year, as in times past here, to the subject of non-restraint, which includes the increase of freedom of the inmates. Some of the gentlemen have been allowed to go out on parole, but there is an obstacle to the extension of this practice, in the proximity of the city, and, in regard to some cases, because of the encompassing lines of railroads very near the buildings. The practice of keeping unlocked during the day, the doors of four, and sometimes of five of the ten wards for ladies, has been continued as for the last eight or ten years. The occupants of these wards thus go freely from one to another, or out into the large, shady garden for the use of the ladies. This garden is enclosed by a fence, which is necessary, if for no other reason, because of the immediate proximity of railroad tracks, and to prevent intrusion from a populous neighborhood. Six of the wards for gentlemen, communicate freely with each other by doors which are never locked by day or night, and, as a rule, the doors of rooms are not locked at night.

Many of the windows of the asylum have large panes of glass, and are protected by ornamental latticed gratings of small iron rods. During the latter part of the year a number of these gratings were removed from windows of parlors and chambers, and the sashes were stopped so as to open only six inches at the top and bottom.

In relation to mechanical restraint, the principle adopted is, to reduce it to a minimum, and never to employ it when other means will do as well. In a small percentage of cases, it may prove to be a proper and useful therapeutic measure.

The usual means of diversion and entertainment have been made use of during the year, such as concerts, readings, and dancing parties, in the newly renovated hall. There have been carriage drives every week-day in good weather, and visits to places of interest and amusement in and about Boston.

The continued attentions of the many friends of the Asylum, are gratefully appreciated and remembered.

Very respectfully,

EDWARD COWLES,
Superintendent.

TABLE No. 2.

Monthly Admissions, Discharges, and Averages.

Months.	Admissions.			Discharges, (Including Deaths.)			Daily Average of Patients in the House.		
	Ma.	Fe.	Total.	Ma.	Fe.	Total.	Ma.	Fe.	Total.
January	1	4	5	1	2	3	65.77	82.93	148.70
February	..	4	4	..	1	1	66.00	86.68	152.68
March	1	..	1	1	2	3	66.16	83.87	150.03
April........	1	2	3	..	2	2	66.10	82.13	148.23
May	1	6	7	1	2	3	67.35	85.55	152.90
June	1	2	3	1	3	4	67.70	86.76	154.46
July........	3	1	4	2	1	3	67.51	85.19	152.70
August......	3	5	8	2	3	5	68.48	89.81	158.29
September...	..	2	2	..	1	1	69.00	86.26	155.26
October......	4	2	6	2	2	4	68.00	83.00	151.00
November....	..	5	5	1	3	4	70.30	80.10	150.40
December....	2	1	3	5	10	15	68.74	84.74	153.48
Total *cases*...	17	34	51	16	32	48	67.59	84.67	152.26
Total *persons.*	..	..	..	15	32	47	..	..	..

TABLE No. 3.

Received on First and Subsequent Admissions.

Number of the Admission.	Cases Admitted.			Times previously Recovered.		
	Males.	Females.	Total.	Males.	Females.	Total.
First...............	6	24	30	..	..	..
Second.............	7	3	10	2	..	. 2
Third..............	2	5	7	1	2	3
Fourth.............	1	..	1	..	..	..
Fifth..............	..	1	1	..	3	3
Sixth..............	..	1	1	..	1	1
Sixteenth..........	1	..	1	15	..	15
Total of *cases*........	17	34	51	18	6	24
Total of *persons*......	17	34	51	..	..	..

These 24 recoveries represent 8 persons, one having recovered 3 and another 15 times.

44

TABLE No. 4.

Ages of Persons admitted for the First Time.

Ages.	At first attack of Insanity.			When Admitted.		
	Males.	Females.	Total.	Males.	Females.	Total.
Fifteen years and less.	..	..	..	..	..	..
From 15 to 20 years..	1	..	1	1	..	1
" 20 to 25 " ..	..	3	3	..	1	1
" 25 to 30 " ..	2	5	7	2	6	8
" 30 to 35 " ..	1	3	4	1	4	5
" 35 to 40 " ..	1	2	3	1	2	3
" 40 to 50 " ..	1	3	4	1	3	4
" 50 to 60 " ..	..	5	5	..	4	4
" 60 to 70 " ..	..	3	3	..	3	3
" 70 to 80 " ..	..	..	..	..	1	1
Trtal of *persons*.. ...	6	24	30	6	24	30

TABLE No. 5.

Residence of Persons Admitted.

Places.	Males.	Females.	Total.
Massachusetts :—			
Suffolk County	9	11	20
Middlesex County	3	11	14
Bristol County	1	1	2
Norfolk County	1	1	2
Worcester County	..	1	1
Essex County	..	1	1
Plymouth County	..	1	1
Maine	..	2	2
New Hampshire	..	2	2
Vermont	1	..	1
Rhode Island	..	1	1
New York	2	1	3
Illinois	..	1	1
Total of *persons*	17	34	51

TABLE No. 6.

Civil Condition of Persons Admitted.

Number of the Admission.	Unmarried.			Married.			Widowed.		
	Ma.	Fe.	Total.	Ma.	Fe.	Total.	Ma.	Fe.	Total.
First........	4	10	14	2	11	13	1	2	3
Second......	2	2	4	4	1	5	1	..	1
Third.......	2	1	3	..	3	3	..	1	1
Fourth......	1	..	1	..	..	..	..	..	..
Fifth........	..	1	1	..	..	..	..	..	..
Sixth........	..	1	1	..	..	..	..	..	..
Sixteenth....	1	..	1	..	..	..	..	..	..
Total *persons*	10	15	25	6	15	21	2	3	5

TABLE No. 7.

Occupations of Persons Admitted.

Occupations.	Males.	Females.	Total.
Housewife....................................	..	15	15
Clerk....	4	..	4
Teacher....................................	..	3	3
Merchant....................................	4	..	4
Farmer....................................	1	..	1
Student....................................	1	..	1
Music Teacher................................	..	1	1
Dress Maker................................	..	1	1
Physician....................................	1	..	1
Stone Mason................................	1	..	1
Clergyman................................	1	..	1
Servant....................................	..	1	1
Seamstress................................	..	1	1
Printer....................................	1	..	1
Civil Engineer................................	1	..	1
No occupation................................	2	12	14
Total of *persons*.............................	17	34	51

TABLE No. 8.

Reported Duration of Insanity Before Last Admission.

Previous Duration.	First Admission to any Hospital.			All other Admissions.			Total.		
	Ma.	Fe.	Total.	Ma.	Fe.	Total.	Ma.	Fe.	Total.
Congenital...	..	..	..	..	..	..	..	..	..
Under 1 month	3	1	4	..	..	..	3	1	4
From 1 to 3 mo.	1	9	10	..	1	1	1	10	11
" 3 " 6 "	..	2	2	2	..	2	2	2	4
" 6 " 12 "	..	6	6	3	..	3	3	6	9
" 1 " 2 yrs.	2	3	5	2	1	3	4	4	8
" 2 " 5 "	..	2	2	2	5	7	2	7	9
" 5 " 10 "	..	1	1	1	2	3	1	3	4
" 10 " 20 "	..	..	..	1	1	2	1	1	2
Total *cases*...	6	24	30	11	10	21	17	34	51
Total *persons*.	..	..	..	..	..	..	17	34	51
Average of known cases, (in years.)	$3\frac{5}{72}$	$1\frac{7}{36}$	$1\frac{19}{360}$	$2\frac{47}{66}$	$4\frac{17}{20}$	$3\frac{46}{63}$			

TABLE No. 9.

Form of Disease in the Cases Admitted.

Form of Disease.	Males.	Females.	Total.
Mania, acute	3	8	11
Mania, chronic	6	9	15
Melancholia, acute	4	13	17
Melancholia, chronic	..	2	2
Dementia, chronic	..	2	2
General Paralysis	4	..	4
Total of *cases*	17	34	51
Total of *persons*	17	34	51

TABLE No. 10.

Alleged Causes of Insanity in Persons Admitted.

Causes.	Males.	Females.	Total.
Mental.			
Overstudy	1	5	6
Grief...	1	..	1
Anxiety	1	1	2
Disappointment...............................	..	1	1
Self-indulgence...............................	..	1	1
Pecuniary trouble.............................	1	..	1
Physical.			
Ill-health.....................................	..	7	7
Overwork.....................................	1	4	5
Constitutional................................	2	2	4
Change of life................................	..	2	2
Child-birth...................................	..	2	2
Domestic trouble..............................	..	1	1
Opium habit..................................	..	1	1
Dissipation...................................	1	..	1
Intemperance.................................	1	..	1
Masturbation.................................	1	..	1
Congenital...................................	1	..	1
Unknown.....................................	6	7	13
Total of *persons*.............................	17	34	51

TABLE No. 11.

Relation to Hospitals of the Persons Admitted.

	Males.	Females.	Total.
Never before in any Hospital.....................	6	24	30
Former inmates of this Hospital.................	6	5	11
Former inmates of other Hospitals in this State:			
Danvers	1	1	2
Taunton.....................................	1	..	1
Worcester	1	..	1
Former inmates of Hospitals in other States	1	1	2
Former inmates of this Hospital and of other Hospitals in this State :			
Danvers......................................	..	2	2
Worcester....................................	1	..	1
Former inmates of this Hospital and of Hospitals in other States.........................	..	1	1
Total of *persons*.............................	17	34	51

TABLE No. 12.

Discharges Classified by Admission and Result.

Admission.	Recovered.			Much Improved.			Improved.			Unimproved.			Died.			Total.		
	Ma.	Fe.	Tot.	Ma.	Fe.	Tot.	Ma.	Fe.	Tot.	Ma.	Fe.	Tot.	Ma.	Fe.	Tot.	Ma.	Fe.	Tot.
First............	4	6	10	2	6	8	2	5	7	1	6	7	2	2	4	11	25	36
Second..........	1	..	1	..	1	1	..	1	1	..	1	1	1	..	1	2	3	5
Third...........	..	..	..	..	..	..	1	..	1	..	..	..	..	1	1	1	1	2
Fourth..........	..	..	..	..	..	..	1	1	2	..	1	1	..	..	..	1	2	3
Ninth...........	..	..	..	..	..	..	..	..	..	..	1	1	..	..	..	..	1	1
Fifteenth.......	1	..	1	..	..	..	..	..	..	..	..	..	..	..	..	1	..	1
Total of *cases*.....	6	6	12	2	7	9	4	7	11	1	9	10	3	3	6	16	32	48
Total of *persons*..........	..	..	..	..	..	..	..	..	..	..	..	..	..	..	..	15	32	47

TABLE No. 13.

Cases Discharged Recovered.—Duration.

Period.	Duration before Admission.			Hospital Residence.			Whole Duration from the Attack.		
	Ma.	Fe.	Total.	Ma.	Fe.	Total.	Ma.	Fe.	Total.
Under 1 month	3	4	7	..	..	..	..	..	..
From 1 to 3 mo.	..	1	1	1	..	1	1	..	1
" 3 " 6 "	..	..	..	1	1	2	1	1	2
" 6 " 12 "	2	1	3	3	1	4	1	1	2
" 1 " 2 yrs.	1	..	1	..	3	3	2	3	5
" 2 " 5 "	..	..	..	1	..	1	1	..	1
" 5 " 10 "	..	..	..	..	..	..	..	..	..
" 10 " 20 "	..	..	..	..	1	1	..	1	1
Total *cases*...	6	6	12	6	6	12	6	6	12
Total *persons*.	5	6	11	5	6	11	5	6	11
Average of known cases, (in months.)	$5\frac{1}{8}$	$1\frac{7}{12}$	$3\frac{17}{48}$	$11\frac{5}{6}$	$30\frac{2}{3}$	$21\frac{1}{4}$	$16\frac{11}{12}$	$32\frac{1}{3}$	$24\frac{5}{8}$

TABLE No. 14.

Cases Resulting in Death.—Duration.

Period.	Duration before Admission.			Hospital Residence.			Whole Duration from the Attack.		
	Ma.	Fe.	Total.	Ma.	Fe.	Total.	Ma.	Fe.	Total.
Under 1 month	1	..	1	..	1	1	..	..	..
From 1 to 3 mo.	1	1	2	..	1	1	..	1	1
" 3 " 6 "	..	..	..	1	..	1	..	..	..
" 6 " 12 "	1	..	1	..	1	1	1	..	1
" 1 " 2 yrs.	..	1	1	..	..	..	..	1	1
" 2 " 5 "	..	1	1	..	..	..	..	1	1
" 5 " 10 "	..	..	..	2	..	2	2	..	2
Total	3	3	6	3	3	6	3	3	6
Average of known cases, (in months.)	$4\frac{3}{4}$	$18\frac{1}{2}$	$11\frac{5}{8}$	$59\frac{2}{3}$	$5\frac{1}{4}$	$32\frac{11}{24}$	$61\frac{5}{16}$	$23\frac{7}{12}$	44

TABLE No. 15.

Cases Discharged by Recovery or Death.

Form of Insanity.	Recoveries.			Deaths.		
	Males.	Females.	Total.	Males.	Females.	Total.
Mania, acute.........	2	4	6	..	..	..
Mania, chronic.......	4	..	4	..	2	2
Melancholia, acute ...	..	1	1	1	1	2
Melancholia, chronic..	..	1	1	..	..	..
Dementia, chronic....	..	..	..	2	..	·2
Total of *cases*.......	6	6	12			
Total of *persons*.....	5	6	11	3	3	6

TABLE No. 16.

Causes of Death.

Causes.	Males.	Females.	Total.
Cerebral Disease.			
Disease of Brain	1	..	1
Exhaustion from Mania......................	..	1	1
Exhaustion from Melancholia..................	1	..	1
Meningo-encephalitis and diffused sclerosis.......	..	1	1
Thoracic Disease.			
Bronchitis and emphysema of lung....	1	..	1
Heart-clot and œdema of lung..................	..	1	1
Totals..	3	3	6

TABLE No. 17.

Deaths, Classified by Results of Previous Admissions.

Number of the Admission.	Recovered.			Unimproved.			Total.		
	Ma.	Fe.	Total.	Ma.	Fe.	Total.	Ma.	Fe.	Total.
First........	1	..	1	..	1	1	1	1	2
Total	1	..	1	..	1	1	1	1	2

TABLE No. 18.

Recoveries, Classified by Results of Previous Admissions.

Number of the Admission.	Recovered.			Total.		
	Males.	Females.	Total.	Males.	Females.	Total.
First...............	1	..	1	1	..	1
Fifteenth...........	1	..	1	1	..	1
Total of *persons*......	2	..	2	2	..	2

TABLE No. 19..

Deaths Classified by Duration of Insanity and of Treatment.

Period.	Duration of Insanity.			Whole known period of Hospital Residence.		
	Males.	Females.	Total.	Males.	Females.	Total.
Congenital...........	..	..	..	..	..	..
Under 1 month.......	..	..	..	..	1	1
From 1 to 3 months..	..	1	1	..	..	..
" 6 to 12 " ..	1	..	1	1	1	2
" 2 to 5 years....	..	2	2	..	1	1
" 5 to 10 "	2	..	2	2	..	2
Total..............	3	3	6	3	3	6
Average of known cases, (in months.)	$64\frac{5}{12}$	$23\frac{7}{12}$	44	$59\frac{2}{3}$	$5\frac{1}{4}$	$32\frac{11}{24}$

TABLE No. 20.

Ages of those who Died.

Ages.	At time of the first attack.			At time of Death.		
	Males.	Females.	Total.	Males.	Females	Total.
From 20 to 25 years..	1	1	2	..	..	..
" 25 to 30 " ..	..	..	..	..	1	1
" 30 to 35 " ..	..	1	1	..	1	1
" 35 to 40 " ..	..	1	1	..	1	1
" 50 to 60 " ..	1	..	1	1	..	1
" 60 to 70 " ..	1	..	1	1	..	1
" 70 to 80 " ..	..	..	..	1	..	1
Total	3	3	6	3	3	6

Table of Admissions, Discharges, and Results, at the McLean Asylum from its opening, October 6, 1818, to December 31, 1880, inclusive.

YEARS.	Admitted.	Discharged	Whole No. under care.	Died.	Much improved, etc.	Recovered	Remaining at end of year.	Average No. of Patients.
1818–25	398	344	623	29	205	110	279	–
1826	47	46	101	5	21	20	55	–
1827	58	56	113	5	17	34	57	–
1828	77	65	134	5	37	23	69	–
1829	73	77	142	9	42	26	65	–
1830	82	78	147	10	34	34	69	–
1831	83	84	152	8	46	30	68	–
1832	94	98	162	10	45	43	64	–
1833	103	100	167	8	50	42	67	–
1834	108	95	174	7	47	41	80	–
1835	83	84	163	11	28	45	77	–
1836	106	112	183	10	38	64	71	–
1837	120	105	191	8	25	72	86	80
1838	138	131	224	12	45	74	93	95
1839	132	117	225	10	38	69	108	112
1840	155	138	263	13	50	75	125	128
1841	157	141	283	11	55	75	142	135
1842	129	138	271	15	43	80	133	143
1843	126	126	260	18	45	63	134	131
1844	158	140	292	20	52	68	152	146
1845	119	120	271	13	33	74	151	149
1846	148	126	299	9	52	65	173	164
1847	170	170	343	33	50	87	173	172
1848	143	155	316	23	50	82	155	171
1849	160	137	321	15	58	64	184	177
1850	173	157	357	28	51	78	200	201
1851	164	173	364	29	69	75	191	195
1852	145	135	336	15	48	72	201	200
1853	114	120	315	17	45	58	195	194
1854	120	120	315	16	45	59	195	195
1855	123	126	318	24	46	56	192	192
1856	149	145	341	19	58	68	196	195
1857	141	159	337	28	60	71	178	191
1858	155	147	333	25	50	72	186	187
1859	131	142	317	28	53	61	175	185
1860	121	109	296	24	46	39	187	185
1861	111	110	298	23	33	54	188	193
1862	82	94	270	18	37	39	176	190
1863	94	69	270	13	20	36	201	191
1864	101	107	302	27	38	42	195	200
1865	82	85	277	17	33	35	192	186
1866	103	98	295	29	23	46	197	197
1867	89	108	286	27	36	45	178	186
1868	92	94	270	23	37	34	176	166
1869	108	100	284	18	31	51	184	187
1870	79	85	263	12	40	33	178	187
1871	75	81	253	13	47	21	172	178
1872	93	101	265	23	63	15	164	173
1873	92	95	256	13	63	19	161	165
1874	75	88	236	10	58	20	148	159
1875	85	83	233	16	51	16	150	156
1876	92	74	242	20	36	18	168	160
1877	110	103	278	20	68	15	175	175
1878	63	84	238	12	66	6	154	168
1879	76	79	230	12	14	19	151	157
1880	51	48	202	6	10	12	154	152
	6456	6302		922	2581	2745		

YEAR.	Total Admitted.	Free.	Paying Board all the time.	Paying part of the time.	Paying Board.	Paying Board part of time.	Free.	Discharged Well.	Percentage on "Total Admitted."	Much Relieved, or Relieved in part.	Not Relieved.	Not Treated, Unfit, Dismissed, &c.	Deaths.	Percentage on "Total Admitted."	Greatest number free at one time.	Greatest number paying at one time.	Greatest total.	Least total.	Average.	Accidents.	Percentage.	Average time of Paying Weeks.	Average time of Free Weeks.	Patients remaining Paying.	Patients remaining Free.	Out-Patients treated.
1821to1843	8748	390	327	34				3391		2902	913	105	624				123	54				4	6			328
1843	385	183	167	15				136	37	115	55	17	41	11		30	56	33	47²		12²	6-7	7 1-7			378
1844	435	250	174	11				183	43	137	41	23	47	11	44	34	71	40	53	55	14	5 4-7	6 6-7			272
1845	413	259	176	12				205	45	130	37	28	45	12	44	28	72	37	56	62	13	3 1-2	4 3-4			294
1846	459	250	182	27				211	46	137	39	33	36	8	82	41	72	37	55	59	11	3 1-7	4 1-2			287
1847	674	354	279	41				340	50	145	54	30	57	8	86	38	123	54	81	74	11	3 1-7	5			248
1848	804	460	283	61				400	50	219	51	39	84	13	89	38	124	94	108	103	13	2 4-7	5 5-7			359
1849	870	543	273	54	49			436	50	218	75	58	76	9	86	33	127	90	112	97	13	2 6-7	6	14	140	477
1850	746	427	242	77	42		1040	383	48	200	56	49	98	10	89	41	136	83	108	98	16	3	6	15	121	645
1851	830	472	298	64	11		1187	387	50	235	52	63	82	11	103	29	141	104	112	123	16	3 1-4	5	16	124	887
1852	826	505	271	85	11		1252	410	46	234	47	66	115	9	93	45	133	108	119	159	17	3 1-6	7	25	120	1574
1853	925	490	335	86	11		1299	431	50	287	66	61	112	12	108	59	142	125	120	212	23 17 3-10	4	11 4-7	24	126	2223
1854	922	414	321	111	11		1448	423	46	267	73	41	117	11	112	48	152	114	123	157	14 17 7-10	3 4-10	5	25	123	3523
1855	515	549	352	147	11		1388	456	50	238	77	51	130	12	107	40	163	120	131	189	17 18 7-10	3.18	5²	45	126	4433
1856	976	543	335	96	43		687	478	49	195	55	71	141	13	119	37	157	91	140	163	18² 8-4	3.67	4 2-3	39	123	4676
1857	1015	718	280	91	21		676	510	50	229	64	71	99	11	120	51	165	92	123	186	17 16 3-10	3.40	6	51	69	4800
1858	920	584	251	49	21		890	514	56	280	54	58	101	7	145	40	162	80	131	212	21 17 2-10	3.00	5 3-4	35	60	4987
1859	1240	937	257	49	45		1658	653	53	305	73	54	102	7-10	135	37	166	102	128	293	16 15 2-10	3.40	4 1-10	25	69	5619
1860	1116	934	201	32	24		1289	698	62	318	73	86	130	6-9³	133	35	162	116	134	247	17 17-10	3.37	4.37	24	96	5366
1861	1611	997	263	22	35		1251	831	51	431	96	70	104	8	139	43	166	110	137	292	17 11-10	3.15	4.85	28	100	6008
1862	1618	1175	283	17	44		1565	861	53	459	84	61	109	7.64	137	44	187	88	138	242	16 9.36	3.28	5.10	30	86	4653
1863	1189	1202	325	45	120		1646	916	57	300	96	74	130	7.46	150	43	183	116	113	140	7.74	2.73	4.26	35	126	6204
1864	1199	564	567	49	88		687	702	60	245	84	141	104	7.75	146	42	173	89	95	132	6.69	2.82	3.50	28	120	6963
1865	1120	626	556	45	88		676	671	60	282	68	84	94	7.69	182	36	199	90	104	113		2.84	4.30	26	126	8767
1866	1296	831	463	24	43		936	678	56	288	62	68	107	10.97	170	41	194	98	102	98		2.80	4.82	19	129	9792
1867	1384	970	632	31	62		1458	757	56	352	78	73	165	7.68	165	31	187	97	118	93		2.84	3.92	11	114	11878
1868	1302	1063	41	24	120		1289	771	59	322	65	86	186	12.46		36	140	111	120	140		2.68	4.36	17	171	13517
1869	1427	1125	472	55	88		1251	780	57	363	78	73	127	7.69		41	183	132	122	178			6.09	17	145	15612
1870	1517	1146	3?8	64	88		1646	880	57	313	66	102	189	10.27		31	199	165	135	259			6.64	17	141	16993
1871	1560	1270	411	43	42		1441	916	62	321	81	144	127	7.68		36	194	165	156	291			6.18		157	17292
1872	1638	1264	384	93	52		1577	1032	62	306	98	130	189			34	187	165	149	234			5.73			18004
1873	1841	1131	308	48	42		1961	930	56	380	92	138	134	7.94		30	188	135	185	285			5.54			18744
1874	1906	12-4	339	38	45			1040	54	502	93	125	143	7.16		35	188	131	165	245			5.27			18960
1875	1667		323	42				1019		505	84		131						163	147			5.16			20566
1876	1794		335	45				1040		422	74		151					156	170	200			4.53			
			354					1186		545										351						235818

Totals: 64429 | | | | | | | | 18302 | | 13878 3122 3301 | | 4739 | | | | | | | | | | | | |

Table of Applications, Admissions, etc., for Seventeen Years,—1864-'80.

Years	Applications (Hospital)	Admissions (Hospital)	Admissions (Asylum)	American (Hospital)	American (Asylum)	Foreign (Hospital)	Foreign (Asylum)	Not Admitted (Hospital)	Discharged, cured, relieved, or improved (Hospital)	Discharged (Asylum)	Percentage of same, on Admissions (Hospital)	Percentage (Asylum)	Died (Hospital)	Died (Asylum)	Accidents	Whole number under care in the year (Hospital)	Whole number (Asylum)	No. of Free patients (Hospital)	Paying all the time (Hospital)	Paying part of the time (Hospital)	Greatest total number at any time (Hospital)	Greatest total (Asylum)	Least total at any one time (Hospital)	Least total (Asylum)	Average (Hospital)	Average (Asylum)	Greatest number at any one time — Free	Greatest number — Paying	Average time in weeks — Paying	Average time — Free	Out Patients (Hospital)
1864	1932	1599	101	654	99	945	2	333	1306	80	8.168	79.1	130	27	242	1749	302	1388	350	11	157	208	110	192	138	200	139	33	3.2	4.4	5619
1865	1430	1199	82	571	80	628	2	231	997	68	8.315	82.9	104	17	140	1347	277	687	592	68	104	195	88	181	113	186	137	72	3.7	4.8	5856
1866	1328	1120	103	542	100	587	3	208	909	69	81.17	66.9	93	29	132	1224	295	556	623	45	109	203	78	192	95	197	62	58	3.4	5.1	5608
1867	1419	1206	89	558	88	648	1	213	958	81	79.43	91.0	94	27	113	1301	218	676	601	24	126	200	72	172	104	186	77	62	3.4	4.8	4653
1868	1174	1265	92	604	92	661	0	209	1015	71	80.08	77.1	85	18	98	1373	284	840	502	31	132	181	69	160	102	160	97	57	3.0	3.5	5264
1869	1633	1390	108	631	108	709	0	243	1123	82	80.03	75.9	107	23	93	1217	342	930	563	24	139	196	90	177	106	166	98	56	3.4	4.3	6953
1870	1706	1302	79	584	76	718	3	404	1083	73	88.20	92.4	85	12	140	1427	253	958	439	30	137	195	98	181	118	187	106	55	3.4	4.8	8767
1871	1781	1427	75	649	75	778	0	354	1143	52	80.09	60.3	109	13	178	1637	265	1066	456	25	164	187	91	167	120	178	126	45	3.1	3.9	9792
1872	1815	1547	93	655	88	882	5	263	1271	52	82.15	55.9	120	23	259	1701	256	1289	396	16	160	179	97	163	122	173	133	43	3.1	4.3	11878
1873	1958	1550	92	640	85	910	7	408	1201	64	77.48	69.5	186	13	291	1700	236	1195	441	64	187	171	129	158	135	165	156	42	3.3	6.0	13517
1874	2153	1630	75	713	68	926	7	514	1342	54	81.88	72	127	10	234	1800	233	1251	394	120	183	167	111	144	150	159	146	44	2.7	5.6	16612
1875	2357	1841	85	709	72	1022	13	516	1412	57	76.70	67	189	16	285	1889	242	1565	336	88	199	165	132	145	149	156	176	41	2.8	5.2	16993
1876	2560	1906	92	900	82	1006	10	654	1621	45	85.04	48.9	150	20	245	2096	278	1696	308	92	210	173	163	148	166	160	182	31	3.2	5.7	17292
1877	2131	1657	110	863	103	794	7	474	1839	57	80.80	51.8	130	20	147	1847	238	1270	339	48	194	184	135	154	185	175	178	36	2.8	5.5	18004
1878	2275	1791	63	946	58	848	5	481	1461	45	81.43	71.4	134	12	200	1950	230	1578	334	38	187	182	132	154	164	168	170	33	2.8	5.2	18744
1879	2310	1813	76	979	63	834	13	497	1462	46	80.63	60.5	143	12	222	1971	202	1677	352	42	188	164	131	150	165	157	165	34	2.3	5.1	18960
1880	2701	2123	51	1117	46	1006	5	578	1731	48	81.53	94.1	161	6	351	2284	202	1864	371	45	188	159	156	146	163	152	165	35	2.5	4.5	20666

Table Showing the Cost of the Principal Stores at the Massachusetts General Hospital.

Articles.	1877.			1878.			1879.			1880.		
	Quantity.	Cost.	Average.	Quantity.	Cost.	Average.	Quantity.	Cost.	Average.	Quantity.	Cost.	Average.
Beef, Sirloin.........lbs.	9,100	$1,927.38	.2118	7,729	$1,610.72	.2084	8,375	$1,716.87	.205	8,815	$1,692.99	.1941
" for Soup........ "	560	23.80	.0425	132	5.28	.04	....	....	....	....	....	....
" Corned........ "	5,889	479.54	.0816	4,378	324.72	.07415	4,123	288.61	.07	4,952	346.64	.07
" Round........ "	9,327	805.85	.0864	11,944	1,016.43	.0851	12,973	1,054.70	.0813	16,414	1,148.98	.07
" Rump........ "	6,882	1,163.05	.169	4,158	635.34	.1528	....	....	....	....	....	....
" Roasting........ "	11,584	1,274.24	.11	14,998	1,349.82	.09	14,141	1,341.98	.0949	16,439	1,643.90	.10
Mutton........ "	18,416	2,509.04	.13624	15,808	1,903.28	.1204	12,592	1,385.12	.11	15,522	1,876.60	.1208
Poultry........ "	13,509	2,475.65	.184	14,079	2,276.57	.1617	14,488	2,433.98	.168	13,682	2,123.44	.1552
Butter........ "	10,056	2,644.72	.263	10,156	2,500.40	.2462	10,526	2,589.39	.246	11,011	3,366.06	.3057
Eggs.........doz.	4,608	967.68	.21	5,495	967.12	.176	4,392	843.26	.192	4,214	866.39	.2056
Flour.........bbls.	40	362.48	9.062	42	323.82	7.71	37	266.80	7.40	51	440.15	8.65
Bread.........lbs.	34,343	1,717.15	.05	35,800	1,790.00	.05	36,556	1,827.80	.05	40,536	2,026.80	.05
Ice.........tons.	180½	627.54	3.48	238½	808.25	3.333	271¾	714.70	2.63	280¼	1,297.56	4.63
Sugar.........lbs.	10,592	982.88	.0928	12,979	1,023.65	.0781	15,462	1,189.32	.769	21,005	2,003.87	.0954
Tea.........	593	222.96	.376	738	254.61	.345	848	337.82	.398	1,134½	471.95	.416
Milk.........qts.	97,594	4,879.70	.05	107,618	5,380.90	.05	96,186	4,934.34	.0513	89,904½	4,495.22½	.05
Potatoes.........bush.	909	915.36	1.007	973	964.61	.77	942	1,010.76	1.073	1,039½	902.58	.868

Table Showing the Cost of Principal Stores at the McLean Asylum.

Articles.	1877. Quantity.	Cost.	Average.	1878. Quantity.	Cost.	Average.	1879. Quantity.	Cost.	Average.	1880. Quantity.	Cost.	Average.
Beef..........lbs.	63,352	$7,261.94	.114	77,166	$8,384.25	.108	58,771½	$7,062.58	.12	57,462	$6,625.64	.115
Mutton and Lamb......... "	21,819	2,769.17	.126	21,411	2,411.63	.112	20,266½	2,055.36	.101	19,794¼	2,107.14	.106
Veal......... "	5,029	651.17	.129	7,636	1,017.22	.133	9,182½	1,045.09	.113	12,288	1,372.34	.111
Poultry......... "	29,321	5,164.12	.176	33,620	5,305.56	.157	25,754⅞	4,148.75	.16	23,714½	3,726.80	.157
Hams, etc.........doz.	13,076	1,477.74	.113	14,966	1,556.23	.103	7,180½	670.81	.093	8,932½	899.85	.1007
Eggs......... "	13,257	2,874.59	.216	13,679	2,508.71	.183	11,270	2,242.03	.198	11,295	2,337.09	.2069
Lard..........lbs.	2,786	310.40	.111	2,256	181.61	.08	1,723	123.00	.071	1,849	159.24	.086
Flour..........bbls.	425	3,952.46	9.299	449	3,440.50	7.662	397	2,709.85	6.825	418	3,296.63	7.886
Butter..........lbs.	19,990	5,105.84	.255	21,240	5,390.49	.253	20,219½	4,873.85	.241	19,511¼	5,405.80	.277
Coffee......... "	5,840	1,670.33	.285	5,066	1,309.89	.258	4,934½	1,271.89	.257	4,124	1,212.62	.294
Tea......... "	1,775	739.44	.416	1,532	626.22	.408	1,383	450.72	.325	1,492½	486.41	.325
Sugar......... "	28,199	3,174.47	.112	28,796	2,716.50	.094	23,759½	2,039.82	.085	24,330	2,290.05	.094
Lights, Gas, etc.........feet	1,250,494⁄2000	4,840.31	....	2,112,100	5,695.42	2.60 ℔mft	2,072,000	5,559.83	2.60 ℔mft	1,158 1620⁄2000	2,515.78	....
Coal..........tons.		6,057.45	4.845	1,064 1020⁄2000	5,407.81	5.08	904 1520⁄2000	4,015.13	4.44		5,972.06	5.15
Wood..........cords.				200		....	15⅘	134.53	8.75	25¾	219.84	8.75
Ice..........tons.	533	1,836.28	3.445	588 200⁄2000	1,958.44	3.33	476 741⁄2000	1,208.34	2.53	462 1500⁄2000	2,069.31	4.47

58

OFFICERS OF THE HOSPITAL.

JAMES H. WHITTEMORE, M.D. . . . . . *Resident Physician.*

GEORGE C. SHATTUCK, M.D. . . .
FRANCIS MINOT, M.D. . . . . .
CALVIN ELLIS, M.D. . . . . . .
SAMUEL L. ABBOT, M.D. . . . . . } *Visiting Physicians.*
BENJAMIN S. SHAW, M.D. . . . . .
GEORGE G. TARBELL, M.D. . . . .

HENRY J. BIGELOW, M.D. . . . .
SAMUEL CABOT, M.D. . . . . . .
RICHARD M. HODGES, M.D. . . .
CHARLES B. PORTER, M.D. . . . . } *Visiting Surgeons.*
JOHN COLLINS WARREN, M.D. . .
HENRY H. A. BEACH, M.D. . . . .

DAVID H. HAYDEN, M.D. . . . .
WILLIAM L. RICHARDSON, M.D.
EDWARD N. WHITTIER, M.D. . .
ELBRIDGE G. CUTLER, M.D. . . } *Physicians to Out-Patients.*
F. GORDON MORRILL, M.D. . . .
FREDERICK C. SHATTUCK, M.D.

THOMAS B. CURTIS, M.D. . . .
JOHN HOMANS, M.D. . . . . } *Surgeons to Out-Patients.*
WM. STURGIS BIGELOW, M.D. .

JAMES C. WHITE, M.D. . . } *Physician to Out-Patients with diseases of the Skin.*

JAMES J. PUTNAM, M.D. . . } *Physician to Out-Patients with diseases of the Nervous System.*

FREDERICK I. KNIGHT, M.D. } *Physicians to Out-Patients with*
S. W. LANGMAID, M.D. . . . } *diseases of the Throat.*

OLIVER F. WADSWORTH, M.D. } *Ophthalmic Surgeon to Out-Patients.*

MANNING K. RAND, D.M.D. . . . . . . *Dental Surgeon.*

REGINALD H. FITZ, M.D. . . } *Microscopist, and Curator of the Pathological Cabinet.*

EDWARD S. WOOD, M.D. . . . . *Chemist.*

HENRY P. QUINCY, M.D. . . . . *Artist.*

WILLIAM N. SWIFT, . . . } *Medical House-Pupils, for*
THOMAS F. SHERMAN, . . }   1880–81.

FRANK B. HARRINGTON, . ⎫
WILLIAM D. HODGES, . . . ⎬ *Surgical House-Pupils, for*
CHARLES P. STRONG, . . . ⎥   1880–81.
CHARLES B. WITHERLEE, . ⎭

MISS G. L. STURTEVANT, ... *Matron.*

JOHN W. PRATT, ... *Apothecary.*

OFFICERS OF THE McLEAN ASYLUM.

EDWARD COWLES, M.D.. . . . . *Superintendent.*

GEORGE T. TUTTLE, M. D., . . . 1st *Assistant Physician.*

FREDERICK M. TURNBULL, M. D., 2nd *Assistant Physician.*

ROYAL WHITMAN, ... *House Pupil.*

JOSEPH H. POTTS, ... *Apothecary.*

RANSOM WILLARD, ... }
MISS LUCIA E. WOODWARD, . } . . . . . . *Supervisors.*

STANDING COMMITTEES.
On Finance.
MESSRS. KIDDER and MORRILL.
On Accounts and Expenditures.
MESSRS. LOTHROP and WOLCOTT.
On Free-Beds.
MESSRS. BOWDITCH and ENDICOTT.
On the Book of Donations.
DR. BEMIS.
On the Warren Fund and Library.
MESSRS. ELIOT and HALE.
On Repairs.
MESSRS. DALTON, DWIGHT, and WARREN.
On Admitting Patients.
MESSRS. WARREN and DWIGHT.

VISITING COMMITTEE.

February and August,	. .	MESSRS.	KIDDER and WOLCOTT.
March and September,	.	"	MORRILL and ENDICOTT.
April and October,	. .	"	DWIGHT and ELIOT.
May and November,	. .	"	BOWDITCH and DALTON.
June and December,	. .	"	HALE and WARREN.
July and January,	. . .	"	BEMIS and LOTHROP.

LADIES' VISITING COMMITTEE.

January,	. . .	Miss E. GRAY,
		Miss ELLEN CARY,
		Miss MARGARET CURTIS.
February,	. . .	Miss GRAY,
		Miss ELIZA GOODWIN,
		Miss SERAFINA LORING.
March,	. . . .	Miss GOODWIN,
		Miss SERAFINA LORING,
		Miss LOUISA LORING.
April,	. . . .	Mrs. JOHN C. PHILLIPS,
		Miss LOUISA LORING,
		Miss MARGARET CURTIS,
		Miss ELIOT.
May,	. . . .	Miss MARGARET CURTIS,
		Miss ELIOT.
June,	. . . .	Mrs. S. ELIOT,
		Miss ELLEN T. PARKMAN.
October,	. . .	Mrs. ELIOT,
		Miss PARKMAN.
November,	. . .	Miss ANNIE W. MORRILL.
		Mrs. H. W. HAYNES.
December,	. . .	Miss MORRILL,
		Mrs. HAYNES.

SIXTY-EIGHTH ANNUAL REPORT

OF THE

TRUSTEES

OF THE

ASSACHUSETTS GENERAL HOSPITAL

1881

Printed at the Expense of the Bowditch History Fund

BOSTON
GEO. H. ELLIS, PRINTER, 141 FRANKLIN STREET
1882

SIXTY-EIGHTH ANNUAL REPORT

OF THE

TRUSTEES

OF THE

MASSACHUSETTS GENERAL HOSPITAL.

1881 .

Printed at the Expense of the Bowditch History Fund

BOSTON
GEO. H. ELLIS, PRINTER, 141 FRANKLIN STREET
1882

REPORT OF THE TRUSTEES

OF THE

MASSACHUSETTS GENERAL HOSPITAL

For the Year 1881.

THE Committee of the Trustees appointed to prepare the Annual Report of the Board to the Corporation, to whom the accounts of the Treasurer and
the reports of the other officials have been referred,
respectfully submit the

SIXTY-EIGHTH ANNUAL REPORT.

Early in the year, Mr. Francis H. Peabody resigned
the office of Treasurer, which he had held for four
years, leaving the Corporation under a heavy obliga-
tion to him for able and successful service. Mr.
David R. Whitney was elected Treasurer in his
place.

At the close of the year, the long connection with
the Board of Trustees of Mr. Charles H. Dalton
terminates by his declining a re-election. Mr. Dalton
became a Trustee of the Hospital in 1866; and to
him, in great measure, are due many important improvements in the buildings, as well as the purchase
of the large tract of land in Belmont, already utilized
by the erection of the Convalescent Cottage, and to
which, at no distant day, it is hoped that the Asylum
may be removed. His faithful and highly efficient
service has been fully appreciated and cordially ac-
knowledged by his associates.

In the last weeks of the year died the aged and honored Dr. Edward Reynolds, a member of the Board of Consultation since 1839, and Dr. Thomas B. Curtis, one of the surgeons to out-patients, who, although still a young man, had already achieved eminence by his scholarly and profound mastery of his profession.

The average number of patients in the Hospital the past year was 166, a slight decrease as compared with the year before. In the Asylum, the average number has been 149 against 152 in 1880.

The Treasurer's account shows an excess of expenses over income from the funds applicable to the expenses of the Hospital of $15,021.81, in part due to the erection of a new entrance-lodge on Blossom Street, which has proved an important aid in the orderly administration of the Hospital, and in part to costly repairs not yet completed at the Asylum.

The Trustees gratefully acknowledge the following

Donations and Legacies.

Bequest of Miss Jane Welles, ...	$5,000.00
Bequest of John C. Gray, ...	25,000.00
Bequest of E. R. Mudge, ...	1,000.00
Bequest of T. D. Quincy, ...	1,000.00
Donation of a grateful patient to Surgical Instrument Fund, ...	100.00
Donation of Sir Moses Montefiore, ...	5.97
From subscribers to Convalescent Home Fund, . .	70,850.83
From subscribers to free beds, ...	10,950.00

It is earnestly hoped that the number of subscribers to free beds may be increased. Death every year makes many vacancies among the older subscribers; and the increased demands of a larger community make it necessary not only to repair these losses, but to add constantly to our resources.

It is a pleasure to report that the whole sum of $100,000, which the public were invited to contribute for the building and maintenance of the Convalescent Cottage at Belmont, has been subscribed; and, with the exception of a small amount, is already in the hands of the Treasurer. A substantial, well-arranged, and picturesque building has been erected, and will be ready for occupancy in the spring. It is believed that this will furnish an important addition to the curative resources of the Hospital. It is estimated that the total cost of preparing the grounds and erecting the cottage will fall within $35,000, leaving the remainder of the amount subscribed to constitute a fund for maintenance as originally intended. But this fund will need considerable increase in order to meet from its income the necessary expenses of the House. The Trustees hope that this will be remembered as one of the wants of the Hospital for a generous community to supply.

The Trustees are firm in the belief that the Asylum should be removed as soon as may be to its new site on the Belmont estate.

It is true that the buildings of the Asylum were justly considered at the time of their erection admirably adapted to their use. It is true that, by the removal of window bars, and by the introduction of female attendants in the gentlemen's wards, much has been done to ameliorate the somewhat gloomy aspect of the place. But it is not less true that the buildings are not well adapted to a proper classification of cases, or to that cheerful and homelike arrangement so conducive to content, if not to cure. To attain these ends, it would be necessary radically to reconstruct the principal building of the Asylum at a heavy cost. This might perhaps be the policy of the Trustees, were they not convinced that the site had ceased to be the best one for the institution. The discordant noises from the encircling railways and neighboring factories are a source of positive suffering to nerves rendered acutely sensitive by disease; and the variety of drives, one of the pleasantest breaks in the monotonous lives of the patients, is far more restricted than would be the case in the country. Except in certain easily distinguished cases of acute mania or delusion, the proportion of positive cures is, and will probably continue to be, distressingly small; but no effort should be spared to make calm and content take the place of excitement and complaining. The fund for the removal of the Asylum now amounts to $131,123.58, and the Trustees hope that the slow process of accretion will be hastened by generous donations and bequests.

It is not impossible that the estate and buildings at Somerville may in the future be found capable of adaptation to other uses. The Trustees believe that, among its many charities, Boston has not yet made sufficient provision for incurables, a class certainly not the least deserving of pity and aid. While suffering from accident or acute disease, the poorest patient can command in our hospitals the best skill which the city affords; but, when his ailment is such that science is impotent to cure it, he is sent back to his home to drag out long years of suffering and possible neglect, which might be made almost painless by healthful surroundings and intelligent care. The Trustees feel it to be their duty to announce that they will receive donations or legacies to be applied, whenever the amount shall be sufficient, in establishing a department for incurables.

Visitors to the Hospital must often be struck by

the air of cheerfulness diffused throughout a ward by the presence of children. The interest and sympathy which they excite among the adult patients; their own buoyant spirits, if suffering is even for a moment allayed; and the power they exert in banishing from their fellow-sufferers that listlessness and depression which are often the worst foes to recovery,— constitute sufficient reasons why they should always be welcome as among the best of curative influences. They become the petted and indulged favorites of the ward ; and the kindly attention they receive reacts upon their own condition, and encourages their recovery. It' is hoped that the ·Hospital may always be allowed to do its share in alleviating the sufferings of little children.

The Trustees have continued their efforts to restrict the service in the Out-Patient Department to the class of suffering poor whom the Hospital was founded to relieve. The practice of exacting a nominal fee from all applicants save the very poor was discontinued early in the year, as it was found not to accomplish the good it was intended to effect, and to be productive of positive ill results. In April, an experienced person was appointed to examine all applicants, in order to ascertain whether their circumstances entitled them to the benefits of a gratuitous charity. The results of his investigations will be found embodied in the report of the Resident Physician. It will be seen that, of 1,250 cases visited at the addresses given, 545 were pronounced undeserving of charitable aid. It is no doubt true that, to a large number of these, the term impostor would be a harsh and unjust one to apply. It may well be feared that the past practice of the Hospital and of similar institutions has tended to disseminate the belief that, whatever the means of the sufferer, sickness entitles him to free advice and treatment. The managers of such institutions in this country and in Europe are now fully awakened to the dangerous influence of such a belief in its tendency to impair the spirit of providence and self-dependence so essential to good citizenship. The aim of such an investigation of cases as that now in force in our Out-Patient Department should be rather to prevent than to detect improper applications for treatment. It is probable that the result will be to diminish in some degree the number of those annually treated, but it is well to remember that to judge of the success of an institution by the number of its patients is to apply the easiest but not the most adequate test. The Trustees feel it to be their duty to check so far as they may the further spread of a tendency which they believe already to have assumed the proportions of a great evil.

ROGER WOLCOTT, *Committee.*
EDMUND DWIGHT,

REPORT OF THE TREASURER

OF THE

MASSACHUSETTS GENERAL HOSPITAL.

To the Board of Trustees:

Gentlemen,— In accordance with the Fifth Article of the By-Laws the report of the accounts of the Massachusetts General Hospital, made up to the last day of December, 1881, is respectfully submitted, to be laid before the Corporation at its annual meeting.

Dr. D. R. WHITNEY, *Treasurer, in account with the* MASSACHUSETTS GENERAL HOSPITAL. *Cr.*

Jan. 1, 1881.

To Cash on hand,—balance from last year,	$1,377.03
" " from Mass. Hospital Life Ins. Co.'s Policies, paid,	83,000.00
" " Mortgages, paid,	196,000.00
" " Railroad bonds, called,	3,000.00
" " Subscriptions for Convalescent Home,	70,850.83
" " Donations,	105.97
" " Legacies,	32,000.00
" " One-third profits Mass. Hospital Life Ins. Co.,	25,000.00
" " Income from investments applicable to Distributive Income, $94,199.47	
" " Income from investments applicable to other purposes, 2.78	94,202.25
" " Paying Patients at the Asylum,	114,247.17
" " Paying Patients at the Hospital,	14,134.97
" " Subscribers for Free Beds for 1881,	10,950.00
" " Subscribers for Free Beds for 1882, in advance,	3,900.00
	$648,768.22

By Cash paid Kidder, Peabody & Co., balance due them Dec. 31, 1880,	$56,161.27
" " Taxes and betterment on land in Chicago,	2,323.69
" " Taxes on land in Waltham,	104.24
" " Taxes on land in Belmont,	496.37
" " Insurance,	551.58
" " Annuitants,	1,813.23
" " For printing Annual Report of 1880,	238.60
" " For gas works at Asylum,	348.08
" " On account of Convalescent Home buildings,	17,072.24
" " For land on Cross Street,	1,819.14
" " For investments,	229,847.75
" " J. H. Whittemore, Resident Physician, balance in account,	941.15
" " E. Cowles, Supt., balance in account,	258.99
" " Expenses at Hospital,	102,153.80
" " Expenses at Asylum,	134,561.14
" " Balance, cash on hand, Dec. 31, 1881,	100,076.95
	$648,768.22

MASSACHUSETTS GENERAL HOSPITAL, BOSTON, Dec. 31, 1881.

E. & O. Ex. D. R. WHITNEY, *Treasurer.*

The expense of carrying on the business of the corporation for the year 1881 has been $237,370.12, namely: —

On account of Hospital Department, ...	$102,403.65
On account of McLean Asylum, ...	134,966.47
	$237,370.12

This expense has been met from: —

Amount charged to patients, ...	$128,382.14
Income from various funds applicable, ...	93,966 17
Deficit drawn from the General Fund, ...	15,021.81
	$237,370 12

Of the deficit drawn from the General Fund, $6,280.16 has been on account of the Hospital Department, and $8,741.65 has been on account of the McLean Asylum Department, as per Tables 1 and 2.

TABLE No. 1.

EXPENSES AND RECEIPTS OF THE HOSPITAL DEPARTMENT.

Disbursements for the year 1881: —

Expenses at Hospital (see Table 3), ...	$102,153 80
Insurance, ...	11.25
Publishing Trustees' Report, ...	238.60
	$102,403.65

Receipts.

Income from Redman Fund (see Table 5), ...	$30,151.26
" " Free Bed Funds (see Table 5), ...	29,142.01
" " Treadwell Library Fund (see Table 5),	331.25
" " Wooden Leg Fund, in part (see Table 8),	225.00
" " Bowditch History Fund, in part (see Table 9), ...	238.60
" " Funds with income unrestricted (see Table 5), ...	2,650.00
" " General Fund (see Table 5), ...	8,300.40
Free Bed Subscriptions (see Table 6), ...	10,950.00
Amount charged to Patients, ...	14,134.97
Deficit from General Fund, ...	6,280.16
	$102,403.65

12

TABLE No. 2.

EXPENSES AND RECEIPTS AT THE McLEAN ASYLUM.

Disbursements for year 1881:—

Expenses at Asylum (see Table 4), ...	$134,561.14	
Insurance, ...	405.33	
		$134,966.47

Receipts.

Income from Fund for Beneficiaries (see Table 5) .	$4,951.05	
Income from Fund for Female Beneficiaries (see Table 5), ...	5,631.25	
Income from Amusement Fund (see Table 5), . .	662.50	
Unused balance of Cabot Fund, ...	732.85	
Amount charged to Patients, ...	114,247.17	
Deficit from General Fund, ...	8,741.65	
		$134,966.47

TABLE No. 3.

EXPENSES OF THE HOSPITAL DEPARTMENT.

For Stores, ...	$34,239.74	
Gas and Oil, ...	2,175.05	
Water, ...	1,547.29	
Wages, ...	23,621.79	
Medicine, ...	2,909.56	
Furniture, ...	6,617.81	
Surgical Instruments, ...	867.02	
Stationery, ...	984.32	
Wines and Liquors, ...	2,004.87	
Library, ...	225.51	
Salaries, ...	4,664.98	
One-half General Expenses, ...	1,137.43	
Fuel, ...	7,664.34	
Wooden Legs, ...	225.00	
Contingencies, ...	767.17	
New Lodge and Repairs, ...	11,802.92	
Ice, ...	699.00	
		$102,153.80

These expenditures have been for account of:—

Library, ...	$225.51
Wooden Legs, ...	225.00
1,678 Free Patients for 7,410 weeks, ...	88,241.17
428 Paying Patients for 1,196 weeks, ...	13,462.12
	$102,153.80

The average number of patients has been, in 1880, .	170½
The average number of patients has been, in 1881, .	166
The average cost per week has been, in 1880, 8,866 weeks, ...	$10.39
The average cost per week has been, in 1881, 8,606 weeks,.	11.87
The total expenses have been, in 1880, ...	92,077.90
The total expenses have been, in 1881, ...	102,153.80

The amount paid for account of free patients has been, ... $88,241.17

The amount received for them has been : —

From Income Free Bed Funds, ... $29,142.01
(See Table 6.)　From 93 Subscribers for this object, 10,950.00

　　　　　　　　　　　　　　　　　　　　　　40,092.01

　　　　　　　　　　　　　　　　　　　　　　$48,149.16

The deficiency has been drawn in part from the income of the various funds applicable to the purpose, and the remainder from the General Fund.

TABLE No. 4.

EXPENSES OF THE ASYLUM DEPARTMENT.

For Stores, ...	$43,932.76
Laundry,.	8,608.81
Fuel, ...	7,130.34
Stationery, ...	415.82
Medicines and Liquors, ...	2,284.24
Contingencies, ...	1,128.27
Furniture, ...	6,038.77
Repairs, ...	11,617.98
Diversions, ...	1,328.72
Water and Ice, ...	2,347.31
Lights, ...	2,771.42
Wages, ...	28,202.96
Salaries, ...	6,098.39
One-half General Expenses, ...	1,137.43
Library, ...	300.00
Stables, ...	4,711 55
Garden, ...	4,156.94
New Sewer, ...	2,245.29
Burial of F. James, ...	97.00
Legal Services, ...	10.00
Farm, ...	289 44
	$134,853.44
Less Cr. Clothing, ...	292.30
	$134,561.14

These expenditures have been for account of: —

Patients paying cost and more, ... $28,321.72
"   "   less than cost, ... 106,239.42
                                                         $134,561.14

The average number of patients has been, in 1880, . $152\frac{97}{100}$
The average number of patients has been, in 1881, . $149\frac{281}{365}$
The average cost per week has been, in 1880, . . . 16.48
The average cost per week has been, in 1881, . . . 16.92
The total expenses have been, in 1880, ... $131,172.69
The total expenses have been, in 1881, ...   134,561.14

The increase was in the items of repairs and cost of new sewer.

The amount expended at the Asylum for patients who
have paid less than cost has been, ... $106,239.42

The amount received has been : —

From patients, 6,134$\frac{2}{7}$ weeks' board, at less than cost, $53,469.27
Income of Funds for Beneficiaries, ... 4,951.05
Income of Funds for Female Beneficiaries, . . 5,631.25
Income of Amusement Fund, ... 662.50
Unused balance of Cabot Fund, ... 732.85
                                                        65,446 92

The deficiency has been drawn in part from patients paying more than cost, and the remainder from the General and other Funds, . . $40,792.50

TABLE No. 5.

The Income from Investments has been:—

From Annuities Receivable,	$10,272.77
City of Boston Bonds,	1,750.00
Mass. Hospital Life Ins. Co. Stock,	8,000.00
Railroad Bonds,	26,815.00
Manufacturing Stocks,	3,647.00
Bank Stocks,	1,627.93
Real Estate, Productive,	20,505.96
Notes Receivable,	19,246.63
Union League Club Bonds,	501.67
Interest,	1,832.51
	$94,199 47

Which has been distributed as follows:—

To Redman Fund,	$30,151.26
Warren Prize Fund,	186.25
Bowditch History Fund,	258.02
Wooden Leg Fund,	366.88
Redman Annuities,	936 00
Clara Barton Annuity,	214 72
Surgical Instrument Fund,	146.81
Amusement Fund,	662.50
Free Bed Funds, { for use, $29,142.01 / for Joy Annuities, 700.00	29,842.01
Beneficiaries at Asylum Funds,	4,951.05
Warren Library Fund,	80 59
Treadwell Library Fund,	331.25
One-half Lincoln Fund,—Female Beneficiaries,	5,631.25
Funds with Income Unrestricted,	2,650.00
General Fund,	8,300.40
Convalescent Fund, Building,	796.19
Convalescent Home Fund,	547.01
Asylum Building Fund,	8,147.28
	$94,199.47

The Income for 1880 was	$76,243.66
The Income for 1881 was	94,199.47

TABLE No. 6.

SUBSCRIBERS FOR FREE BEDS.

Theodore Lyman, ...	$100	*Amount brought up*, . . .	$5,700
William Amory, ...	100	J. Huntington Wolcott, . . .	100
Fitchburg Railroad Co., . .	100	Henry S. Shaw, ...	100
J. C. Gray, ...	100	Amory A. Lawrence, . . .	100
Miss Mary Wigglesworth, . .	200	J. Amory Lowell, ...	100
Miss Anne Wigglesworth, . .	200	W. O. Grover, ...	100
Union Railway Co., ...	100	Eastern Railroad Co., . . .	100
Boston & Providence R.R. Co.,	100	Charles Merriam, ...	100
Miss Mary Pratt, ...	100	Martin Brimmer, ...	100
George Higginson, . . .	100	W. D. Pickman	100
T. Jefferson Coolidge, . . .	100	C. H. Dalton, ...	100
H. P. Kidder, ...	200	Mrs. L. G. Wadsworth, . . .	100
F. H. Peabody, . . . ' . .	100	Nathaniel Thayer, ...	500
Boston & Maine Railroad Co.,	100	Henry Saltonstall, ...	100
S. D. Warren, ...	100	H. H. Fay, ...	100
Mrs. Gorham Brooks, . . .	100	Otis E. Weld, ...	100
James L. Little, ...	100	F. Gordon Dexter, ...	100
Shepherd Brooks, ...	100	W. Powell Mason, ...	100
Miss C. A. Brewer, ...	100	Thomas D. Quincy, ...	100
W. W. Tucker, ...	100	Greely S. Curtis, ...	100
J. G. Cushing, ...	100	R. C. Greenleaf, ...	100
Mrs. Anna C. Lodge, . . .	100	Henry Woods, ...	100
Moses Williams, ...	100	J. F. Anderson, ...	100
J. B. Glover, ...	100	Sarah S. Fay, ...	200
P. C. Brooks, Jr., ...	100	J. R. Coolidge, donation, . .	50
J. L. Gardner, Jr., ...	100	R. W. Hooper, ...	100
Mrs. Peter C. Brooks, . . .	100	Miss Josephine May, . . .	100
Miss Eunice Hooper, ...	100	J. G. Kidder, ...	100
Mass. Humane Society, . . .	600	Joseph Sawyer, ...	100
Mrs. E. B. Bowditch, . . .	200	Mrs. Ozias Goodwin, . . .	100
Samuel Johnson, ...	100	Miss Eliza Goodwin, ...	100
William Endicott, Jr., . . .	100	Mrs. Charles Merriam, . . .	100
Mrs. Charlotte A. Johnson, .	100	Miss Madeleine C. Mixter, ⎱	
George A. Gardner, ...	100	Miss Helen K. Mixter, ⎰ .	100
Miss A. W. Davis, ...	100	J. M. Sears, ...	100
Geo. W. Wales, ...	100	J. T. Coolidge, Jr., ...	100
J. L. Bremer, ...	100	J. Putnam Bradlee, ...	100
Dr. C. E. Ware, ...	100	F. L. Higginson, ...	100
George Dexter, . . . : .	200	Pacific Mills Board of Relief, .	200
F. R. Sears, ...	100	J. P. Squire & Co., ...	100
Mrs. Samuel Cabot, ...	100	W. S. Adams, ...	100
S. R. Payson, ...	100	Children of Mrs. H. Winsor,	
Henry B. Rogers, ...	100	donation, ...	400
Mrs. Edward Wigglesworth, .	100	Mrs. James Lawrence, . . .	100
Samuel Eliot, ...	100	Boston Gaslight Co., . . .	100
C. J. Morrill, ...	100	C. W. Amory, ...	100
Geo. D. Howe, . . ' . . .	100	Sarah B. Fay, ...	100
Amount carried up, . . .	$5,700		$10,950

Total Free Bed Subscriptions (96) in 1880, ... $11,300.00
Total Free Bed Subscriptions (93) in 1881, ... 10,950.00

TABLE No. 7.

LIBRARY ACCOUNT.

Paid for Books, ...	$525.51
Income Treadwell Library Fund, ...	331.25
Deficiency from General Fund, ...	$194.26

TABLE No. 8.

WOODEN LEG ACCOUNT.

The amount received for this purpose has been Income of the Wooden Leg Fund, ...	$366.88
The amount expended for Artificial Limbs has been, .	225.00
The surplus is credited to the fund, ...	$141.88

TABLE No. 9.

THE BOWDITCH HISTORY FUND.

Balance, December 31, 1880 : —		
Principal, ...	$2,000.00	
Income, ...	1,894.42	
		$3,894.42
Amount of Income received, ...	$258.02	
Amount of Income expended, ...	238.60	
		19.42
		$3,913.84
Balance, December 31, 1881 : —		
Principal, ...	$2,000.00	
Income, ...	1,913.84	
		$3,913.84

TABLE No. 10.

GENERAL FUND.

Balance, December 31, 1880, ...	$966,574.77	
Add one-third profits Mass. Hospital Life Ins. Co., . .	25,000.00	
Add donations and legacies, ...	27,005.97	
		$1,018,580.74
Less balance of premiums paid for Railroad Bonds and Bank Stocks, ...	$9,197.75	
Taxes on land at Belmont and Waltham, ...	600.61	
Transfer to Fund for Beneficiaries at Asylum, . . .	10.00	
Balance of Expenses over Income, ...	15,021.81	
		24,830.17
Balance, December 31, 1881, ...		$993,750.57

TABLE No. 11.

Income devoted to Free Beds:—

The Joy Fund, being a bequest from Miss Nabby Joy,	$20,000.00
Belknap Fund, being a bequest from Jeremiah Belknap,	10,000.00
Wm. Phillips Fund, being a bequest from Wm. Phillips,	5,000.00
Williams Fund, being a bequest from John D. Williams, of estate No. 17, Blackstone Street,	19,600.00
Bromfield Fund, being half of a bequest from John Bromfield,	20,000.00
Miss Townsend Fund, being a donation from the Executors of the will of Miss Mary P. Townsend,	11,486.50
Brimmer Fund, being a bequest from Miss Mary Ann Brimmer,	5,000.00
Wilder Fund, being a bequest from Charles W. Wilder,	12,000.00
Sever Fund, being a bequest from Miss Martha Sever,	500.00
Thompson Fund, being a bequest from S. B. Thompson,	500.00
Tucker Fund, being a bequest from Miss Margaret Tucker,	3,312.37
Davis Fund, being a bequest from Mrs. Eleanor Davis,	900.00
Loring Fund, being a bequest from Abigail Loring,	5,000.00
Nichols Fund, being a bequest from B. R. Nichols,	6,000.00
Gray Fund, being a donation from John C. Gray,	1,000.00
Dowse Fund, being a bequest from Thomas Dowse,	5,000.00
Todd Fund, being a bequest from Henry Todd,	5,000.00
J. Phillips Fund, being a bequest from Jonathan Phillips,	10,000.00
Greene Fund, being a bequest from Benj. D. Greene,	5,000.00
Percival Fund, being a bequest from John Percival,	950.00
Pickens Fund, being a bequest from John Pickens,	1,676.75
Treadwell Fund, being part of a bequest from J. G. Treadwell,	38,703.91
Raymond Fund, being a bequest from E. A. Raymond,	2,820.00
Amount carried forward,	$189,449.53

19

Amount brought forward, ...	$189,449.53
Harris Fund, being part of a bequest from Charles Harris, ...	1,000.00
Mason Fund, being a bequest from Wm. P. Mason,	9,400.00
Sawyer Fund, being part of a bequest from M. P. Sawyer, ...	7,000.00
J. L. Gardner Fund, being a donation from J. L. Gardner, ...	20,000.00
B. T. Reed Fund, being a donation from Benj. T. Reed, ...	1,000.00
Wm. Reed Fund, being a bequest from Wm. Reed,	5,233.92
McGregor Fund, being half of a donation and bequest from James McGregor, ...	7,500.00
Miss Rice Fund, being a bequest from Miss Arabella Rice, ...	5,000.00
Templeton Fund, being half of a bequest from John Templeton, ...	5,000.00
Mrs. J. H. Rogers Fund, being a donation from J. H. Rogers, ...	1,177.50
Beebe Fund, being a bequest from J. M. Beebe, .	50,000.00
Lincoln Fund, being half of a bequest from Mrs. F. W. Lincoln, ...	85,000.00
Blanchard Fund, being a bequest from Mrs. M. B. Blanchard, ...	4,000.00
George Gardner Fund, being a donation from George Gardner, ...	1,000.00
Hemenway Fund, being a donation from the Executors of the will of Augustus Hemenway, .	20,000.00
Jessup Fund, being part of a bequest from Dr. Chas. A. Jessup, ...	1,000.00
Tufts Fund, being a bequest from Quincy Tufts, .	10,000.00
Read Fund, being half of a bequest from Jas. Read,	1,000.00
Parker Fund, being a bequest from Jno. Parker, Jr.,	10,000.00
Miss Shaw Fund, being a donation and bequest from Miss M. Louisa Shaw, ...	5,500.00
Eliza Perkins Fund, being a donation from Mrs. H. B. Rogers, ...	1,000.00
Dwight Fund, being a donation from Mrs. T. Bradford Dwight, ...	1,000.00
Hunnewell Fund, being a donation from H. H. Hunnewell, ...	10,000.00
R. M. Mason Fund, being a bequest from R. M. Mason, ...	5,000.00
Anna Lowell Cabot Fund, being a donation from Dr. Samuel Cabot, ...	1,000.00
Welles Fund, being a donation from Miss Jane Welles, ...	5,000.00
Amount carried forward, ...	$462,260.95

Amount brought forward, ... $462,260.95

Income devoted to Beneficiaries at Asylum : —

The Bromfield Fund, being half of a bequest from
    John Bromfield, ... $20,000.00
Read Fund, being half of a bequest from Jas. Read,   1,000.00
Appleton Fund,
    $10,010 being a bequest from Sam'l Appleton,
    $20,000 being a donation from Wm. Appleton,   30,010.00
McGregor Fund, being half of a donation and
    bequest from James McGregor, ...   7,500.00
Austin Fund, being part of a bequest from Mrs.
    Agnes Austin, ...   5,000.00
Kittredge Fund, being a bequest from Rufus
    Kittredge, ...   5,500.00
Templeton Fund, being half of a bequest from
    John Templeton, ...   5,000.00
                             74,010.00

Income devoted to Female Beneficiaries at Asylum : —

The Lincoln Fund, being half of a bequest from Mrs.
    F. W. Lincoln, ...   85,000.00

Income unrestricted : —

The Waldo Fund, being a bequest from Daniel Waldo,   40,000.00

Income devoted to any purpose except buildings : —

The Redman Fund, being a bequest from John Redman,   455,113.34

Income devoted to a Triennial Prize : —

The Warren Prize Fund, being a bequest from Dr.
    J. M. Warren, ...   2,299.61

Income devoted to the Library : —

The Treadwell Library Fund, being part of a bequest
    from J. G. Treadwell, ...   5,000.00

Income devoted to Books for Patients : —

The Warren Library Fund, being a donation from
    Dr. J. C. Warren, ...   1,000.00

Income and Principal devoted to the publication of a History of the Hospital : —

The Bowditch History Fund, being a bequest from
    N. I. Bowditch, ...   2,000.00
        Amount carried forward, ... $1,126,683.90

Amount brought forward, ...	$1,126,683.90

Income devoted to Amusements at the Asylum: —

The Amusement Fund, $5,000 being a bequest from Miss Mary Louisa Shaw; $5,000 being a donation from Mrs. Quincy A. Shaw and other Ladies, ...   10,000.00

Income devoted to Special Surgical Instruments: —

The Surgical Instrument Fund, being a donation from Dr. H. J. Bigelow, $1,250 ; donation of Mr. R. M. Moore, $100, ...   1,350.00

The Wooden Leg Fund: —

Being a bequest from N. I. Bowditch, ...   5,000.00

The Convalescent Home Fund, . .   11,709.83

The Convalescent Home Building Fund, ...   85,038.85

Permanent Free Beds: —

Miss Marian Hovey, ...	$1,000.00	
Mrs. Fanny H. Morse,.	1,000.00	
Henry S. Hovey, ...	1,000.00	
Edward Woodman, ...	1,000.00	
		4,000.00

Redman Annuities, ...   15,600.00

Clara Barton Annuity, ...   3,241.00

Asylum Building Fund, ...   119,547.31

Add unused income at credit of

The Warren Prize Fund, ...	$698.06	
Warren Library Fund, ...	297.12	
Bowditch History Fund, ...	1,913.84	
Surgical Instrument Fund, ...	1,012.77	
Wooden Leg Fund, ...	679.69	
Convalescent Home Fund, ...	844.81	
Convalescent Home Fund Building, ...	1,014.31	
Asylum Building Fund, ...	11,576.27	
		18,036.87
Total of Restricted Funds, ...		$1,400,207.76

TRIAL BALANCE, Dec. 31, 1881.

Dr.

	Principal.
Land and Buildings for Asylum,	$320,794.75
Land and Buildings for Hospital,	485,472.73
Land at Belmont,	45,000.00
Buildings at Belmont,— Convalescent Home,	23,346.14
Land at Waltham,	11,200.00
Land at Chicago,	3,330.87
Annuities Receivable,	160,000.00
City of Boston Loan,	35,000.00
Insurance Stocks,	50,000.00
Delaware Mutual Insurance Co.'s Scrip,	365.00
Railroad Bonds,	480,600.00
Union League Club Bonds,	12,000.00
Manufacturing Stocks,	41,400.00
Bank Stocks,	38,250.00
Real Estate Productive,	352,391.64
Notes Receivable,	214,600.00
Cash in Bank, at Interest,	100,076.95
Edward Cowles, Superintendent,	33,249.39
J. H. Whittemore, Resident Physician,	1,818.35
Reversions (see item "Suspense" on Cr. side),	9.00
	$2,408,904.82

Cr.

	Principal.	Income.
Redman Fund,	$455,113.34	
Warren Prize Fund,	2,299.61	$698.06
Bowditch History Fund,	2,000.00	1,913.84
Wooden Leg Fund,	5,000.00	679.69
Redman Annuities,	15,600.00	
Clara Barton Annuity,	3,241.00	37.49
Surgical Instrument Fund,	1,350.00	1,012.77
Amusement Fund,	10,000.00	
Free Bed Funds,	462,260.95	
Warren Library Fund,	1,000.00	297.12
Beneficiaries at Asylum Funds,	74,010.00	
Treadwell Library Fund,	5,000.00	
Lincoln Fund,	85,000.00	
Funds with Income Unrestricted,	40,000.00	
Asylum Building Fund,	119,547.31	11,576.27
Fund for Convalescents, Miss Russell,	11,709.83	844.81
Convalescent Building Fund,	85,033.85	1,014.31
General Fund,	993,750.57	
Permanent Free Beds,	4,000.00	
Suspense (see item "Reversions" on Dr. side),	9.00	
Notes Payable,	11,000.00	
Subscribers for Free Beds, 1882,	3,900.00	
	2,390,830.46	
	$2,408,904.82	

Property on hand belonging to the Corporation, invested as follows : —

INVESTMENTS PRODUCING NO INCOME.

Asylum. —	Land and Buildings occupied for Asylum,	$320,794.75	
	Land in Belmont, ...	45,000.00	
	Buildings at Belmont, ...	23,346.14	
	Steward's balance, consisting of uncollected board bills, ...	33,249.39	
			$422,390.28
Hospital. —	Land and Buildings occupied for Hospital,	$485,472.73	
	Steward's balance, ...	1,818.35	
			487,291.08
Sundries. —	Land in Waltham, ...	$11,200.00	
	Memorandum of expectancies, ...	9.00	
	Land in Chicago, ...	3,330.87	
			14,539.87
			$924,221.23

INVESTMENTS PRODUCING INCOME.

Policies Mass. Hospital Life Insurance Co., ...	$160,000.00
500 Shares Mass. Hospital Life Insurance Co., . . .	50,000.00
$35,000 City of Boston Bonds, ...	35,000.00
$21,000 Eastern Railroad Bonds @ 70, ...	14,700.00
$1,000 Kansas City and Cameron Railroad Bonds, . .	1,000.00
$5,000 Boston and Lowell Railroad 7 ℛ cent. Bonds, .	5,000.00
$5,000 Boston and Albany Railroad 7 ℛ cent. Bonds, .	5,000.00
$100,000 Chicago, Bur. & Quincy R.R. 7 ℛ c. Bonds, .	100,000.00
$11,000 Chicago, Bur. & Quincy R.R. 5 ℛ c. Bonds @ 90,	9,900.00
$12,000 Union League Club Bonds, ...	12,000.00
$100,000 Atchison, Topeka & Santa Fé 7s., ...	100,000.00
$100,000 Atchison, Topeka & Santa Fé 4½s., ...	100,000.00
$100,000 Oregon R.R. & Navigation Co. 6s., ...	100,000.00
$22,000 Bur. & Mo. River R.R. in Neb. Non-Ex. 6s., .	22,000.00
$10,000 Atchison Land Grant 7s., ...	10,000.00
$10,000 Kan. City, Top. & Western R.R. 1st. M. 7s., .	10,000.00
$3,000 Old Colony Railroad 6s., ...	3,000.00
14 Shares Merrimack Manufacturing Co., ...	14,000.00
1 Share Appleton " "	1,000.00
9 Shares Amoskeag " "	9,000.00
9 " Amory ··	900.00
9 " Stark Mills	9,000.00
25 " Great Falls Manufacturing Co., ...	2,500 00
5 " Boston " "	5,000.00
100 " National Union Bank, ...	10,000.00
70 " Tremont National Bank, ...	7,000.00
50 " Old Boston " "	2,500.00
25 " Suffolk " "	2,500 00
Amount carried forward, ...	$801,000.00

Amount brought forward, ...	$801,000.00
100 Shares Columbian National Bank, ...	10,000.00
30 " Merchants " "	3,000.00
20 " New England National Bank, ...	2,000.00
5 " Massachusetts National Bank, ...	1,250.00
Land and Store, 17 Blackstone Street, ...	19,600.00
" " " 168 Washington Street, ...	45,000.00
" " House, 61 Dartmouth Street, ...	10,000.00
Hospital Wharf, ...	62,000.00
Redman Mansion Estate, Washington Street, . . .	106,000.00
Land and Houses on Warrenton Street, ...	17,700.00
" " Store, 496 Washington Street, ...	55,500.00
" " Houses, Chambers Street, ...	23,900.00
" " " 42–50 Cross Street, ...	12,691.64
Notes secured by Mortgage, ...	194,600.00
$20,000 Note of Phila , Wilmington & Balt. R.R., . .	20,000.00
$365 Scrip Delaware Mutual Insurance Co., ...	365.00
Cash deposited in bank at interest, ...	100,076.95

Investments producing Income, ...	$1,484,683.59
Investments producing no Income, ...	924,221.23
The exact foot of Trial Balance, ...	$2,408,904.82

D. R. WHITNEY, *Treasurer.*

TABLE OF THE EXPENSES OF THE HOSPITAL AND
ASYLUM FOR TWENTY YEARS,— 1862 TO 1881.

ORDINARY EXPENSES.

Year.	Cost of Paying Patients.	Cost of Free Patients.	Other Charities.	Total Expenses of	
	Hospital.	Hospital.	Hospital.	Hospital.	Asylum.
1862	$6,628.65	$35,072.01	$414.15	$42,114.81	$71,823.46
1863	6,151.27	40,575.14	695.30	. 47,421.71	69,300.63
1864	10,224.81	49,286.53	648.21	60,159.55	101,484.38
1865	23,119.62	34,131.83	717.35	57,968.80	120,885.84
1866	30,086.08	37,538.12	1,162.60	68,786.80	126,015.83
1867	26,086.67	33,758.02	1,164.53	61,009.22	133,844.14
1868	23,663.50	42,481.71	1,419.26	67,564.47	142,535.36
1869	20,128.86	40,736.44	1,373.30	62,238.60	138,132.02
1870	15,844.35	46,087.42	883.05	62,814.82	134,339.63
1871	15,266.51	47,126.12	1,133.74	63,526.37	146,191.23
1872	12,664.70	56,537.74	1,497.86	70,700.30	153,327.60
1873	16,681.66	69,109.97	2,135.29	87,926.92	165,023.79
1874	14,198.41	64,266.27	2,634.60	81,099.28	161,934.11
1875	10,677.72	71,447.23	1,761.59	83,886.54	165,660.47
1876	11,344.58	82,033.60	1,312.94	94,691.12	164,973.80
1877	10,833.10	72,678.63	279.16	83,790.89	143,148.94
1878	11,252.42	85,102.61	588.98	96,944.01	136,394.36
1879	11,564.44	77,216.88	514.25	89,295.57	117,250.02
1880	10,529.35	81,085.73	462.82	92,077.90	131,172.69
1881	13,462.12	88,241.17	450.51	102,153.80	134,561.14

Year.	Average cost per week per patient.		Cost over Board.	
	Hospital.	Asylum.	Hospital.	Asylum.
1862	$6.04	$7.27	$36,260.92	$6,640.81
1863	6.66	6.98	41,109.46	2,170.56
1864	8.38	9.76	52,445.01	4,523.85
1865	9.86	12.49	43,121.53	9,507.86
1866	13.88	12.30	53,809.36	558.19
1867	11.28	13.84	44,291.54	....
1868	12.74	16.51	52,893.02	14,642.07
1869	10.14	14.21	48,811.90	....
1870	10.05	13.83	50,811.01	....
1871	9.96	15.80	52,447.68	9,996.88
1872	10.10	16.93	59,547.91	14,917.57
1873	10.29	19.23	72,435 94	26,404.27
1874	10.13	19.59	67,548.81	2,750.66
1875	9.72	21.07	71,989.93	11,872.47
1876	9.41	19.72	82,027.86	13,019.51
1877	9.47	15.66	72,957.79	....
1878	9.87	15.55	83,516.61	....
1879	10.54	14.30	73,440.58	....
1880	10.39	16.48	79,280.61	10,078.33
1881	11.87	16.92	88,268.68	20,719.30

20 years, ... | $1,227,016.15 | $147,802.33

ANNUAL REPORT OF THE RESIDENT PHYSICIAN

OF THE

MASSACHUSETTS GENERAL HOSPITAL.

For the Year 1881.

Number of Patients in the Hospital, January 1, 1881.

Paying, ... 17

Free, ... 157

    Total, ... 174

Admitted from January 1, 1881, to January 1, 1882.

	Males.	Females.	Total.
Patients paying board, ...	279	123	402
Patients paying board part of the time, .	16	10	26
Patients entirely free, ...	1,073	605	1,678
	1,368	738	2,106

	Medical.	Surgical.
Males (Boys, 121), ...	434	934
Females (Girls, 50), ...	396	342
	830	1,276

Of these, 1 paid $52.50 per week; 7 paid $50; 2 paid $40; 13 paid $35; 1 paid $31.50; 3 paid $30; 2 paid $28; 4 paid $25; 57 paid $21; 1 paid $15; 9 paid $14; 1 paid $12; 74 paid $10.50; 11 paid $10; 1 paid $9; 1 paid $8; 1 paid $7.50; 167 paid $7; 5 paid $6; 33 paid $5; 12 paid $4.50; 12 paid $4; 3 paid $3.50; 4 paid $3; 4 paid $2.

Whole number of patients treated during the year: paying, 419; paying a part of the time, 26; free, 1,835; total, 2,270.

Discharged During the Year.

	Medical.	Surgical.	Male.	Female.	Total.
Well,	422	901	888	436	1,324
Much relieved,	132	102	133	100	233
Relieved,	100	94	118	78	196
Not relieved,	47	23	38	32	70
Not treated,	42	62	53	50	103
Dead,	93	97	138	51	189
Insane and eloped,	1	9	9	1	10
	837	1,288	1,377	748	2,125

Number of Patients remaining December 31, 1881.

Males,	102
Females,	53
Total,	155

Paying,	15
Free,	140
Total,	155

Medical,	54
Surgical,	101
Total,	155

Proportion of deaths to whole number of results, 8.89 per cent.

Number of patients received on account of accidents, 391.

The greatest number of paying patients at any one time was 39; in private rooms, 8; the greatest number of free patients, 168; the greatest total, 195. The least number of paying patients at any one time was 13; in private rooms, 1; the least free, 121; the least total, 139. The proportion of ward beds occupied by free patients was 81 per cent.; by paying patients, 19 per cent.; about 2.32 per cent. of the paying patients occupied private rooms.

The average number of patients was 166: males, 108; females, 58.

The average number of paying patients was 23: Americans, 16.1; foreigners, 6.9.

The average number in private rooms was 4.85.

The average number of free patients was 143: Americans, 68; foreigners, 75.

The average time of paying patients was 2.79 weeks, and that of free patients 4.41.

Residences.

Boston, ...	978
Massachusetts (excepting Boston), ...	970
Maine, ...	34
New Hampshire and Vermont, ...	49
Rhode Island and Connecticut, ...	19
Other States, ...	38
British Provinces, ...	18

Birthplaces.

Boston, ...	138
Massachusetts (excepting Boston), ...	531
Maine, ...	120
New Hampshire, ...	93
Vermont, ...	48
Rhode Island and Connecticut, ...	38
New York, ...	35
Southern and Western States, ...	71
Total Americans, ...	1,074

British Provinces, ...	252
Great Britain, ...	111
Ireland, ...	501
Germany, ...	37
Norway and Sweden, ...	39
France, ...	10
Western Islands, ...	7
Belgium and Holland, ...	2
Italy, ...	5
Switzerland, ...	1
Other places, ...	67
Total foreigners, ...	1,032

Occupation.

Males.	Paying.	Free.	Partial Payment.
Mechanics, ...	33	87	3
Laborers, ...	60	563	3
Farmers, ...	19	29	4
Minors, ...	18	120	2
Seamen, ...	25	43	
Clerks, ...	22	45	1
Teamsters, ...	12	24	
Traders, ...	12	36	2
Servants, ...	1	41	
Lawyers, ...	4	1	
Clergymen, ...	1		
Physicians, ...	6	2	
Merchants, ...	16	6	1
Students, ...	8	6	
Other professions, ...	42	70	
	279	1,073	16

Total males, 1,368. Of these, 71 were in private rooms.

Females.	Paying.	Free.	Partial Payment.
Domestics, ...	17	270	2
Minors, ...	11	43	
Wives, ...	58	161	4
Widows, ...	14	25	
Seamstresses, ...	9	32	1
Spinsters, ...	9	20	
Operatives, ...	1	14	
Teachers, ...	1	3	2
Clerks, ...	2	6	
Nurses, ...	1	31	1
	123	605	10

Total females, 738. Of these, 21 were in private rooms.

Sixteen per cent. of the free patients were female domestics; thirty-three per cent. were laborers; five per cent. were mechanics; and nine per cent. were minors.

Admissions Refused.

Phthisis (Consumption),	78
Syphilis,	31
Chronic Ulcers,	35
Scrofula and Abscesses,	14
Insanity and Delirium Tremens,	12
Hip and Spine,	38
Debility and Senility,	21
Chronic Rheumatism,	38
Paralysis,	38
Epilepsy,	11
Cancer,	18
Uterine,	23
Injuries,	8
Of skin,	21
Contagious,	29
Other diseases,	265
Total,	680

Males,	391
Females,	289
Americans,	426
Foreigners,	254
Residents of Boston,	248
Residents of Massachusetts,	344
Residents of other places,	88

Out-Patients.

Number of new patients,	18,443
Men,	6,745
Women,	7,730
Children,	3,968
Americans,	10,128
Foreigners,	8,315
Residents of Boston,	12,088
Of other places,	6,355
Medical department for women,	3,462
Medical department for men and children,	3,454
Surgical department,	4,599
Ophthalmic department,	462
Dental department,	4,048
Department for diseases of the skin,	1,089
Department for diseases of the nervous system,	426
Department for diseases of the throat,	903
Total attendance,	35,136

Average daily attendance, ... 114
Fractures and dislocations, ... 344
Wounds, ... 277
Sprains and injuries, ... 896
Abscesses, ... 378
Ulcers, ... 260
Felons, ... 217
Tumors, ... 256
Diseases of hip, ... 64
Diseases of spine, ... 61
Genito-urinary, ... 229
Club-foot, ... 11
Specific, ... 257
Hernia, ... 84
Necrosis, ... 33
Fistula in Ano, ... 33
Diseases of joints, ... 44
Referred, ... 419
Miscellaneous, ... 736

Of the dental patients, 758 had 1,229 teeth filled,
3,246 had 4,807 teeth extracted.

Whole number of new patients in the Out-Patient De-
partment in 1880, ... 20,566
Whole number of new patients in 1881, ... 18,443
Decrease in the number, ... 2,123

The new lodge at the Hospital entrance on Blossom Street, which was commenced in the early part
of the year, was completed and ready for use November 1. The result of this change at the entrance
to the Hospital has been most satisfactory, and
added much to the quiet and order of the house, as
people are now easily directed to the department
they seek, and do not wander blindly over the whole
institution.

Acting upon instructions received from the Board
of Trustees, I employed, on the first of April, a competent and experienced man to investigate the condi-

tion of every person who applied for admission to the Out-Patient Department for treatment, and with the following results : —

Number of applications for admission,	10,612
Number admitted,	9,220
Number refused,	1,392
Number of visits of investigation,	1,250
Number found deserving of charity,	705
Number found undeserving of charity,	545
Number sent to physicians' offices,	791

The greatest consideration for all applicants has been exercised, and no one excluded who did not themselves give sufficient proof that they were not objects of charity.

The Young Men's Christian Union has given us seventy-five "Drives for Patients," taking out three hundred and seventy-one individuals. Many other friends have often and in various ways most kindly remembered us. To all of them, we are very grateful.

Respectfully submitted,

JAMES H. WHITTEMORE,
Resident Physician.

BOSTON, Jan. 1, 1882.

THE AMBULANCE

OF THE

MASSACHUSETTS GENERAL HOSPITAL,

accompanied by a Medical Officer, will be despatched to any point north of Dover and Berkeley Streets, for the conveyance of cases of *accident* or *urgent sudden sickness, not contagious*, to this Hospital, or elsewhere, upon notice from a Physician, the Police, or other responsible source, subject to the approval of the undersigned.

In cases requiring gratuitous treatment, no charge will be made.

By order of the Board of Trustees.

JAMES H. WHITTEMORE,
Resident Physician,
Mass. Gen. Hospital, Blossom Street.

34

TABLE SHOWING THE COST OF THE PRINCIPAL STORES AT THE MASSACHUSETTS GENERAL HOSPITAL.

Articles.	1877.			1878.			1879.			1880.			1881.		
	Quantity.	Cost.	Average.	Quantity.	Cost.	Average.	Quantity.	Cost.	Average.	Quantity.	Cost.	Average.	Quantity.	Cost.	Average.
Beef, Sin, . . lbs.	9,100	$1,927.38	.2118	7,729	$1,610.72	.2084	8,375	$1,716.87	.205	8,815	$1,692.99	.1941	8,658	$1,792.20	.207
" for Soup, . "	560	23.80	.0425	132	5.28	.04	...	...	...	...	...	...	...	...	...
" Corned, . "	5,889	479.54	.0816	4,378	324.72	.07415	123	288.61	.07	4,952	346.64	.07	5,183	367.99	.07
" Round, . "	9,327	805.85	.0864	11,944	1,016.43	.0851	12,973	1,054.70	.0813	16,414	1,148.98	.07	19,477	1,636.06	.084
" Rump, . "	6,882	1,163.05	.169	4,158	635.34	.1528	14,141	1,341.98	.0949	16,439	1,643.90	.10	16,438	1,758.86	.107
" Roasting, . "	11,584	1,274.24	.11	14,998	1,349.82	.09	12,592	1,385.12	.11	15,522	1,876.60	.1208	21,093	2,720.99	.129
Mn, . . "	18,416	2,509.04	.13624	15,808	1,903.28	.1204	14,488	2,433.98	.168	13,682	2,123.44	.1552	13,562	2,278.41	.168
Poultry, . . "	13,509	2,475.65	.184	14,079	2,276.57	.1617	10,526	2,589.39	.246	11,011	3,366.06	.3057	11,129	3,505.63	.315
Veal, . . "	10,056	2,644.72	.263	10,156	2,500.40	.2462	4,392	843.26	.192	4,214	866.39	.2056	4,401	1,188.27	.26
Eggs, . . doz.	4,608	967.08	.21	5,495	967.12	.176	37	266.80	7.40	51	440.15	8.65	49	468.73	9.565
Flour, . . bbls.	40	362.48	9.062	42	323.82	7.71	36,556	1,827.80	.05	40,536	2,026.80	.05	34,892	1,744.60	.05
Bread, . . lbs.	34,343	1,717.15	.05	35,800	1,790.00	.05	271¾	714.70	2.63	280½	1,297.56	4.63	306	887.55	2.91
Ice, . . tons	180½	627.65	3.48	238½	808.25	3.333	15,462	1,189.32	.769	21,005	2,003.87	.0954	20,552	1,901.06	.09
Sugar, . . lbs.	10,592	982.88	.0928	12,979	1,023.65	.0781	848	337.82	.398	1,134½	471.95	.416	555	244.22	.44
Ta, . . "	593	222.96	.376	738	254.61	.345	96,186	4,934.34	.0513	89,904½	4,495.22½	.05	92,350	4,617.50	.05
Milk, . . qts.	97,594	4,879.70	.05	107,618	5,380.90	.05	942	1,010.76	1.073	1,039½	902.58	.868	981	1,101.66	1.125
Potatoes, . . bush.	909	915.36	1.007	973	964.61	.77									

SIXTY-FOURTH ANNUAL REPORT

OF THE

SUPERINTENDENT OF THE MCLEAN ASYLUM FOR THE INSANE,

TO THE

TRUSTEES OF THE MASS. GENERAL HOSPITAL,

For the Year 1881.

TO THE TRUSTEES OF THE MASSACHUSETTS GENERAL HOSPITAL:

Gentlemen, — The following report, with tabular statements relating to the number and condition of the patients treated in the Asylum during the year 1881, is respectfully presented: —

TABLE No. 1.

GENERAL STATISTICS OF THE YEAR.

	Males.	Females.	Total.
Patients in the Asylum, Jan. 1, 1881, ...	67	87	154
Admissions within the year, ...	29	37	66
Whole number of *cases* within the year, ...	96	124	220
Discharged within the year, ...	33	32	65
Namely,— as Recovered, ...	6	8	14
Much improved, ...	3	3	6
Improved, ...	10	7	17
Unimproved, ...	7	7	14
Deaths, ...	7	7	14
Patients remaining Dec. 31, 1881, } supported as private patients, }	63	92	155
Number of different *persons* within the year, . .	94	121	215
" " " " admitted, ...	29	34	63
" " " " recovered, ...	5	8	13
Daily average number of patients, ...	62.84	86.93	149.77

During the year, one woman was twice, another three times, admitted. One man and one woman were each twice discharged, and one man was discharged and readmitted. There were two hundred and twenty cases treated, representing two hundred and fifteen persons.

Of the sixty-three persons admitted, forty were regarded as recent cases, and twenty-three as chronic or as incurable at the time of admission.

Forty-six persons, nineteen men and twenty-seven women, had never before been in any hospital. Of the remaining twenty cases, nine, five men and four women, were admitted for the second time; three, one man and two women, for the third time; two, one man and one woman, for the fifth time; one man for the eighth; one woman for the ninth, tenth, and eleventh times respectively; one man for the seventeenth, and one for the twentieth time. These twenty cases represent seventeen persons, as the nine second admissions represent eight persons, and the ninth, tenth, and eleventh admissions were of one and the same individual. Of these seventeen persons, eight, four men and four women, had formerly been inmates of this Asylum.

There were fifteen more admissions, seventeen more discharges, and eighteen more cases under treatment than during the year 1880; and the number present was one more at the end than the beginning of the year.

Of those discharged, eleven, seven men and four women, were transferred to other hospitals,— four men and three women to Danvers and three men and one woman to private asylums. Of the thirteen persons discharged recovered, eight had never before been inmates of any hospital, and five had been inmates of this Asylum.

Of the fourteen deaths during the year, nine were of elderly persons, from fifty-nine to eighty-three years of age. Some had been long resident in the

Asylum, and most of them died from causes other than cerebral disease. Of the more recently admitted cases of those resulting in death, only one, terminating by exhaustion from mania, gave any promise of recovery when admitted.

Nine persons were admitted and discharged recovered within the year. In general, it may be said that there were more persons admitted, and a much larger proportion of them were acute cases, than during the preceding year.

The work of renovation and repairs, for the purpose of putting all parts of the Asylum in a thoroughly comfortable condition, has been diligently carried on during the past year, notwithstanding the purpose of building a new asylum elsewhere in the near future. Not only this, but, as the work proceeds, all practicable alterations of construction, with the introduction of modern improvements for increasing the comfort and attractiveness of the wards, are being made. For example, one of the oldest of the women's wards in the Asylum, being a long and rather dark hall, with a window at one end and rooms on either side, has been changed in its whole aspect, and made cheerful and pleasant by the use of bright colors in its decoration, by plants and birds and by an alcove in place of one of the rooms on the sunny side of the house. A window as wide as the alcove, and extending from floor to ceiling, has panes of ordinary glass 17x29 inches in dimensions, and is so arranged as to be opened both at top and bottom twenty-nine inches. These open spaces are covered by outside screens of fine wire gauze, such as is customarily used in the windows of private houses, in the summer season. Some windows of other wards and rooms have, during the past two years, been protected in the same way, in place of the iron guards which have been removed. The objection to the common plan in foreign asylums, of limiting the opening of windows to five or six inches, which is inadmissible during the hot summer months in this climate, is thus overcome.

The dining-room of the reconstructed ward above described has been decorated in bright colors, and the iron guards removed from the windows, which have been fitted with large panes of glass, together with some small colored ones, giving a pleasing effect. A similar change is being made in the chambers of the ward, as to the removal of guards and use of large glass in the windows, which are here provided with concealed shutters, for use in cases requiring them, but so constructed that the windows may be left fully open and the fresh air may freely enter the rooms during the night in hot weather.

Similar alterations, introducing alcoves, changing windows, etc., are in progress in other wards, to the effect of letting in more sunlight and fresh air, and greatly increasing the cheerfulness and comfort of the house.

Some progress has been made in the direction of enlarging the freedom of patients. A door leading from the five principal wards for men has been fitted with an ordinary handle, and remains unlocked nearly all day, permitting free egress of the occupants of those wards to the large garden, which is not a secure enclosure. Two persons only have taken advantage of this opportunity to escape, and one of these returned voluntarily in a few days.

Since early in the year, the door of the Appleton ward for gentlemen has been left unlocked during the day. This building stands upon the open grounds of the Asylum; and, though its door is unlocked and some of its windows are without guards, no trouble has arisen in consequence.

As usual, during the year a number of patients have been placed on parole, with the privilege of going outside the Asylum grounds. Permission has been freely given for patients to make short visits to their friends at home, with beneficial results; and very little restriction has been placed upon their receiving the visits of their friends at the Asylum.

In regard to the attendance upon the patients, some experiments, that have been tried during the past two years, have given gratifying results. Ward-maids are now employed, after the manner of the training schools for nurses in general hospitals, in all the female wards of the house. As a consequence, the attendants, being relieved of a good deal of their former work, have more time to devote to the patients, and are made more strictly nurses and companions of the sick.

In the male wards also, some important results have been gained. On a few occasions heretofore, the wife of a supervisor has been allowed to reside here, and has had some special duty given her. A few years ago, a nurse was placed in one of the wards, where she had the care of the dining-room and some association with the patients, and the results gave some favorable indications.

During the past year, the plan of employing female nurses in the men's wards has been successfully developed and its possibilities established. The difficulties that have been supposed to exist in the way of doing all that is desirable in this direction are two-fold:—first, the possible impropriety in associating female nurses with insane men; and, second, a practical difficulty in administration, in accommodating the duties of male and female attendants, the one to the other, in a harmonious way. I found these generally regarded as controlling objections by the superintendents of some fifteen or more of the English, Scotch, and French hospitals, which I had the privilege of visiting two years ago, when I made this subject one of my special points of inquiry, having then already determined to carry out such a plan here. It was granted that it would be a good thing, but nowhere had the plan been put to a complete practical test in the general wards of an asylum. Dr. Bayley at Northampton, England, employed a few women as " bed-makers "; and Dr. Batty Tuke, at Saughton Hall in Scotland, was just then trying the experiment of employing a lady to act in a social capacity among the gentlemen in his private asylum.

My plan is to choose a matronly, ladylike, discreet, and amiable woman, and to place in her charge all the housekeeping duties of two adjoining wards. These duties include the sole and undivided control of two dining-rooms, the charge of the ordinary housekeeping, care of the wards themselves, and their appurtenances, and of the chambers, the bed-making, etc. She is assisted by one or more wardmaids, whom she directs in their work, and by the assistant male attendants. She presides at the table, and contributes to the social life of the wards as if she were *mistress* of the house. There is a head attendant, however, who is *master* of the ward, who has general control of its affairs, the immediate charge of the patients and of his assistants. The nurse takes her turn in watching the ward when other attendants are absent, and thus in many ways satisfactorily fills the place of a male attendant.

It is found that, by thus defining the duties and making the arrangement conform to that of the ordinary way of life in a private household, matters go on smoothly, with proper persons in charge.

There are now four women employed in the male wards, whose duties require their presence there at all times of the day and evening. From the experience gained here in associating nurses with insane men, I am able to say that there is no reason why this cannot be done with great benefit in all our wards, excepting one for some special cases.

The results gained are better than were expected. Not only is the more obvious advantage derived of giving the place the homelike appearance due to woman's presence, and its consequent influence upon the patients, which is directly curative in leading them to practice better self-control, but the influence upon the male attendants is equally marked as making them more considerate and gentlemanly in their deportment.

Much attention has been given to the subject of the occupation of the patients, which, for those of the class in this Asylum, is with difficulty extended beyond some form of recreation. The usual variety of entertainments, concerts, exhibitions, and dancing parties attended by both ladies and gentlemen have been given. Open air concerts were given in the evening every two weeks during the summer, in the large garden, and were greatly enjoyed by all the inmates of the Asylum. Picnic parties and boating parties to Spot Pond were of frequent occurrence during the summer. Later in the season, parties have been sent to afternoon concerts and other entertainments in Boston. The customary carriage excursions for ladies and gentlemen have been sent out twice daily in all pleasant weather, during the year; and some of the patients are accustomed to take daily drives in private conveyances furnished them.

In other ways, the gentlemen find occupation in walking, reading, playing games, and in the billiard-room and bowling alley, where some gymnastic appliances are soon to be introduced. The ladies are more readily employed in sewing, knitting, embroidery, reading, playing billiards, etc. Classes in drawing and singing have recently been formed, which are well attended, and have aroused a good deal of interest.

The introduction of medical internes, a year and a half ago, has proved a very satisfactory and valuable addition to the medical staff. Two such officers act as clinical clerks, make daily visits to the wards, and do other clinical work, such as is required in general hospitals.

To the friends of the Asylum, who have manifested their continued interest in its welfare and progress, sincere and grateful thanks are due.

Very respectfully,

EDWARD COWLES,
Superintendent.

TABLE No. 2.

MONTHLY ADMISSIONS, DISCHARGES, AND AVERAGES.

Months.	Admissions.			Discharges (including Deaths).			Daily Average of Patients in the House.		
	Males.	Females.	Total.	Males.	Females.	Total.	Males.	Females.	Total.
January, .	1	3	4	2	2	4	66.09	87.52	153.61
February, .	2	3	5	5	2	7	64.93	86.39	151.32
March, . .	3	2	5	1	3	4	63.19	88.81	152.00
April, . .	2	5	7	..	1	1	65.30	87.60	152.90
May, . .	2	3	5	3	4	7	63.49	89.74	153.23
June, . .	2	4	6	4	8	12	61.30	89.03	150.33
July, . . .	1	..	1	1	2	3	60.36	84.48	144.84
August, . .	3	3	6	4	2	6	59.26	84.87	144.13
September,	5	1	6	2	..	2	61.23	84.47	145.70
October, .	3	2	5	1	4	5	61.89	83.56	145.45
November, .	2	6	8	2	1	3	63.73	85.70	149.43
December, .	3	5	8	8	3	11	63.39	90.93	154.32
Total *cases*,	29	37	66	33	32	65	62.84	86.93	149.77
Total *persons*,	29	34	63	32	31	63	....	....	....

TABLE No. 3.

RECEIVED ON FIRST AND SUBSEQUENT ADMISSIONS.

Number of the Admission.	Cases Admitted.			Times previously Recovered.		
	Males.	Females.	Total.	Males.	Females.	Total.
First, ...	19	27	46	..	..	..
Second.	5	4	9	1	2	3
Third, ...	1	2	3	..	4	4
Fifth, ...	1	1	2	..	3	3
Eighth, ...	1	..	1	6	..	6
Ninth, ...	..	1	1	..	..	..
Tenth, ...	..	1	1	..	..	..
Eleventh, ...	..	1	1	..	..	..
Seventeenth, ...	1	..	1	16	..	16
Twentieth, ...	1	..	1	..	..	..
Total of *cases*, . . .	29	37	66	23	9	32
Total of *persons*, . .	29	34	63	..	..	..

These 32 recoveries represent 8 persons, 2 having recovered 2, one 3, one 6, and another 16 times.

TABLE No. 4.

AGES OF PERSONS ADMITTED FOR THE FIRST TIME.

Ages.	At first attack of Insanity.			When admitted.		
	Males.	Females.	Total.	Males.	Females.	Total.
Fifteen years and less,	1	..	1	1	..	1
From 15 to 20 years,	..		3	..	1	1
" 20 to 25 "	1		6	1	6	7
" 25 to 30 "	3		6	2	2	4
" 30 to 35 "	2		4	2	3	5
" 35 to 40 "	5		11	6	6	12
" 40 to 50 "	2		7	2	5	7
" 50 to 60 "	3	8	6	3	4	7
" 70 to 80 "	1	..	1	1	..	1
" 80 to 90 "	1	..	1	1	..	1
Total of *persons*, .	19	27	46	19	· 27	46

TABLE No. 5.

RESIDENCE OF PERSONS ADMITTED.

Places.	Males.	Females.	Total.
Massachusetts: —			
Suffolk County, ...	7	13	20
Middlesex County,.	7	9	16
Bristol County, ...	1	1	2
Norfolk County, ...	1	1	2
Worcester County, ...	..	1	1
Essex County, ...	5	2	7
Plymouth County, ...	..	2	2
Maine, ...	1	..	1
New Hampshire, ...	2	1	3
Rhode Island, ...	1	..	1
New York, ...	..	1	1
South Carolina, ...	..	1	1
Wisconsin, ...	1	..	1
California, ...	..	1	1
Nova Scotia, ...	2	..	2
Canada, ...	1	..	1
Peru, ...	..	1	1
Total of *persons*, ...	29	34	63

TABLE No. 6.

CIVIL CONDITION OF PERSONS ADMITTED.

Number of the Admission.	Unmarried.			Married.			Widowed.		
	Males.	Females.	Total.	Males.	Females.	Total.	Males.	Females.	Total.
First, . .	5	8	13	12	16	28	2	2	4
Second, . .	2	2	4	3	2	5	..	..	..
Third, . .	1	1	2	..	1	1	..	..	..
Fifth, . .	1	1	2	..	..	..	..	..	..
Eighth, . .	1	..	1	..	..	..	..	..	..
Ninth, . .	..	..	..	..	..	..	..	1	1
Seventeenth,	1	..	1	..	..	..	..	..	..
Twentieth,	1	..	1	..	..	..	..	..	..
Total *persons*,	12	12	24	15	19	34	2	3	5

TABLE No. 7.

OCCUPATIONS OF PERSONS ADMITTED.

Occupations.	Males.	Females.	Total.
Housewife, ...	..	17	17
Clerk, ...	5	..	5
Publisher, ...	1	..	1
Merchant, ...	8	..	8
Farmer, ...	2	..	2
Stenographer, ...	1	..	1
Artist, ...	..	1	1
Milliner, ...	..	1	1
Mechanic, ...	2	..	2
Machinist, ...	2	..	2
Servant, ...	..	3	3
Seamstress, ...	..	1	1
Civil Engineer, ...	1	..	1
No occupation, ...	7	11	18
Total of *persons*, ...	29	34	63

TABLE No. 8.

REPORTED DURATION OF INSANITY BEFORE LAST ADMISSION.

Previous Duration.	First Admission to any Hospital.			All other Admissions.			Total.		
	Males.	Females.	Total.	Males.	Females.	Total.	Males.	Females.	Total.
Congenital, .	..	..	..	2	..	2	2	.	2
Under 1 mo.,	6	5	11	..	..	..	6	5	11
Fr. 1 to 3 mo.,	3	11	14	..	..	..	3	11	14
" 3 " 6 "	3	5	8	1	1	2	4	6	10
" 6 " 12 "	2	2	4	..	1	1	2	3	5
" 1 " 2 yrs.,	2	2	4	1	2	3	3	4	7
" 2 " 5 "	2	2	4	2	3	5	4	5	9
" 5 " 10 "	..	..	..	3	..	3	3	..	3
"10 " 20 "	1	..	1	1	..	1	2	..	2
"20 " 30 "	..	..	..	..	3	3	..	3	3
Total cases, .	19	27	46	10	10	20	29	37	66
Total persons,	..	..	..	10	8	18	29	34	63
Average of known persons (in years).	1.45	.52	.98	8.9	4.7	6.8			

TABLE No. 9.

FORM OF DISEASE IN THE CASES ADMITTED.

Form of Disease.	Males.	Females.	Total.
Mania, acute, ...	9	14	23
Mania, chronic, ...	4	1	5
Mania, hysterical, ...	..	3	3
Mania, puerperal, ...	..	1	1
Mania, recurrent, ...	..	1	1
Melancholia, acute, ...	6	11	17
Melancholia, chronic, ...	1	4	5
Dementia, chronic, ...	1	1	2
General Paralysis, ...	4	1	5
Epilepsy, ...	2	..	2
Imbecility, ...	2	..	2
Total of cases, ...	29	37	66
Total of persons, ...	29	34	63

TABLE No. 10.

ALLEGED CAUSES OF INSANITY IN PERSONS ADMITTED.

Causes.	Males.	Females.	Total.
Mental.			
Overstudy, ...	2	1	3
Grief, ...	..	1	1
Anxiety, ...	4	4	8
Spiritualism, ...	..	1	1
Physical.			
Ill-health, ...	3	5	8
Over-work, ...	1	4	5
Constitutional, ...	2	3	5
Change of life, ...	..	2	2
Child-birth, ...	..	2	2
Blow on the head, ...	2	..	2
Hemiplegia, ...	2	..	2
Epilepsy, ...	1	..	1
Syphilis, ...	1	..	1
Sunstroke, ...	1	..	1
Masturbation, ...	1	..	1
Congenital, ...	3	..	3
Unknown, ...	6	11	17
Total of *persons*, ...	29	34	63

TABLE No. 11.

RELATION TO HOSPITALS OF THE PERSONS ADMITTED.

	Males.	Females.	Total.
Never before in any Hospital, ...	19	27	46
Former inmates of this Hospital, ...	4	4	8
Former inmates of other Hospitals in this State : —			
Danvers, ...	1	..	1
South Boston, ...	..	1	1
Worcester, ...	..	1	1
Former inmates of Hospitals in other States, . .	1	..	1
Former inmates of this Hospital and of other Hospitals in this State : —			
Danvers, ...	1	..	1
South Boston, ...	1	..	1
Former inmates of this Hospital and of Hospitals in other States, ...	2	4	6
Total of *cases*, ...	29	37	66
Total of *persons*, ...	29	34	63

TABLE No. 12.

DISCHARGES CLASSIFIED BY ADMISSION AND RESULT.

Admission.	Recovered.			Much Improved.			Imp'd.			Imp'd.			Died.			Total.		
	Males.	Females.	Total.	Males.	Females.	Total.	Males.	Females.	Total.	Mos.	Females.	Total.	Males.	Females.	Total.	Males.	Females.	Total.
First,	4	4	8	1	1	2	8	4	12	6	6	12	7	5	12	26	20	46
Second,	..	..	..	1	..	1	2	2	4	..	1	1	..	2	2	3	5	8
Third,	..	2	2	..	1	1	..	..	..	1	..	1	..	..	..	1	3	4
Fourth,	..	1	1	..	..	..	..	..	..	..	..	..	..	..	..	..	1	1
Fifth,	..	1	1	..	..	..	..	..	..	..	..	..	..	..	..	..	1	1
Eighth,	..	..	..	1	..	1	..	..	..	..	..	..	..	..	..	1	..	1
Tenth,	..	..	..	..	1	1	..	..	..	..	..	..	..	..	..	..	1	1
Eleventh,	..	..	..	..	..	..	..	1	1	..	..	..	..	..	..	..	1	1
Sixteenth,	1	..	1	..	..	..	..	..	..	..	..	..	..	..	..	1	..	1
Seventeenth,	1	..	1	..	..	..	..	..	..	..	..	..	..	..	..	1	..	1
Total of *cases*,	6	8	14	3	3	6	10	7	17	7	7	14	7	7	14	33	32	65
Total of *persons*,	5	8	13	3	2	5	..	..	..	..	..	..	..	..	..	32	31	63

49

TABLE No. 13.

CASES DISCHARGED RECOVERED.— DURATION.

Period.	Duration before Admission.			Hospital Residence.			Whole Duration from the Attack.		
	Males.	Females.	Total.	Males.	Females.	Total	Males.	Females	Total.
Under 1 month	4	5	9	2	1	3	2	..	2
From 1 to 3 mo.	1	2	3	2	3	5	1	3	4
" 3 " 6 "	1	..	1	1	1	2	2	2	4
" 6 " 12 "	..	..	..	1	2	3	..	1	1
" 1 " 2 years	..	1	1	..	1	1	1	1	2
" 2 " 5 "	..	..	..	..	..	..	..	1	1
Total *cases* . .	6	8	14	6	8	14	6	8	14
Total *persons* .	5	8	13	5	8	13	5	8	13
Average of known cases (in months).	1.35	2.85	2.1	2.76	5.06	3.91	4.11	7.92	6.01

TABLE No. 14.

CASES RESULTING IN DEATH.— DURATION.

Period.	Duration before Admission.			Hospital Residence.			Whole Duration from the Attack.		
	Males.	Females.	Total.	Males.	Females.	Total.	Males.	Females.	Total.
Under 1 month	2	1	3	1	1	2	..	..	..
From 1 to 3 mo.	..	2	2	2	..	2	1	1	2
" 3 " 6 "	2	..	2	..	1	1	..	..	..
" 6 " 12 "	1	2	3	1	2	3	2	1	3
" 1 " 2 years	1	..	1	..	1	1	1	1	2
" 2 " 5 "	..	2	2	1	1	2	..	3	3
" 5 " 10 "	..	..	..	..	1	1	..	1	1
" 20 " 25 "	1	..	1	1	..	1	1	..	1
" 25 " 30 "	..	..	..	..	..	..	1	..	1
" 30 " 35 "	..	..	..	1	..	1	1	..	1
Total	7	7	14	7	7	14	7	7	14
Average of known cases (in months).	7.39	10.93	9.16	105.86	19.21	62.53	152.50	30.14	91.32

TABLE No. 15.

CASES DISCHARGED BY RECOVERY OR DEATH.

Form of Insanity.	Recoveries.			Deaths.		
	Males.	Females.	Total.	Males.	Females.	Total.
Mania, acute, ...	4	4	8	3	1	4
Mania, chronic, ...	..	..	..	2	1	3
Mania, hysterical, ...	..	2	2	..	..	..
Melancholia, acute, ...	2	2	4	..	..	..
Melancholia, chronic, ...	..	..	.	..	3	3
Dementia, chronic, ...	..	..	..	1	2	3
General Paralysis, ...	..	..	..	1	..	1
Total of *cases*, ...	6		14	7	7	14
Total of *persons*, ...	5	8	13	..	..	..

TABLE No. 16.

CAUSES OF DEATH.

Causes.	Males.	Females.	Total.
Cerebral Disease.			
General Paralysis, ...	1	..	1
Chronic Arachnitis, ...	..	1	1
Exhaustion from Mania, ...	2	1	3
Cerebral Hemorrhage, ...	1	..	1
Thoracic Disease.			
Phthisis Pulmonalis, ...	..	3	3
Heart Disease, ...	..	1	1
Pneumonia, ...	1	..	1
Other Causes.			
Senile Gangrene, ...	1	..	1
Cirrhosis of the Liver, ...	1	..	1
Burns (suicidal), ...	..	1	1
Totals, ...	7	7	14

TABLE No. 17.

DEATHS, CLASSIFIED BY RESULTS OF PREVIOUS ADMISSIONS.

Number of the Admission.	Recovered.			Unimproved.			Total.		
	Males.	Females.	Total.	Males.	Females.	Total.	Males.	Females.	Total.
First, . .	..	1	1	..	1	1	..	2	2
Total, . .	..	1	1	..	1	1	..	2	2

TABLE No. 18.

RECOVERIES, CLASSIFIED BY RESULTS OF PREVIOUS ADMISSIONS.

Number of the Admission.	Recovered.			Much Improved.			Improved.			Total.		
	Ma.	Fe.	Tot.	Ma.	Fe.	Tot.	Ma.	Fe.	Tot.	Ma.	Fe.	Tot.
Third, ...	..	1	1	..	1	1	..	..	..	..	2	2
Fourth, ...	..	1	1	..	..	..	..	..	..	..	1	1
Fifth, ...	..	..	..	..	..	..	..	1	1	..	1	1
Sixteenth, ...	1	..	1	..	..	..	..	..	..	1	..	1
Seventeenth, . . .	1	..	1	..	..	..	..	..	..	1	..	1
Total of *persons*, .	2	2	4	..	1	1	..	1	1	2	4	6

TABLE No. 19.

DEATHS, CLASSIFIED BY DURATION OF INSANITY AND OF TREATMENT.

Period.	Duration of Insanity.			Whole known period of Hospital Residence.		
	Males.	Females.	Total.	Males.	Females.	Total.
Congenital, ...	..	..	..	..	..	..
Under 1 month, . .	..	..	..	1	1	2
From 1 to 3 months,	1	1	2	2	..	2
" 3 to 6 " .	1	..	1	..	1	1
" 6 to 12 " .	1	1	2	1	2.	3
" 1 to 2 years, .	1	1	2	..	1	1
" 2 to 5 " .	..	3	3	1	1	
" 5 to 10 " .	..	1	1	..	1	1
" 20 to 30 " .	2	..	2	1	..	1
" 30 to 40 " .	1	..	1	1	..	1
Total, ...	7	7	14	7	7	14
Average of known cases (in months).	153	29.55	91.27	105.86	19.21	62.53

TABLE No. 20.

AGES OF THOSE WHO DIED.

Ages.	At time of the first attack.			At time of Death.		
	Males.	Females.	Total.	Males.	Females.	Total.
From 20 to 25 years .	..	1	1	..	..	..
" 25 to 30 " .	1	2	3	1	..	1
" 30 to 35 " .	.	..		..	2	2
" 35 to 40 " .	2	..	2	1	..	1
" 40 to 50 " .	1	1	2	..	1	1
" 50 to 60 " .	1	1	2	..	2	2
" 60 to 70 " .	..	2	2	1	2	3
" 70 to 80 " .	1	..	1	2	..	2
" 80 to 90 " .	1	..	1	2	..	2
Total, ...	7	7	14	7	7	14

TABLE OF ADMISSIONS, DISCHARGES, AND RESULTS AT THE McLEAN ASYLUM,

FROM ITS OPENING, OCTOBER 6, 1818, TO DECEMBER 31, 1881, INCLUSIVE.

Years.	Ad-mitted.	Dis-charged.	Whole No. under care.	Died.	Much im-proved, etc.	Re-covered.	Remaining at end of year.	Average No. of Patients.
1818–25	398	344	623	29	205	110	279	· ·
1826	47	46	101	5	21	20	55	· ·
1827	58	56	113	5	17	34	57	· ·
1828	77	65	134	5	37	23	69	· ·
1829	73	77	142	9	42	26	65	· ·
1830	82	78	147	10	34	34	69	· ·
1831	83	84	152	8	46	30	68	· ·
1832	94	98	162	10	45	43	64	· ·
1833	103	100	167	8	50	42	67	· ·
1834	108	95	174	7	47	41	80	· ·
1835	83	84	163	11	28	45	77	· ·
1836	106	112	183	10	38	64	71	· ·
1837	120	105	191	8	25	72	86	80
1838	138	131	224	12	45	74	93	95
1839	132	117	225	10	38	69	108	112
1840	155	138	263	13	50	75	125	128
1841	157	141	283	11	55	75	142	135
1842	129	138	271	15	43	80	133	143
1843	126	126	260	18	45	63	134	131
1844	158	140	292	20	52	68	152	146
1845	119	120	271	13	33	74	151	149
1846	148	126	299	9	52	65	173	164
1847	170	170	343	33	50	87	173	172
1848	143	155	316	23	50	82	155	171
1849	160	137	321	15	58	64	184	177
1850	173	157	357	28	51	78	200	201
1851	164	173	364	29	69	75	191	195
1852	145	135	336	15	48	72	201	200
1853	114	120	315	17	45	58	195	194
1854	120	120	315	16	45	59	195	195
1855	123	126	318	24	46	56	192	192
1856	149	145	341	19	58	68	196	195
1857	141	159	337	28	60	71	178	191
1858	155	147	333	25	50	72	186	187
1859	131	142	317	28	53	61	175	185
1860	121	109	296	24	46	39	187	185
1861	111	110	298	23	33	54	188	193
1862	82	94	270	18	37	39	176	190
1863	94	69	270	13	20	36	201	191
1864	101	107	302	27	38	42	195	200
1865	82	85	277	17	33	35	192	186
1866	103	98	295	29	23	46	197	197
1867	89	108	286	27	36	45	178	186
1868	92	94	270	23	37	34	176	166
1869	108	100	284	18	31	51	184	187
1870	79	85	263	12	40	33	178	187
1871	75	81	253	13	47	21	172	178
1872	93	101	265	23	63	15	164	173
1873	92	95	256	13	63	19	161	165
1874	75	88	236	10	58	20	148	159
1875	85	83	233	16	51	16	150	156
1876	92	74	242	20	36	18	168	160
1877	110	103	278	20	68	15	175	175
1878	63	84	238	12	66	6	154	168
1879	76	79	230	12	48	19	151	157
1880	51	48	202	6	30	12	154	152
1881	66	65	220	14	37	14	155	150
	6,522	6,367		936	2,672	2,759		

TABLE OF APPLICATIONS, ADMISSIONS, ETC., FOR EIGHTEEN YEARS,—1864–1881.

Years	Applications (Hosp.)	Admissions (Hosp.)	Admissions (Asyl.)	American (Hosp.)	American (Asyl.)	Foreign (Hosp.)	Foreign (Asyl.)	Not Admitted (Hosp.)	Discharged, cured, relieved, or improved (Hosp.)	Discharged (Asyl.)	Percentage on Adm. (Hosp.)	Percentage on Adm. (Asyl.)	Died (Hosp.)	Died (Asyl.)	Accidents	Whole no. under care (Hosp.)	Whole no. under care (Asyl.)	No. free patients (Hosp.)	Paying all the time (Hosp.)	Paying part of the time (Hosp.)	Greatest total (Hosp.)	Greatest total (Asyl.)	Least total (Hosp.)	Least total (Asyl.)	Average (Hosp.)	Average (Asyl.)	Greatest no. Free	Greatest no. Paying	Avg. time Paying	Avg. time Free	Out-Patients (Hosp.)
1864	1932	1599	101	654	99	945	2	333	1306	80	81.68	79.1	130	27	242	1749	302	1388	350	11	157	208	110	192	138	200	139	33	3.2	4.4	5619
1865	1430	1199	82	571	80	628	2	231	997	68	83.15	82.9	104	17	140	1347	277	687	592	68	164	195	88	181	113	186	137	72	3.7	4.8	5356
1866	1328	1120	103	542	100	587	3	208	900	69	81.17	66.9	96	29	132	1224	295	556	623	45	109	203	78	192	95	197	62	58	3.4	5.1	5608
1867	1419	1206	89	558	88	709	1	213	958	81	79.43	91.0	94	27	113	1373	286	676	601	45	126	200	72	172	104	186	69	62	3.4	4.3	4553
1868	1474	1265	92	604	92	661	0	209	1015	71	80.03	77.1	85	23	98	1217	218	840	502	31	132	181	69	160	102	166	97	77	3.0	3.5	5264
1869	1633	1390	108	681	108	778	0	243	1083	82	80.80	75.9	107	18	93	1427	284	958	439	24	139	196	90	177	118	187	98	56	3.4	4.3	6953
1870	1706	1302	79	584	76	718	3	401	1123	73	83.20	92.4	85	12	140	1537	342	1056	563	30	137	195	98	181	120	181	106	45	3.4	4.8	8767
1871	1781	1427	78	649	75	982	0	354	1143	52	80.09	69.3	109	13	178	1700	253	1289	396	25	154	187	91	167	122	178	126	43	3.1	3.9	9792
1872	1815	1547	93	605	88	910	5	268	1271	52	82.15	55.9	120	23	259	1800	265	1195	441	16	160	179	97	163	135	173	133	42	3.1	4.3	11878
1873	1958	1550	92	640	85	1022	7	408	1201	64	81.88	69.5	186	13	291	1847	256	1565	394	64	187	171	129	158	156	165	156	44	4.3	6.0	13517
1874	2153	1639	75	713	68	1006	7	514	1342	54	76.70	72	127	10	234	1989	236	1251	339	120	183	167	111	144	149	159	146	41	3.3	5.6	15612
1875	2357	1841	85	799	72	794	13	516	1412	57	76.80	67	189	16	285	2096	233	1696	336	88	199	165	132	145	166	156	176	31	2.7	5.2	16993
1876	2560	1906	110	900	82	848	10	654	1021	45	81.43	48.9	150	20	245	1950	242	1270	308	92	210	173	163	148	185	160	182	36	2.8	5.7	17292
1877	2131	1657	63	853	103	834	7	474	1339	57	80.63	71.4	130	12	147	1971	238	1578	334	48	194	184	135	154	166	175	170	33	3.2	5.5	18004
1878	2275	1794	76	946	58	1006	13	481	1461	45	81.53	60.5	134	12	200	2284	230	1577	334	38	187	182	132	168	165	168	178	34	2.8	5.2	18744
1879	2310	1813	51	979	63	1032	3	497	1462	46	82.19	62.7	143	6	222	2270	202	1864	352	42	188	164	131	150	163	157	105	30	2.8	5.1	18960
1880	2701	2123	66	1117	46		5	578	1731	32		56	151	14	351		220	1835	371	45	188	159	156	146	170	152	165	35	2.5	4.5	20566
1881	2786	2106		1074	57		9	680	1853	37			189		391				419	26	195	161	139	147	166	150	168	39	2.79	4.41	18443

TABLE SHOWING THE COST OF PRINCIPAL STORES AT THE McLEAN ASYLUM.

Articles.	1878. Quantity.	Cost.	Average.	1879. Quantity.	Cost.	Average.	1880. Quantity.	Cost.	Average.	1881. Quantity.	Cost.	Average.
Beef, lbs.,	77,166	$8,384.25	.108	58,771½	$7,062.58	.12	57,462	$6,025.64	.115	56,835½	$6,467.14	.1137
Mutton and Lamb, lbs.	21,411	2,411.63	.112	20,266¾	2,055.36	.101	19,794½	2,107.14	.106	23,583	2,308.16	.0978
Veal, lbs.,	7,636	1,017.22	.133	9,182¼	1,045.09	.113	12,288	1,372.34	.111	19,707	1,846.00	.094
Poultry, lbs.,	33,620	5,305.56	.157	25,754¾	4,148.75	.16	23,714½	3,726.80	.157	20,052¾	3,517.55	.175
Hams, etc.,	14,966	1,556.23	.103	7,180½	670.81	.093	8,932½	899.85	.1007	10,148¼	1,087.55	.107
Eggs, doz.,	13,679	2,508.71	.183	11,270	2,242.03	.198	11,295	2,337.09	.2069	11,523	3,084.19	.269
Lard, lbs.,	2,256	181.61	.08	1,723	123.00	.071	1,849	159.24	.086	2,093	244.44	.1167
Flour, bbls.,	449	3,440.50	7.662	397	2,709.85	6.825	418	3,296.63	7.886	413	3,219.16	7.794
Butter, lbs.,	21,240	5,390.49	.253	20,219½	4,873.85	.241	19,511½	5,405.80	.277	21,979¾	6,163.79	.2804
Coffee, lbs.,	5,066	1,309.89	.258	4,934½	1,271.89	.257	4,124	1,212.62	.294	3,841	945.95	.246
Tea, lbs.,	1,532	626.22	.408	1,383	450.72	.325	1,492½	486.41	.325	1,609	513.58	.319
Sugar, lbs.,	28,796	2,716.50	.094	23,759½	2,039.82	.085	24,330	2,290.05	.094	24,932	2,338.88	.0938
Lights, Gas, etc., feet,	2,112,100	5,695.42	2.60 ℔ M ft.	2,072,000	5,559.83	2.60 ℔ M ft.	....	2,515.78	....	....	2,771.42	....
Coal, tons,	1,064 10/2000	5,407.81	5.08	904 1530/2000	4,015.13	4.44	1,158 1620/2000	5,972.06	5.15	1,099 350/2000	6,635.44	6.036
Wood, cords,	2/2000	....	....	15 8/2000	134.53	8.75	25 1/2000	219.84	8.75	15	140.70	9.38
Ice, tons,	588 200/2000	1,058.44	3.33	476 741/2000	1,208.34	2.53	462 1560/2000	2,069.31	4.47	366 300/2000	849.88	2.33

SEPT. 3, 1821, TO DEC. 31, 1881.

Year	Total Admitted	Free	Pay'ng Board all the time	Paying part of the time	Whole No. treated: Paying Board	Whole No. treated: Paying Board part of time	Whole No. treated: Free	Discharged well	Percentage on "Total Admitted."	Much Relieved, or Relieved in part	Not Relieved	Not Treated, Unfit, Dismissed, etc.	Deaths	Percentage on "Total Admitted."	Greatest number free at one time	Greatest number paying at one time	Greatest total	Least total	Average	Accidents	Percentage	Average time of Paying Weeks	Average time of Free Weeks	Patients remaining — Paying	Patients remaining — Free	Out-Patients treated
1821 to 1843	8743	330	327	34				3991		2902	913	105	624				123	54								
1843									37	115	55	23										4	7 1-7			
1844	365		174					136	37	137	55	28		11			56		53	55		3 6-7	6 6-7			
1845	433	183	16½	11				183	43	130	41	33		11	44	41	71	33	56	62		5 4-7	6			
1846	453	250	174	12				205	45	137	37	30	41	11	82	34	72	40	55	59		3 1-2	4 3-4			
1847	459	265	176	27				211	46	145	37	39	47	12	86	30	72	37	47*	74		3 1-7	4 1-2			328
1848	674	250	182	41				340	50	219	54	58	54	8	89	38	123	37	53	103		3 1-7	5			378
1849	804	354	279	61				400	50	218	64	49	54	8	103	30	56	54	56	97		2 4-7	5 5-7			272
1850	870	400	283	64				436	50	200	65	47	57	13	82	34	71	58	55	98		2 6-7	6			294
1851	746	543	273	77				363	48	235	75	58	103	9	86	41	124	90	81	123		3	6			237
1852	839	427	242	83				387	46	234	56	49	84	10	89	38	127	83	108	132		3 1-4	5			248
1853	826	472	296	85				410	50	287	47	63	76	11	93	33	136	77	112	159		3 1-6	5			358
1854	925	505	271	111				431	46	257	52	66	82	10	105	48	141	104	108	212		4	7			477
1855	922	490	321	147				423	46	238	70	41	82	9	108	41	133	108	108	167		3	10			645
1856	915	414	352	96				456	50	230	73	51	115	12	112	39	142	108	119	189	12*	3 3-7	11 4-7			887
1857	976	546	352	91				478	49	195	59	71	112	11	114	45	152	125	112	163	14	3	5			1574
1858	920	549	280	49		49		510	55	229	57	66	117	12	119	59	153	114	133	186	13	2 2-3	5			2223
1859	1015	718	91	85		49		514	50	280	65	50	130	14	120	40	157	91	134	212	11	4	7*			3523
1860	1240	934	257	111		42		653	53	305	54	94	127	13	145	31	165	92	128	233	12*	4	4 2-3	14	140	4433
1861	1240	997	201	147	287	32		698	56	318	73	58	141	11	149	37	162	80	131	297	11	4	6	15	121	4676
1862	1416	1131	253	96	255	11		831	59	305	79	57	99	9¼	135	33	166	102	128	271	13	4	5 3-4	16	124	4800
1863	1611	1175	425	91	268	17	1040	843	52	459	77	77	101	7	133	45	165	102	140	292	15	4	4 1-10	25	120	4987
1864	1648	1348	326	49	441	11	1137	856	52	390	96	61	162	6¼	133	60	162	116	134	242	16	3.18	4.37	24	128	5619
1865	1199	1262	567	42	308	68	1252	916	57	295	94	74	130	9¼	130	33	166	110	138	140	17	3.67	4.85	25	123	5366
1866	1190	564	578	35	350	45	1299	702	59	82	68	74	104	8¼	137	72	158	88	113	132	23	3.40	5.10	45	59	5608
1867	1206	626	556	11	692	24	1468	677	56	283	62	68	94	8½	62	62	157	78	95	113	17 3-10	3.37	4.26	45	50	4553
1868	1265	834	463	11	601	31	1388	757	60	258	64	63	85	7	97	62	164	72	102	98	19	3.00	3.50	39	69	5264
1869	1390	858	532	68	302	24	687	771	55½	352	78	62	57	7.7	98	57	109	69	104	93	17 7-10	3.40	4.30	31	96	6953
1870	1302	970	414	24	763	30	676	780	60	303	65	78	85	6.45	106	56	132	69	118	140	17	3.37	4.82	25	100	8767
1871	1427	1163	432	31	439	25	840	821	57½	322	68	65	116	7.64	126	55	132	90	120	178	21	3.12	3.92	24	86	9792
1872	1647	1075	368	24	456	16	930	958	62	313	76	68	120	7.75	133	46	137	98	91	259	18 7-10	3.15	4.35	28	126	11878
1873	1550	1125	394	30	396	64	958	880	57	321	66	76	120	12	156	43	154	91	120	291	16 3-4	3.28	6.09	28	120	13517
1874	1639	1445	411	16	429	120	1289	946	57½	396	81	86	127	7.69	146	42	187	97	135	234	17 7-10	2.73	5.64	35	126	15612
1875	1841	1532	308	120	336	88	1251	1032	56	380	89	102	189	10.27	176	41	183	129	140	285	17 5-10	2.82	5.18	28	120	16993
1876	1906	1270	282	88	358	92	1565	1019	53½	502	91	144	100	7.86	182	31	199	111	166	245	15 2-10	3.22	5.73	26	164	17292
1877	1657	1433	339	48	308	42	1696	930	50	409	92	130	130	7.68	178	36	210	132	166	147	11 7-10	2.84	5.54	19	171	18004
1878	1794	1436	323	38	334	38	1441	956	50	505	94	138	130	7.46	170	33	187	135	164	290	11 7-10	2.80	5.27	11	145	18744
1879	1813	335	335	42	352	43	1577	1040	57	422	84	125	143	7.94	165	30	188	131	163	222	9.36	2.84	5.16	17	141	18960
1880	2123	1724	354	45	371	45	1864	1186	54	545	74	150	151	7.16	165	35	188	156	170	351	7.74	2.58	4.53	17	157	20666
1881	2106	1678	402	26	419	26	1835	1324	62	429	70	103	189	8.96	168	39	195	139	166	391	6.69	2.79	4.41	15	140	18443

OFFICERS OF THE INSTITUTION.

1882.

President.

HENRY B. ROGERS.

Vice-President.

NATHANIEL THAYER.

Treasurer.

DAVID R. WHITNEY, 60 State Street.

Secretary.

THOMAS B. HALL, 75 State Street.

Trustees.

SAMUEL ELIOT, *Chairman*, 44 Brimmer Street.
* CHARLES V. BEMIS, Medford, Mass.
E. FRANCIS BOWDITCH, Framingham, Mass.
EDMUND DWIGHT, 60 State Street.
* WILLIAM ENDICOTT, Jr., 10 Mt. Vernon Street.
GEORGE S. HALE, 39 Court Street.
* HENRY P. KIDDER, 40 State Street.
THORNTON K. LOTHROP, 8 Congress Street.
CHARLES J. MORRILL, 11 Arlington Street.
NATHANIEL THAYER, Jr., 21 Sears Building.
* SAMUEL D. WARREN, 67 Mt. Vernon Street.
ROGER WOLCOTT, 8 Pemberton Square.

Board of Consultation.

HENRY I. BOWDITCH, M.D.   CHARLES E. WARE, M.D.
ALGERNON COOLIDGE, M.D.   MORRILL WYMAN, M.D.
D. H. STORER, M.D.   SAMUEL CABOT, M.D.

* Appointed by the Governor of the Commonwealth.

OFFICERS OF THE HOSPITAL.

Resident Physician.
JAMES H. WHITTEMORE, M.D.

Visiting Physicians.

GEORGE C. SHATTUCK, M.D.   SAMUEL L. ABBOT, M.D.
FRANCIS MINOT, M.D.   BENJAMIN S. SHAW, M.D.
CALVIN ELLIS, M.D.   GEORGE G. TARBELL, M.D.

Visiting Surgeons.

HENRY J. BIGELOW, M.D.   JOHN COLLINS WARREN, M.D.
RICHARD M. HODGES, M.D.   HENRY H. A. BEACH, M.D.
CHARLES B. PORTER, M.D.   . . . .

Physicians to Out-Patients.

DAVID H. HAYDEN, M.D.   ELBRIDGE G. CUTLER, M.D.
WILLIAM L. RICHARDSON, M.D.   F. GORDON MORRILL, M.D.
EDWARD N. WHITTIER, M.D.   FREDERICK C. SHATTUCK, M.D.

Surgeons to Out-Patients.

JOHN HOMANS, M.D.   ARTHUR T. CABOT, M.D.
. . . .

Physician to Out-Patients with diseases of the Skin.
JAMES C. WHITE, M.D.

Physician to Out-Patients with diseases of the Nervous System.
JAMES J. PUTNAM, M.D.

Physicians to Out-Patients with diseases of the Throat.
FREDERICK I. KNIGHT, M.D.   S. W. LANGMAID, M.D.

Ophthalmic Surgeon to Out-Patients.
OLIVER F. WADSWORTH, M.D.

Dental Surgeon.
MANNING K. RAND, D.M.D.

59

Microscopist, and Curator of the Pathological Cabinet.
REGINALD H. FITZ, M.D.

Chemist.
EDWARD S. WOOD, M.D.

Artist.
HENRY P. QUINCY, M.D.

Medical House Officers, 1881–1882.
FREDERIC W. TAYLOR.   HERMON F. VICKERY.

Surgical House Officers, 1881–1882.
JOHN HOMANS, 2d.   OTIS K. NEWELL.
F. HOWARD LOMBARD.   ALLEY T. WAKEFIELD.

Matron.
Miss G. L. STURTEVANT.

Apothecary.
JOHN W. PRATT.

***

OFFICERS OF THE McLEAN ASYLUM.

Superintendent.
EDWARD COWLES, M.D.

1st Assistant Physician.
GEORGE T. TUTTLE, M.D.

2d Assistant Physician.
FREDERICK M. TURNBULL, M.D.

Medical Internes.
ROYAL WHITMAN.   HENRY F. ADAMS.

Apothecary.
CHARLES L. CURTIS.

Supervisors.
RANSOM WILLARD.   Miss LUCIA E. WOODWARD.

VISITING COMMITTEE.

February and August.
Messrs. MORRILL and ENDICOTT.

March and September.
Messrs. DWIGHT and BOWDITCH.

April and October.
Messrs. ELIOT and THAYER.

May and November.
Messrs. HALE and WARREN.

June and December.
Messrs. BEMIS and LOTHROP.

July and January.
Messrs. KIDDER and WOLCOTT.

LADIES' VISITING COMMITTEE.

January.

Miss E. GRAY.   Miss E. CARY.
Miss M.. CURTIS.

February.

Miss GRAY.   Miss E. GOODWIN.
Miss S. LORING.

March.

Miss GOODWIN.   Miss L. LORING.
Miss S. LORING.   Miss H. THAYER.

April.

Miss L. LORING.   Miss CURTIS.
Miss THAYER.   Miss ELIOT.

May.

Miss CURTIS.   Miss ELIOT.

June and October.

Mrs. S. ELIOT.   Miss E. T. PARKMAN.

November and December.

Mrs. H. W. HAYNES.   Miss A. W. MORRILL.

STANDING COMMITTEES.

On Admitting Asylum Patients.
Messrs. WARREN and DWIGHT.

On Finance.
Messrs. KIDDER and MORRILL.

On Accounts and Expenditures.
Messrs. WOLCOTT and THAYER.

On Buildings and Repairs.
Messrs. DWIGHT, WARREN, and ELIOT.

On Free Beds.
Messrs. BOWDITCH and ENDICOTT.

On the General Library and Warren Fund.
Messrs. ELIOT and HALE.

On the Book of Donations.
Dr. BEMIS.

SIXTY-NINTH ANNUAL REPORT

OF THE

TRUSTEES

OF THE

MASSACHUSETTS GENERAL HOSPITAL

AND

McLEAN ASYLUM,

1882.

Printed at the Expense of the Bowditch History Fund.

BOSTON:

GEO. H. ELLIS, PRINTER, 141 FRANKLIN STREET.

381

REPORT OF THE TRUSTEES

OF THE

MASSACHUSETTS GENERAL HOSPITAL

For the Year 1882.

THE Committee of the Trustees appointed to prepare the Annual Report of the Board to the Corporation, to whom the accounts of the Treasurer and the reports of the other officials have been referred, respectfully submit the

SIXTY-NINTH ANNUAL REPORT.

The average number of patients in the Hospital was one hundred and sixty-eight against one hundred and sixty-six the year before.

In the Asylum, one hundred and fifty-six against one hundred and forty-nine last year.

The Treasurer's account shows for the year ending Dec. 31, 1882, an excess of expenditure over income of $37,280.17, which has been charged to the General Fund. The average deficiency for the past two years has been $26,150.99.

On June 1st, Mr. David R. Whitney resigned the office of Treasurer during a temporary absence in Europe; and Mr. Edmund Dwight was elected in his place. It is to be hoped that Mr. Whitney will resume the position on his return.

In May, Dr. Samuel Cabot, a member of the Board of Visiting Surgeons since 1854, resigned, leaving the

Hospital indebted to him for many years of faithful and valuable service.

The Trustees gratefully acknowledge the following donations and legacies: —

Donations and Legacies.

Bequest of Miss Mary Pratt, ...	$20,000.00
Received of the executors of Eben Wright (being an assignment of their legacies by the children of T. Jefferson Coolidge, Esq., for the formation of a fund for the support of free beds, to be known as the Eben Wright Fund), ...	14,000.00
Received from a friend, to be known as the George H. Gay Fund, ...	25,000.00
Bequest of Miss Mary Wigglesworth, to be applied as the Trustees see fit, ...	5,000.00

It was voted December 15 to add the above bequest to the Asylum Building Fund.

Bequest of Edwin Fiske, ...	50.00
From subscribers to Convalescent Home Fund, . .	5,225.00
From subscribers to free beds, ...	10,265.00

It is to be regretted that the subscriptions for free beds has fallen off $700. The demand for their use becomes greater every year, and it is to be hoped that the interest taken in so noble a charity may increase.

The Convalescent Home was dedicated May 5. Since that time, it has been in constant use, and has more than fulfilled the benefits that were anticipated from it.

The situation has proved to be a most admirable one in every respect, combining, as it does, not only quiet and pure air, but also great accessibility. Frequent trains to and from Boston add very much to the convenience of carrying it on. It is only two minutes' walk from the Waverly station on the Fitchburg road.

It has been used by surgical and medical cases, and both alike have derived great benefit from their sojourn there.

The Trustees decided during the past year to put up a new building to be used exclusively by the nurses. They have for a long time felt that the accommodations provided for the nurses were altogether insufficient, and not at all suitable for the class of women who are now taking up the profession. For the last five years, all our nurses have come from the Training School for Nurses; and the result has been that we are continually getting not only much better trained nurses, but also a class of women much superior in every respect to those who formerly performed the service.

Plans for the building were submitted about a year ago; and it was finally decided to erect a building 155 feet long on the line of Allen Street, at a cost of about $35,000.

It is intended that each nurse shall have a room to herself, and a large sitting-room has been placed on the lower floor. The following resolution was adopted March 31, 1882: —

Voted, That in grateful recognition of the long expressed good will and generous contributions to the Hospital by Nathaniel Thayer, Esq., the new building be called the " Thayer Building." It will be ready for use by March.

The Trustees still further carefully considered the question of service in the "Out Patient Department."

On June 16, a petition was presented to the Trustees from the surgeons in the special department for out patients, complaining that the personal investigation of applicants instituted a year ago was depriving them of many interesting and instructive cases, and asking that all cases hereafter be admitted, regardless of the pecuniary circumstances of the applicant. The petition was referred to a Committee of the Trustees, who reported October 13 that, while they cannot recommend a change of the policy of questioning every applicant to determine whether their means are such as to entitle them to gratuitous treatment, yet on the other hand every effort shall be made to enlarge the usefulness of the Hospital by adding to medical knowledge as well as to the relief of suffering.

The Committee, therefore, recommended that liberal regard should be paid to the written recommendations of physicians that cases are proper ones for admission by reason of the obscurity and educational value of the disease as well as by reason of the poverty of the applicant.

A friend of the late Dr. George H. Gay has given us $25,000 as a memorial of him. After full consideration, the Trustees voted to apply the money for a building for the "Out Patient Department," believing that to be the greatest need of the Hospital.

This will supply a most pressing want, as our present accommodations have long been totally inadequate for the needs of that department; and very much of the work so faithfully and gratuitously given has been done under most inconvenient and unfavorable surroundings.

Your Trustees cannot express too strongly the hope that they will soon be able to move the Asylum from Somerville to Belmont.

This they consider their most pressing need, and it is to be hoped that this object will be especially borne in mind by the generous public.

The present quarters are probably as well adapted to the purpose as any large building of the kind well can be, and many improvements have been made in them during the past few years which have added very materially to their comfort and attractiveness ;

but, according to modern requirements, they are still cramped and inconvenient, and it is impossible to separate the different stages of insanity so as to bring about the best results. A large class of our patients are most unfavorably affected by being brought in contact with those more insane than themselves, and by the feeling of restraint and confinement that is inseparably connected with a large Asylum Building. The more closely we can approach to that of a large family living in different houses, the better the result we can hope to attain.

Our purpose is to build a number of small cottages surrounding a large one that would be used for administration purposes.

Each cottage would be occupied by a family consisting of a number of patients graded according to their mental condition and their necessary attendants. A cottage would then become a community in itself, and would have its own varied interests.

Aside from all these advantages, the grounds at Belmont are beautifully wooded, and the drives in every direction are much pleasanter and more varied than those which they are now compelled to use, and the whole manner of life would be much better adapted to persons suffering from mental disease.

N. THAYER, Jr., } *Committee.*
ROGER WOLCOTT, }

REPORT OF THE TREASURER

OF THE

MASSACHUSETTS GENERAL HOSPITAL.

To the Board of Trustees:

Gentlemen,— In accordance with the Fifth Article of the By-Laws, the report of the accounts of the Massachusetts General Hospital, made up to the last day of December, 1882, is respectfully submitted, to be laid before the · Corporation at its annual meeting.

Dr.   EDMUND DWIGHT, *Treasurer, in account with the* MASSACHUSETTS GENERAL HOSPITAL.   **Cr.**

Jan. 1, 1882.			By Cash paid, taxes on land in Chicago,	$1,630.40
To Cash on hand,	$100,076.95		" " " " " " Waltham,	.80
" Railroad ... called and paid,	3,000.00		" " Insurance,	248.53
" Dues,	44,275.00		" " Annuitants,	1,816.00
" Legacies,	27,000.00		" " Annual Report, 1881,	237.53
" One-third Profits Mass. Hospital Life Ins. Co.,	10,000.00		" " ... Building,	11,366.88
" Income from investments,	82,698.22		" " Improvements at Belmont,	7,780.59
" Board of paying ... at ...	120,316.15		" " Expenses ...	108,590.43
" Board of paying patients at Hospital,	12,905.48		" " Expenses Asylum,	138,488.36
" Subscribers for Free Beds ($80) additional received for this ... in 1881),	6,315.00		" " Expenses Convalescent's Home,	8,365.94
" Subscribers for Free Beds, for 1882 in advance,	3,050.00		" " Thayer Building,	25,604.61
" City of Boston ... due,	11,000.00		" " ...	101,373.20
" J. H. Whittemore, Resident Physician, balance in account,	61.90		" " Library,	212.88
" Edw. Cox, Superintendent, balance in account,	1,614.95		" " ... Legs,	350.00
			" " Net ...	7,500.00
			" " Balance Cash on hand,	8,847.50
	$422,313.65			$422,313.65

MASSACHUSETTS GENERAL HOSPITAL, BOSTON, Dec. 31, 1882.

E. & O. EX.

EDMUND DWIGHT, *Treasurer.*

The expense of carrying on the business of the Corporation for the year 1882 has been $255,693.26, namely : —

On account of Hospital Department,	$108,620.43
" " " McLean Asylum,	138,518.36
" " " Convalescent's Home,	8,554.47
	$255,693 26

This expense has been met from : —

Amount charged to patients,	$133,221.63
Income from various funds applicable,	85,191.46
Deficit drawn from the General Fund,	37,280.17
	$255,693.26

Of the deficit drawn from the General Fund, $25,208.37 has been on account of the Hospital Department, $8,906.66 has been on account of the McLean Asylum Department, and $3,165.14 has been on account of Convalescent's Home, as per Tables 1, 2, and 3.

TABLE No. 1.

EXPENSES AND RECEIPTS OF THE HOSPITAL DEPARTMENT.

Disbursements for the year 1882 : —

Expenses at Hospital (see Table 4),	$108,590 43	
Insurance,	30.00	
		$108,620.43

Receipts.

Income from Redman Fund (see Table 7),	$25,031.23	
" " Free Bed Funds (see Table 7),	26,704.35	
" " Funds with income unrestricted (see Table 7),	2,200.00	
" " General Fund (see Table 7),	6,356.00	
Free Bed Subscriptions (see Table 8),	10,215.00	
Amount charged to Patients,	12,905.48	
Deficit from General Fund,	25,208.37	
		$108,620.43

TABLE No. 2.

EXPENSES AND RECEIPTS AT THE McLEAN ASYLUM.

Disbursements for year 1882 —:

Expenses at Asylum (see Table 5), ...	$138,488 36	
Insurance, ...	30.00	
		$138,518.36

Receipts.

Income from Fund for Beneficiaries (see Table 7), .	$4,070.55	
Income from Fund for Female Beneficiaries (see Table 7), ...	4,675.00	
Income from Amusement Fund (see Table 7), . . .	550.00	
Amount charged to Patients, ...	120,316.15	
Deficit from General Fund, ...	8,906.66	
		$138,518 36

TABLE No. 3.

EXPENSES AND RECEIPTS AT CONVALESCENT'S HOME.

Disbursements for year 1882 : —

Expenses at Convalescent's Home (see Table 6), . .	$8,365.94	
Insurance, ...	188.53	
		$8,554.47

Receipts.

Income from Convalescent's Home Funds, 1880, . .	$515.92	
" " " " " 1881, . .	1,343.20	
" " " " " 1882, . .	3,530.21	
Deficit from General Fund, ...	3,165.14	
		$8,554.47

TABLE No. 4.

EXPENSES OF THE HOSPITAL DEPARTMENT.

For Stores, ...	$39,979.27	
Gas and Oil, ...	2,379.44	
Water, ...	1,951.43	
Wages, ...	24,731 84	
Medicine, ...	3,742.03	
Furniture, ...	7,648.58	
Surgical Instruments, ...	1,517.64	
Stationery, ...	581.10	
Wines and Liquors, ...	1,674.86	
Salaries, ...	5,353 00	
One-half General Expenses, ...	995.71	
Fuel, ...	8,162.68	
Contingencies, ...	2,495 17	
Repairs, ...	7,377.68	
		$108,590.43

12

These expenditures have been for account of : —

1,725 Free Patients for 7,644 weeks, ...	$95,642.45	
421 Paying Patients for 1,092 weeks, ...	12,947.98	
	$108,590.43	
The average number of patients has been, in 1881, .	166	
The average number of patients has been, in 1882, .	168	
The average cost per week has been, in 1881, 8,606 weeks, ...	$11.87	
The average cost per week has been, in 1882, 8,736, weeks, ...	12 43	
The total expenses have been, in 1881, ...	102,153.80	
The total expenses have been, in 1882, ...	108,590 43	
The amount paid for account of free patients has been,		$95,642.45
The amount received for them has been : —		
From Income Free Bed Funds, ...	26,704.35	
(See Table 8.) From 80 Subscribers for this object,	10,215.00	
		36,919.35
		$58,723.10

The deficiency has been drawn in part from the income of the various funds applicable to the purpose, and the remainder from the General Fund.

TABLE No. 5.

EXPENSES OF THE ASYLUM DEPARTMENT.

For Stores, ...	$46,495.88	
Laundry, ...	8,620.61	
Fuel, ...	7,705.28	
Stationery, ...	337.08	
Medicines and Liquors, ...	2,612.79	
Contingencies, ...	1,381.40	
Furniture, ...	7,023.27	
Repairs, ...	10,479.90	
Diversions, ...	1,652.24	
Water and Ice, ...	3,284 30	
Lights, ...	3,858.49	
Wages, ...	28,701.53	
Salaries, ...	6,373.33	
One-half General Expenses, ...	995.68	
Library, ...	300.00	
Stables, ...	4,715.97	
Garden, ...	3,572.47	
New Sewer, ...	50.00	
Farm, ...	648.31	
		$138,808.53
Less Cr. Clothing, ...	320.17	
		$138,488.36

These expenditures have been for account of : —

Patients paying cost and more, ...	$30,836.21	
" " less than cost, ...	107,652.15	
		$138,488.36
The average number of patients has been, in 1881, . .	149$\frac{281}{365}$	
The average number of patients has been, in 1882, . .	155$\frac{329}{365}$	
The average cost per week has been, in 1881, . . .	$16.92	
The average cost per week has been, in 1882, . . .	17.02	
The total expenses have been, in 1881, ...		$134,561.14
The total expenses have been, in 1882, ...		138,518.36
The amount expended at the Asylum for patients who		
have paid less than cost has been, ...		107,682.15
The amount received has been : —		
From patients, 6,222$\frac{2}{7}$ weeks' board, at less than cost,	$56,219.31	
Income of Funds for Beneficiaries, ...	4,070.55	
Income of Funds for Female Beneficiaries, . .	4,675.00	
Income of Amusement Fund, ...	550.00	
		65,514.86

The deficiency has been drawn in part from patients paying more than cost, and the remainder from the General and other Funds, . . $42,167.29

TABLE No. 6.

EXPENSES OF THE CONVALESCENT'S HOME.

For Stores, ...	$1,919.69	
Gas and oil, ...	19.90	
Medicine, ...	35.85	
Furniture, ...	3,920.75	
Wages, ...	1,417.10	
Fuel, ...	518.48	
Stationery, ...	46.05	
Surgical Instruments, ...	37.86	
Wines, Spirits, and Malt Liquors, ...	24.89	
Repairs, ...	242.62	
Contingencies, ...	182.75	
		$8,365.94
Whole number of patients admitted from April 19 to		
December 31, males, ...	62	
Whole number of patients admitted from April 19 to		
December 31, females, ...	39	
		101
Whole number discharged during same time, . . .		86
Remaining, Jan. 1, 1883, males, ...	9	
" " " females, ...	6	

TABLE No. 7.

INCOME FROM INVESTMENTS.

The Income from Investments has been: —

From Annuities Receivable,	$6,400.00
City of Boston Bonds,	1,475 00
Mass. Hospital Life Ins. Co. Stock,	5,000.00
Railroad Bonds,	29,784.67
Manufacturing Stocks,	3,719.00
Bank Stocks,	5,135.76
Real Estate, Productive,	16,699.71
Notes Receivable,	13,295.81
Union League Club Bonds,	600.00
Interest,	539 37
Delaware Mutual Ins. Co.'s Scrip Interest,	48.90
	$82,698.22

Which has been distributed as follows: —

To G. H. Gay Fund,		$275.00
Redman Fund,		25,031.23
Warren Prize Fund,		126.48
Bowditch History Fund,		110.00
Wooden Leg Fund,		275.00
Redman Annuities,		936.00
Clara Barton Annuity,		178.25
Surgical Instrument Fund,		74.25
Amusement Fund,		550.00
Free Bed Funds, { for use, $26,704.35 / for Joy Annuities, 700.00		27,404.35
Beneficiaries at Asylum Funds,		4,070.55
Warren Library Fund,		55.00
Treadwell Library Fund,		275.00
One-half Lincoln Fund,— Female Beneficiaries,		4,675.00
Funds with Income Unrestricted,		2,200.00
General Fund,		6,356.80
Convalescent Fund, Building,		2,855.92
Convalescent Home Fund,		674.29
Asylum Building Fund,		6,575.10
		$82,698.22
The Income for 1880 was		$76,243.66
The Income for 1881 was		94,199.47
The Income for 1882 was		82,698.22

15

TABLE No. 8.

SUBSCRIBERS FOR FREE BEDS.

Mrs. Susan O. Brooks,	$100	*Amount brought up*,	$5,515
D. R. Whitney, donation,	640	Henry B. Rogers,	100
S. S. Langley, donation,	25	Mrs. Edward Wigglesworth,	100
Peleg Howland, donation,	50	Samuel Eliot,	100
Alden Speare,	100	C. J. Morrill,	100
Chas. P. Curtis,	100	Jas. H. Howe,	100
Sidney Bartlett,	100	Abbott Lawrence,	100
Theodore Lyman,	100	Jos. S. Fay,	100
William Amory,	100	Mrs. G. H. Shaw,	200
Fitchburg Railroad Co.,	100	A. A. Lawrence,	100
Miss Mary Wigglesworth,	200	R. C. Winthrop, Jr.,	100
Miss Anne Wigglesworth,	200	Mrs. B. S. Rotch,	100
Union Railway Co.,	100	Charles Merriam,	100
Boston & Providence R.R. Co.,	100	C. H. Dalton,	100
George Higginson,	100	Ida M. Mason,	100
T. Jefferson Coolidge,	100	Nathaniel Thayer,	500
H. P. Kidder,	200	Henry Saltonstall,	100
F. H. Peabody,	100	H. H. Fay,	100
Boston & Maine Railroad Co.,	100	Otis E. Weld,	100
S. D. Warren,	100	F. Gordon Dexter,	100
Shepherd Brooks,	100	W. Powell Mason,	100
Miss C. A. Brewer,	100	Greely S. Curtis,	100
W. W. Tucker,	100	R. C. Greenleaf,	100
Mrs. J. G. Cushing,	100	Henry Woods,	100
Mrs. Anna C. Lodge,	100	J. F. Anderson,	100
Moses Williams,	100	Sarah S. Fay,	200
J. B. Glover,	100	R. W. Hooper,	100
P. C. Brooks,	100	J. G. Kidder,	100
J. L. Gardner, Jr.,	100	Mrs. Ozias Goodwin,	100
Mrs. Peter C. Brooks,	100	Miss Eliza Goodwin,	100
Miss Eunice Hooper,	100	Mrs. Caroline Merriam,	100
Mass. Humane Society,	600	Miss Madeline C. Mixter, }	100
Mrs. E. B. Bowditch,	200	Miss Helen K. Mixter, }	
Samuel Johnson,	100	J. M. Sears,	200
William Endicott, Jr.,	100	J. T. Coolidge, Jr.,	100
Mrs. Charlotte A. Johnson,	100	Pacific Mills Board of Relief,	200
George A. Gardner,	100	J. P. Squire & Co.,	100
Miss A. W. Davis,	100	W. S. Adams,	100
Geo. W. Wales,	100	Mrs. James Lawrence,	100
Dr. C. E. Ware,	100	Boston Gaslight Co.,	100
George Dexter,	200	C. W. Amory,	100
Amount carried up,	$5,515		$10,215

Total Free Bed Subscriptions (93) in 1881, ... 10,950.00
Total Free Bed Subscriptions (80) in 1882, ... 10,215 00

TABLE No. 9.

LIBRARY ACCOUNT.

Paid for Books,	$212.88
Income Treadwell Library Fund,	275.00
The surplus is credited to the Fund,	$62.12

TABLE No. 10.

WOODEN LEG ACCOUNT.

The amount received for this purpose has been Income of the Wooden Leg Fund, ...	$275.00
The amount expended for Artificial Limbs has been, .	350.00
The deficiency is charged to the accrued income of the fund, ...	$75.00

TABLE No. 11.

THE BOWDITCH HISTORY FUND.

Balance, December 31, 1881 : —		
Principal, ...	$2,000.00	
Income, ...	1,913.84	
		$3,913.84
Amount of Income received, ...	$110.00	
Amount of Income expended, ...	237.53	
		127.53
		$3,786.31
Balance, December 31, 1882 : —		
Principal, ...	$2,000.00	
Income, ...	1,786.31	
		$3,786.31

TABLE No. 12.

GENERAL FUND.

Balance, December 31, 1881, ...	$993,750.57	
Add one-third profits Mass. Hospital Life Ins. Co., . .	10,000.00	
Add donations and legacies, ...	20,050.00	
		$1,023,800.57
Less balance of premiums paid for Railroad Bonds and Bank Stocks, ...	$8,123.20	
Balance of Expenses over Income, ...	37,280 17	
		45,403.37
Balance, December 31, 1882, ...		$978,397.20

17

TABLE No. 13.

RESTRICTED FUNDS.

Income devoted to Free Beds:—

The Joy Fund, being a bequest from Miss Nabby Joy,	$20,000.00
Belknap Fund, being a bequest from Jeremiah Belknap,	10,000.00
Wm. Phillips Fund, being a bequest from Wm. Phillips,	5,000.00
Williams Fund, being a bequest from John D. Williams, of estate No. 17, Blackstone Street,	19,600.00
Bromfield Fund, being half of a bequest from John Bromfield,	20,000.00
Miss Townsend Fund, being a donation from the Executors of the will of Miss Mary P. Townsend,	11,486.50
Brimmer Fund, being a bequest from Miss Mary Ann Brimmer,	5,000.00
Wilder Fund, being a bequest from Charles W. Wilder,	12,000.00
Sever Fund, being a bequest from Miss Martha Sever,	500.00
Thompson Fund, being a bequest from S. B. Thompson,	500.00
Tucker Fund, being a bequest from Miss Margaret Tucker,	3,312.37
Davis Fund, being a bequest from Mrs. Eleanor Davis,	900.00
Loring Fund, being a bequest from Abigail Loring,	5,000.00
Nichols Fund, being a bequest from B. R. Nichols,	6,000.00
Gray Fund, being a donation from John C. Gray,	1,000.00
Dowse Fund, being a bequest from Thomas Dowse,	5,000.00
Todd Fund, being a bequest from Henry Todd, .	5,000.00
J. Phillips Fund, being a bequest from Jonathan Phillips,	10,000.00
Greene Fund, being a bequest from Benj. D. Greene,	5,000.00
Percival Fund, being a bequest from John Percival,	950.00
Pickens Fund, being a bequest from John Pickens,	1,676.75
Treadwell Fund, being part of a bequest from J. G. Treadwell,	38,703.91
Raymond Fund, being a bequest from E. A. Raymond,	2,820.00
Harris Fund, being part of a bequest from Charles Harris,	1,000.00
Mason Fund, being a bequest from Wm. P. Mason,	9,400.00
Sawyer Fund, being part of a bequest from M. P. Sawyer,	7,000.00
J. L. Gardner Fund, being a donation from J. L. Gardner,	20,000.00
Amount carried forward,	$226,849.53

Amount brought forward, ...	$226,849.53
B. T. Reed Fund, being a donation from Benj. T. Reed, ...	1,000.00
Wm. Reed Fund, being a bequest from Wm. Reed,	5,233.92
McGregor Fund, being half of a donation and bequest from James McGregor, ...	7,500.00
Miss Rice Fund, being a bequest from Miss Arabella Rice, ...	5,000.00
Templeton Fund, being half of a bequest from John Templeton, ...	5,000.00
Mrs. J. H. Rogers Fund, being a donation from J. H. Rogers, ...	1,177 50
Beebe Fund, being a bequest from J. M. Beebe, .	50,000.00
Lincoln Fund, being half of a bequest from Mrs. F. W. Lincoln, ...	85,000.00
Blanchard Fund, being a bequest from Mrs. M. B. Blanchard, ...	4,000.00
George Gardner Fund, being a donation from George Gardner, ...	1,000.00
Hemenway Fund, being a donation from the Executors of the will of Augustus Hemenway, .	20,000 00
Jessup Fund, being part of a bequest from Dr. Chas. A. Jessup, ...	1,000.00
Tufts Fund, being a bequest from Quincy Tufts, .	10,000 00
Read Fund, being half of a bequest from Jas. Read,	1,000 00
Parker Fund, being a bequest from Jno. Parker, Jr.,	10,000 00
Miss Shaw Fund, being a donation and bequest from Miss M. Louisa Shaw, ...	5,500.00
Eliza Perkins Fund, being a donation from Mrs. H. B. Rogers, ...	1,000.00
Dwight Fund, being a donation from Mrs. T. Bradford Dwight, ...	1,000 00
Hunnewell Fund, being a donation from H. H. Hunnewell, ...	10,000.00
R. M. Mason Fund, being a bequest from R. M. Mason, ...	5,000.00
Anna Lowell Cabot Fund, being a donation from Dr. Samuel Cabot, ...	1,000.00
Welles Fund, being a donation from Miss Jane Welles, ...	5,000.00
Black Fund, being a bequest from Miss Marianna Black, ...	2,000.00
Eben Wright Fund, being an assignment of legacies by the children of T. Jefferson Coolidge,	14,000.00
Amount carried forward, ...	$478,260.95

Amount brought forward, ... $478,260.95

Income devoted to Beneficiaries at Asylum: —

The Bromfield Fund, being half of a bequest from
John Bromfield, ... 20,000.00
   Read Fund, being half of a bequest from Jas. Read,   1,000.00
   Appleton Fund,
     $10,010 being a bequest from Sam'l Appleton,
     $20,000 being a donation from Wm. Appleton,   30,010 00
   McGregor Fund, being half of a donation and
     bequest from James McGregor, ...   7,500.00
   Austin Fund, being part of a bequest from Mrs.
     Agnes Austin, ...   5,000.00
   Kittredge Fund, being a bequest from Rufus
     Kittredge, ...   5,500.00
   Templeton Fund, being half of a bequest from
     John Templeton, ...   5,000.00
                                    $74,010.00

Income devoted to Female Beneficiaries at Asylum: —

The Lincoln Fund, being half of a bequest from Mrs.
F. W. Lincoln, ...   85,000.00

Income unrestricted: —

The Waldo Fund, being a bequest from Daniel Waldo,   40,000.00

Income devoted to any purpose except buildings: —

The Redman Fund, being a bequest from John Redman,   455,113.34

Income devoted to a Triennial Prize: —

The Warren Prize Fund, being a bequest from Dr.
J. M. Warren, ...   2,299.61

Income devoted to the Library : —

The Treadwell Library Fund, being part of a bequest
from J. G. Treadwell, ...   5,000.00

Income devoted to Books for Patients: —

The Warren Library Fund, being a donation from
Dr. J. C. Warren, ...   1,000.00

Income and Principal devoted to the publication of a History of the Hospital: —

The Bowditch History Fund, being a bequest from
N. I. Bowditch, ...   2,000.00
          Amount carried forward, ... $1,142,683 90

Amount brought forward, ...		$1,142,683.90

Income devoted to Amusements at the Asylum: —

The Amusement Fund, $5,000 being a bequest from Miss Mary Louisa Shaw, $5,000 being a donation from Mrs. Quincy A. Shaw and other Ladies, ... — 10,000.00

Income devoted to Special Surgical Instruments: —

The Surgical Instrument Fund, being a donation from Dr. H. J. Bigelow, $1,250; donation of Mr. R. M. Moore, $100, ... — 1,350.00

The Wooden Leg Fund: —

Being a bequest from N. I. Bowditch, ... 5,000.00

The Convalescent's Home Fund, . . 12,334.83

The Convalescent's Home Building Fund, ... 89,638.85

Permanent Free Beds: —

Miss Marian Hovey, ...	$1,000 00	
Mrs. Fanny H. Morse, ...	1,000.00	
Henry S. Hovey, ...	1,000.00	
Edward Woodman, ...	1,000.00	4,000.00

Redman Annuities, ... 15,600.00

Clara Barton Annuity, ... 3,241.00

Asylum Building Fund, ... 124,547.31

G. H. Gay Fund, ... 25,000.00

Add unused income at credit of

The Warren Prize Fund, ...	$824.54	
Warren Library Fund.	352.12	
Bowditch History Fund, ...	1,786.31	
Surgical Instrument Fund, ...	1,087.02	
Wooden Leg Fund.	604.69	
G. H. Gay Fund, ...	275.00	
Treadwell Library Fund, ...	62.12	
Asylum Building Fund, ...	18,151.37	
Clara Barton Annuity, ...	35.74	
		23,178.91
Total of Restricted Funds, ...		$1,456,574.80

TRIAL BALANCE, Dec. 31, 1882.

Dr.		Cr.		
Land and Buildings for Asylum,	$320,794.75	Redman Fund,	$455,113.34	$821.54
Land and Buildings for Hospital,	485,472.73	Warren Prize Fund,	2,299.61	
Thayer Building,	25,504.61	Bowditch History Fund,	2,000.00	1,786.31
Land and Improvements at Belmont,	52,780.59	Wooden Leg Fund,	5,000.00	604.69
Buildings at Belmont,—Convalescent's Home,	34,713.02	Redman Annuities,	15,600.00	
Land at Waltham,	11,200.00	Clara Barton Annuity,	3,241.00	35.71
Land at Chicago,	4,961.27	Surgical Instrument Fund,	1,350.00	1,087.02
Annuities Receivable,	160,000.00	Amusement Fund,	10,000.00	
City of Boston Loan,	24,000.00	Free Bed Funds,	478,260.95	
Insurance Stocks,	50,000.00	Warren Library Fund,	1,000.00	352.12
Delaware Mutual Insurance Co.'s Scrip,	365.00	Beneficiaries at Asylum Funds,	74,010.00	
Railroad Bonds,	487,600.00	Treadwell Library Fund,	5,000.00	62.12
Union League Club Bonds,	12,000.00	Lincoln Fund,	85,000.00	
Manufacturing Stocks,	41,400.00	Funds with Income Unrestricted,	40,000.00	
Bank Stocks,	67,500.00	Asylum Building Fund,	124,547.31	18,151.37
Real Estate Productive,	352,391.64	Fund for Convalescents, Miss Russell,	12,354.83	
Notes Receivable,	268,600.00	Convalescent's Building Fund,	89,638.85	275.00
Cash,	8,847.50	G. H. Gay Fund,	25,000.00	
Edward Cowles, Superintendent,	31,634.44	General Fund,	978,397.20	
J. H. Whittemore, Resident Physician,	1,756.45	Permanent Free Beds,	4,000.00	
Reversions (see item "Suspense" on Cr. side),	9.00	Suspense (see item "Reversions" on Dr. side),	9.00	
		Notes Payable,	2,500	
		Subscribers for Free Beds, 1883,	3,050	
	$2,441,531.00		2,418,352.09	
				$2,441,531.00

Trial Balance at Close of Business, Dec. 31, 1882.

Property on hand belonging to the Corporation invested as follows: —

INVESTMENTS PRODUCING NO INCOME.

Asylum.— Land and Buildings occupied for Asylum,	$320,794.75	
Steward's balance,	31,634.44	
		$352,429.19
Hospital.— Land and Buildings occupied for Hospital,	$485,472.73	
Steward's balance,	1,756.45	
Thayer Building,	25,504.61	
		512,733.79
Convalescent's Home.— Land and Buildings occupied for Convalescent's Home,		87,493.61
Sundries.— Land in Waltham,	$11,200.00	
Land in Chicago,	4,961.27	
Memorandum of expectancies,	9.00	
		16,170.27
		$968,826.86

INVESTMENTS PRODUCING INCOME.

Policies Mass. Hospital Life Ins. Co.,	$160,000.00
500 shares Mass. Hospital Life Ins. Co.,	50,000.00
$24,000 City of Boston Bonds,	24,000.00
$21,000 Eastern Railroad Bonds @ 70,	14,700.00
$1,000 Kansas City & Cameron Railroad Bonds,	1,000.00
$5,000 Boston & Lowell Railroad 7 ℁ c. Bonds,	5,000.00
$5,000 Boston & Albany Railroad 7 ℁ c. Bonds	5,000.00
$100,000 Chicago, Bur. & Quincy R.R. 7 ℁ c. Bonds,	100,000.00
$11,000 Chicago, Bur. & Quincy R.R. 5 ℁ c. Bonds @ 90	9,900.00
$12,000 Union League Club Bonds,	12,000.00
$100,000 Atchison, Topeka & Santa Fé 7s.,	100,000.00
$100,000 Atchison, Topeka & Santa Fé 4½s.,	100,000.00
$100,000 Oregon R.R. & Navigation Co. 6s.,	100,000.00
$29,000 Bur. & Mo. River in Neb., Non-Ex. 6s,	29,000.00
$10,000 Atchison Land Grant 7s.,	10,000.00
$10,000 Kansas City, Topeka & Western R.R. 1st M. 7s.,	10,000.00
$3,000 Old Colony Railroad 6s.,	3,000.00
14 Shares Merrimack Manufacturing Co.,	14,000.00
1 " Appleton " "	1,000.00
9 " Amory " "	900.00
9 " Amoskeag " "	9,000.00
25 " Great Falls " "	2,500.00
5 " Boston,	5,000.00
9 " Stark Mills,	9,000.00
100 " National Union Bank,	10,000.00
70 " Tremont National Bank,	7,000.00
50 " Old Boston " "	2,500.00
100 " Suffolk " "	10,000.00
10 " State " "	1,000.00
Amount carried forward,	$805,500.00

Amount brought forward, ...		$805,500.00
100 Shares Columbian National Bank, ...		10,000.00
100 " Merchants " "		10,000.00
20 " New England " "		2,000.00
40 " Massachusetts " "		10,000.00
50 " Eagle " "		5,000.00
Land and Store, 17 Blackstone Street, ...		19,600.00
" " " 168 Washington Street, ...		45,000.00
" " House, 61 Dartmouth Street, ...		10,000.00
Hospital Wharf, ...		62,000.00
Redman Mansion Estate, Washington Street, . . .		106,000.00
Land and Houses on Warrenton Street, ...		17,700.00
" " Store, 496 Washington Street, ...		55,500.00
" " Houses on Chambers Street, ...		23,900.00
" " " 42–50 Cross Street, ...		12,691.64
Notes secured by Mortgage, ...		214,600.00
$20,000 Notes Phila., Wilmington & Balt. R.R., . .		20,000.00
$34,000 Notes Stark Mills, ...		34,000.00
$365 Scrip. Delaware Mutual Insurance Co., ...		365.00
Cash deposited in bank at interest, ...		8,847.50
Investments producing Income, ...	.	$1,472,704.14
Investments producing no Income, ...		968,826.86
The exact foot of Trial Balance, ...		$2,441,531.00

EDMUND DWIGHT, *Treasurer.*

OF THE

MASSACHUSETTS GENERAL HOSPITAL

For the Year 1882.

***

Number of Patients in the Hospital, January 1, 1882.

Paying, ... 15
Free, ... 140

     Total, ... 155

Admitted from January 1, 1882, to January 1, 1883.

	Males.	Females.	Total.
Patients paying board, ...	259	140	399
Patients paying board part of the time, .	7	5	12
Patients entirely free, ...	1,102	634	1,736
	1,368	779	2,147

	Medical.	Surgical.
Males (Boys, 149), ...	412	956
Females (Girls, 62), ...	384	395
	796	1,351

Of these, 6 paid $50 per week; 18 paid $35; 2 paid $28; 4 paid $25; 59 paid $21; 1 paid $15; 2 paid $14; 5 paid $12; 117 paid $10.50; 3 paid $10; 2 paid $8; 147 paid $7; 2 paid $6; 23 paid $5; 8 paid $4; 7 paid $3; 1 paid $2.50; 3 paid $2; 1 paid $1.50.

Whole number of patients treated during the year: paying, 414; paying a part of the time, 12; free, 1,876; total, 2,302.

Discharged during the Year.

	Medical.	Surgical.	Male.	Female.	Total.
Well, ...	402	910	878	434	1,312
Much relieved, ...	140	133	166	107	273
Relieved, ...	88	102	115	75	190
Not relieved, ...	41	18	37	22	59
Not treated, ...	35	78	50	63	113
Dead, ...	87	90	126	51	177
Insane and eloped, . . .	2	11	8	5	13
	795	1,342	1,380	757	2,137

Number of Patients remaining December 31, 1882.

Males, ...	93
Females, ...	72
Total, ...	165

Paying, ...	24
Free, ...	141
Total, ...	165

Medical, ...	65
Surgical, ...	100
Total, ...	165

Proportion of deaths to whole number of results, 8.28 per cent.

Number of patients received on account of accidents, 348.

The greatest number of paying patients at any one time was 35; in private rooms, 8: the greatest number of free patients, 167; the greatest total, 195. The least number of paying patients at any one time was 13; in private rooms, 1; the least free, 125; the least total, 143. The proportion of ward beds occupied by free patients was 85 per cent.; by paying patients, 15 per cent. About 2.87 per cent. of the paying patients occupied private rooms. The average number of patients was 168: males, 108; females, 60.

The average number of paying patients was 21: Americans, 15.5; foreigners, 5.5.

The average number in private rooms was 4.

The average number of free patients was 147: Americans, 72; foreigners, 75.

The average time of paying patients was 2.84 weeks; and that of free patients, 4.41.

Residences.

Boston, ...	951
Massachusetts (excepting Boston), ...	1,012
Maine, ...	44
New Hampshire and Vermont, ...	51
Rhode Island and Connecticut, ...	26
Other States, ...	47
British Provinces, ...	16
	2,147

Birthplaces.

Boston, ...	163
Massachusetts (excepting Boston), ...	599
Maine, ...	114
New Hampshire, ...	84
Vermont, ...	33
Rhode Island and Connecticut, ...	29
New York, ...	43
Southern and Western States, ...	62
Total Americans, ...	1,127
British Provinces, ...	219
Great Britain, ...	122
Ireland, ...	564
Germany, ...	36
Norway and Sweden, ...	26
France, ...	6
Western Islands, ...	10
Belgium and Holland, ...	1
Italy, ...	7
Switzerland, ...	3
Other places, ...	26
Total foreigners, ...	1,020

Occupations.

Males.	Paying.	Free.	Partial Payment.
Mechanics, ...	26	95	
Laborers, ...	55	613	3
Farmers, ...	22	35	
Minors, ...	17	148	
Seamen, ...	19	40	3
Clerks, ...	20	32	1
Teamsters, ...	5	26	
Traders, ...	11	17	
Servants, ...	1	19	
Lawyers, ...		2	
Clergymen, ...	2	1	
Physicians, ...	5	4	
Merchants, ...	22	8	
Students, ...	7	10	.
Other professions, ...	47	52	
	259	1,102	7

Total males, 1,368. Of these, 61 were in private rooms.

Females.	Paying.	Free.	Partial Payment.
Domestics, ...	14	243	1
Minors, ...	12	57	
Wives, ...	85	183	2
Widows, ...	11	36	
Seamstresses, ...	1	18	
Spinsters, ...	11	44	1
Operatives, ...	1	13	
Teachers, ...	1	6	
Clerks, ...	2	8	
Nurses, ...	2	26	
	140	634	5

Total females, 779. Of these, 37 were in private rooms.

Fourteen per cent. of the free patients were female domestics; thirty-five per cent. were laborers; five per cent. were mechanics; and eleven per cent. were minors.

28

Admissions Refused.

Phthisis (Consumption),	41
Syphilis,	33
Chronic Ulcers,	26
Scrofula and Abscesses,	20
Insanity and Delirium Tremens,	16
Hip and Spine,	47
Debility and Senility,	16
Chronic Rheumatism,	22
Paralysis,	23
Epilepsy,	10
Cancer,	14
Uterine,	15
Injuries,	12
Of skin,	12
Contagious,	9
Other diseases,	124
Total,	440
Males,	273
Females,	167
Americans,	263
Foreigners,	177
Residents of Boston,	154
Residents of Massachusetts,	227
Residents of other places,	59

Out-Patients.

Number of new patients,	16,304
Men,	5,659
Women,	7,219
Children,	3,426
Americans,	8,993
Foreigners,	7,311
Residents of Boston,	10,773
Of other places,	5,531
Medical department for women,	3,047
Medical department for men and children,	2,693
Surgical department,	4,070
Ophthalmic department,	327
Dental department,	3,973
Department for diseases of the skin,	961
Department for diseases of the nervous system,	437
Department for diseases of the throat,	796
Total attendance,	33,604

Average daily attendance,	109
Fractures and dislocations,	296
Wounds,	452
Sprains and injuries,	654
Abscesses,	267
Ulcers,	198
Felons,	97
Tumors,	273
Diseases of hip,	60
Diseases of spine,	52
Genito-urinary,	259
Club-foot,	22
Specific,	140
Hernia,	77
Necrosis,	0
Fistula in Ano,	24
Diseases of joints,	197
Referred,	325
Miscellaneous,	677

Of the dental patients, 899 had 1,197 teeth filled, 3,062 had 4,849 teeth extracted.

Whole number of new patients in the Out-Patient Department in 1880,	20,566
Whole number of new patients in 1881,	18,443
Whole number of new patients in 1882,	16,304
Whole number refused admission in 1882,	1,947
Whole number of visits of investigation,	1,974
Whole number found deserving of charity,	1,080
Whole number found undeserving of charity,	894

Convalescent's Home.

The Convalescent's Home at Waverly was opened for the admission of patients on April 19, 1882, and from that time to January 1, 1883, there have been: —

	Males.	Females.	Total.
Admitted,	62	39	101
Discharged,	53	33	86
Remaining January 1, 1883,	9	6	15

The anticipated benefits of the Home have been fully realized in the case of every person admitted; and, in a very short time after admission, the beneficial effects of the change to this attractive and healthy locality become apparent, and continue through the residence there. Improved health and abundant gratitude from those sent there have been the rewards for the privileges enjoyed.

The Home has been very generously remembered by many kind friends, who have sent us a cabinet organ, framed pictures, books, magazines, illustrated papers, and money in small sums, to provide needed small articles. All of which have contributed directly to the comfort and entertainment of the patients.

The Young Men's Christian Union has given seventy-seven "Drives for Patients," taking out four hundred and six individuals. This, and the various other acts of kindness from many different sources, are highly appreciated, and aid the Hospital in its usefulness.

I am especially indebted to Dr. J. B. Swift and the resident officers for their efficient and devoted services to the Hospital during my prolonged absence last summer.

Respectfully submitted,

JAMES H. WHITTEMORE,
Resident Physician.

BOSTON, Jan. 1, 1883.

TABLE SHOWING THE COST OF THE PRINCIPAL STORES AT THE MASSACHUSETTS GENERAL HOSPITAL.

Articles.	1877 Quantity	1877 Cost	1877 Average	1878 Quantity	1878 Cost	1878 Average	1879 Quantity	1879 Cost	1879 Average	1880 Quantity	1880 Cost	1880 Average	1881 Quantity	1881 Cost	1881 Average	1882 Quantity	1882 Cost	1882 Average
Beef, Sirloin, lbs.	9,100	$1,927.38	.2118	7,729	$1,610.72	.2084	8,375	$1,716.87	.205	8,815	$1,692.90	.1941	8,658	$1,792.20	.207	7,856	$1,931.95	.245
" for Soup, "	560	23.80	.0425	132	5.28	.04	.....	.....	.....	.....	.....	.....	.....	.....	.....	.....	.....	.....
" Corned, "	5,889	479.54	.0816	4,378	324.72	.07415	4,123	288.61	.07	4,952	346.64	.07	5,183	361.99	.07	6,522	673.76	.103
" Round, "	9,327	805.85	.0864	11,944	1,016.43	.0851	12,973	1,054.70	.0813	16,411	1,148.98	.0813	19,477	1,636.06	.084	19,705	1,976.68	.103
" Rump, "	6,882	1,163.05	.169	4,158	635.34	.1528	.....	.....	.....	.....	.....	.....	.....	.....	.....	.....	.....	.....
" Roasting, "	11,584	1,274.24	.11	14,498	1,349.82	.09	14,141	1,341.98	.0949	16,439	1,643.90	.10	16,438	1,758.86	.107	16,221	2,159.07	.13½
Mutton, "	18,416	2,509.04	.1362¼	15,808	1,903.28	.1204	12,592	1,385.13	.11	15,522	1,876.60	.1208	21,083	2,720.19	.129	16,365	2,216.01	.135
Poultry, "	13,509	2,476.65	.184	14,079	2,276.57	.1617	14,488	2,433.98	.168	13,682	2,123.44	.1552	12,082	2,278.41	.168	12,082	2,348.41	.195
Butter, "	10,006	2,644.72	.263	10,156	2,500.40	.2462	10,526	2,689.39	.246	11,011	3,366.06	.3057	11,129	3,565.63	.315	16,843	3,765.97	.221
Eggs, doz.	4,608	967.68	.21	5,495	967.12	.176	4,392	843.26	.192	4,214	866.39	.2056	4,401	1,188.27	.26	5,234	1,470.59	.281
Fish, bbls.	40	362.48	9.062	42	323.82	7.71	37	266.80	7.40	51	440.15	8.65	49	468.73	9.565	49	459.25	9.357
Bread, lbs.	34,343	1,717.15	.05	35,800	1,790.00	.05	36,566	1,827.80	.05	40,536	2,026.80	.05	34,892	1,744.60	.05	35,340	1,941.70	.05
Ice, tons.	180½	627.54	3.48	242½	808.25	3.333	271½	714.70	2.63	280½	1,297.56	4.63	305	887.55	2.91	352½	737.72	2.209
Sugar, lbs.	10,592	982.88	.0928	12,979½	1,023.65	.0781	15,462	1,189.32	.769	21,005	2,003.87	.0954	20,552	1,901.06	.09	22,192	2,021.67	.091
Tea, lbs.	593	222.95	.376	738	254.61	.345	848	337.82	.398	1,114½	471.95	.43	555	244.22	.44	1,114	446.85	.401
Milk, qts.	97,594	4,879.70	.05	96,186	5,380.90	.05	96,186	4,934.34	.0513	89,904½	4,495.22½	.05	92,350	4,617.50	.05	95,358	5,07.70	.052
Potatoes, bush.	909	915.36	1.007	942	964.61	.77	942	1,010.76	1.073	981	902.58	.868	981	1,101.66	1.125	1,005	1,374.72	1.368

SIXTY-FIFTH ANNUAL REPORT

OF THE

SUPERINTENDENT OF THE MCLEAN ASYLUM FOR THE INSANE,

TO THE

TRUSTEES OF THE MASS. GENERAL HOSPITAL,

For the Year 1882.

To the Trustees of the Massachusetts General Hospital:

Gentlemen,— The following report, with tabular statements relating to the number and condition of the patients treated in the Asylum during the year 1882, is respectfully presented : —

TABLE No. 1.

GENERAL STATISTICS OF THE YEAR.

	Males.	Females.	Total.
Patients in the Asylum, Jan. 1, 1882,	63	92	155
Admissions within the year,	42	40	82
Whole number of *cases* within the year,	105	132	237
Discharged within the year,	31	39	70
Namely,—as Recovered,	11	15	26
Much improved,	1	6	7
Improved,	7	7	14
Unimproved,	6	9	15
Deaths,	6	2	8
Patients remaining Dec. 31, 1882, supported as private patients,	74	93	167
Number of different *persons* within the year,	105	130	235
" " " " admitted,	42	40	82
" " " " recovered,	11	15	26
Daily average number of patients,	66.41	89.50	155.91

During the year, no person was twice admitted. Two women were discharged, recovered, and readmitted, both returning upon voluntary requests without commitment.   One of them was not insane, returning at nearly the end of the year for a brief residence as a matter of precaution on her part. Thus there were two hundred and thirty-seven cases treated, representing two hundred and thirty-five persons.

Of the eighty-two persons admitted, fifty-three were regarded as recent cases, and twenty-nine as chronic or as incurable, at the time of admission.

Sixty-two persons, twenty-eight men and thirty-four women, had never been in any hospital. Of the remaining twenty persons, ten, nine men and one woman, were admitted for the second time ; six, four men and two women, for the third time; two women for the fourth time, one woman for the eleventh time, and one man for the eighteenth time. Of these twenty persons, ten, seven men and three women, had been former inmates of this asylum.

Eleven persons, four men and seven women, were admitted as voluntary patients, upon their written applications for treatment in accordance with an act of the Legislature of 1881. Three men were cases of temporary mental disturbance : two recovered, and one discharged improved, subsequently died of Bright's disease. One woman, not insane, was discharged after a few weeks' residence; and the remainder, one man and six women, remain as patients. Four of these voluntary patients had formerly been inmates of the asylum.

There were sixteen more admissions, five more discharges, and seventeen more cases under treatment than during the year 1881 ; and the number present was twelve more at the end than at the beginning of the year.

Of the seventy persons discharged, including deaths, eleven were transferred to other hospitals,— two men and seven women to those in this State, and one man and one woman to the New Hampshire asylum. Of the twenty-six persons discharged recovered, eighteen had never before been inmates of any hospital; and, of the remaining eight persons, seven had been in this asylum. These eight persons had previously made twenty-nine recoveries, four of which were at other hospitals.

The average duration, from the beginning of attack, of all cases recovered was 10.54 months, and the average duration of their hospital residence was 8.86 months.

The percentage of recoveries on admissions was 30.48. The number of recoveries was larger by five than in any year since 1870. Danvers Hospital, now being full, receives fewer than formerly of the acute cases from the region that naturally contributes to this asylum. Thus there is an increase of such cases here, and therefore of recoveries.

Of the eight deaths during the year, one was of an elderly person who had been many years in the asylum. Three persons died of general paralysis, one of chronic Bright's disease, and three were inmates of the asylum but a short time and gave no promise of recovery on admission.

In view of the removal to a new asylum within a few years, it is with reluctance that expenditures are recommended to be made upon the buildings now occupied. But, to keep them in a condition of proper cleanliness and comfort, certain things need to be done in the way of repairing, painting, etc.; and this work has been carried on during the past year. In the process of doing this necessary work, experiments can be made with comparatively little added expense, in alterations of construction, as of windows and of arrangements of wards and rooms, that will be of value in preparation for perfecting plans of new buildings.

In last year's report, a description was given of the alterations made in one of the oldest of the women's wards on the lower floor, by which a sunny alcove was added at its dark end, with a broad window fitted with large panes of glass, the window being arranged to open widely to admit the summer breezes, and being guarded only by fine wire gauze, such as is commonly used in private dwellings. Similar alterations are approaching completion in the two wards on the second and third floors of the same building. Each of the wards is also being divided midway of its length into two smaller ones of five rooms each by a partition with wide folding doors filled with colored glass, and thus a valuable addition is being made to the means of classifying the patients. The ventilation of all these wards, before defective, has been made satisfactory by the introduction of an ample supply of warmed air in each of the alcoves, and by large ventilating fiues that have been inexpensively constructed in the corners of the wards. They are thus .made to fulfil the requirements of hospital wards for the proper treatment of the sick, while they are rendered more homelike and attractive by their smaller size and by bright and cheerful decorations. These wards are thus also made to conform with the homelike aspect characteristic of the other parts of the asylum. In various places, the windows are being improved by inexpensive alterations, permitting the use of large panes of glass, and the substitution for the former guards of the slight protection, necessary when the windows are widely opened, afforded by wire netting, as before described. The appearance of the chapel has been greatly improved by such a change of the windows and the use of some colored glass.

A covered promenade, about seventy feet long by eight feet wide, recently built in one of the gardens, already proves useful in permitting the more insane female patients to take out-door exercise in winter and in stormy weather.

These things are being done for the purpose of providing good conditions for active hospital work in the treatment of the sick, in a way consistent with proper economy, by arrangements of construction that at the same time shall be homelike and agreeable to persons ill with a malady that requires long residence under treatment. A most important principle is involved in this, in regard to giving due prominence to the moral treatment of the insane and to individualizing the cases.

There has, of late, been much discussion of the question of the curability of insanity; and the results of the treatment of the insane in large and well-managed hospitals, like those in Massachusetts, are still disappointing as compared with results reported to be gained in the early days of the older and smaller hospitals. A reduction from 75 per cent. to 20 per cent. of recoveries is perhaps due to something more than the errors of the older statistics. It is probably true that the majority of the insane can be best and most practicably treated away from their homes and in hospitals, and these are not yet accomplishing what has been hoped of them in curative results. Instead, however, of treating this fact in terms of reproach, it should not be forgotten that mental disease involves the disorder of an organ of a highly complex and delicate structure, and comparisons between its diseases and those of other organs of the body should not be drawn unfairly. It has its own physiological and pathological laws; and, at the best, its diseases may have to be regarded as largely incurable. The fact that the insane are treated mostly in hospitals and become burdens upon the State gives them prominence because of their economic relations. Let us suppose that tubercular diseases are to be regarded as infectious, and that their subjects are to be put into hospitals. What public alarm would be aroused by the great number and fatality of cases of this disease, now unrealized, or by the burden of the care of its chronic forms; and how soon would it become the fashion to reproach those who treat it because of its incurability?

The insane must be cared for with due regard to public and private economy, and the system now common to all civilized countries of collecting them in large hospitals is held to be on trial. It is, at all events, imperative that no possible effort should be spared to get curative results from the treatment of the insane. Curability certainly diminishes with duration of mental disease, and its earliest stages should be most thoroughly studied and treated. The smaller hospitals are endowed with greater facilities for individualizing cases, and for treatment; and, therefore, a great responsibility lies with them for making the best use of those facilities. They should encourage the admission of acute cases, and devote their best energies to their study and care. It seems to me that in such hospitals, where the means and the opportunity are liberally given, while due regard is to be had to a proper conservatism, it is a special duty to explore new paths, if any there be, beyond the beaten ways of procedure in the management of the insane. To stand still is to fail, when progress is demanded and is possible; for even negative results are valuable. It is also a duty to report experiments for the later tests of criticism and experience, and hence this may be deemed a fitting time and place for putting on record some of the results of the study of the problems of hospital management in this asylum during the past three years.

Developing a homelike aspect of the hospital, destroying the suggestion of insanity as differing from other disease, individualizing the patients, and perfecting the conditions for moral treatment are of prime importance. The truth goes further, and includes the essential fact that we are treating sick people, and are, after all, dealing with a hospital.

One of the first considerations, therefore, was the quality of the nursing of the sick. The aim has been to introduce the best methods of the general hospitals, by promoting the growth of the spirit that prompts devotion to the sick; requiring constant personal attention to them as individuals, by compauionship as well as nursing; introducing ward-maids to perform duties that distract the attention of nurses from more important ones; increasing the number of nurses on duty at night, so that most of the patients can have the doors of their rooms unlocked, and all noteworthy events can be observed and systematically reported; employing experienced night supervisors to see that all medical directions are properly carried out, and that everything is done to promote the comfort and cure of the sick; in short, by providing a service qualified for the task of treating a houseful of acute cases. This is the beginning of what it is believed can be accomplished as the result of the recent employment of a superintendent of nurses, and of a systematic course of training and instruction which is to be adopted for them. To one who has employed in hospital wards intelligent and well-trained nurses who have an interest in their work as a profession, their value in the companionship as well as the care and treatment of the insane needs no commendation.

In the direction of developing the hospital element of the work, the employment of an ample medical

staff has given increased satisfaction during the past
year. An assistant physician for each service, male
and female, is a liberal allowance for a total of one
hundred and seventy patients; but, in an asylum of
this kind, much attention must, or can well be,
bestowed upon individuals. The continued employment of a house-pupil for each service, to do the
work of clinical clerks, as in general hospitals, is a
valuable addition to the organization. It is understood that the time thus gained by the assistant physicians from clerical and other duty shall be employed
in professional work. And, to facilitate this, a room
has been fitted up for a laboratory and the use of the
microscope; and a systematic course of study, begun
a year ago, is now going on under the direction of
Dr. Gannett, of Boston, who is also employed as the
pathologist of the asylum.

A consideration of the moral treatment of insanity
of course leads over ground that is not new, but it
may be permitted to restate a few propositions. It is
important, at the outset, to establish the principle
which shall serve as a basis for the moral treatment
of the insane person as an individual. The underly-
ing principle in the whole matter is that the patient
should be treated as a reasoning being. In other
words, from the moment he enters the hospital, it
should be assumed that he will understand more or
less correctly all that is said or done to him. Therefore, he should be treated as if he were expected to
act rationally, and led to see that, after his failure
to do what is expected of him, he brings upon himself
friendly advice, criticism, reproof, and, if need be,
restriction. On the part of others, while the attitude
toward him of physicians and nurses should be as
toward a rational man, the fact of his illness and
mental obscuration should be kept in view; and the

conditions of his daily life should be made easy by conforming them as nearly as possible to those of his ordinary experience. His clouded and perverted understanding should be given as few unaccustomed problems for comprehension as possible in his new mode of life in the hospital.

The physiological basis of all moral treatment of the insane is the fact that the normal functions of the cerebral organ may be only temporarily disturbed or only partially impaired, whether by temporary disorder or pathological change, and the consequent fact that in most cases some degree of normal function remains. This principle cannot be better stated than by Dr. Gairdner, in his presidential address to the British Medico-Psychological Association last August. Speaking of the improved treatment of the insane, begun in the time of. Pinel and Tuke, he says it has gradually come to· be regarded as the truth that "the unsound mind, like the unsound body, can only be regarded as an instance of disordered function; and that, however great the disorder, the functions are still there, and may be roused into more or less healthy activity by exactly the same physiological stimuli as are available in the state of health" He would name as the most important gain of modern physiology and pathology for the healing art, the modern conception or theory of disease,— that "disease is, for the most part, normal function acting under abnormal conditions." He argues, therefore, that the insane mind is not *aliena mens*, but has like passions and emotions with the sound mind; and that the sound elements still remaining must be carefully respected, strengthened, and built up again, if possible.

All moral treatment, then, should be addressed to the purpose of calling into normal exercise the rational part of the disordered mind. The patient should be assumed to be capable of some degree of understanding of the fact that he is ill; and all the conduct of others toward him should frankly and consistently declare this, before as well as after his entering the hospital. The fact should be made as plain as possible to him that his commitment by the court is according to law, and based upon medical opinion outside of the hospital. There are few patients who cannot be beneficially impressed in this way, however much they may contest the correctness of the judgment upon them.

Once within the hospital, the conduct of physicians and nurses toward the patient should show that he is regarded as simply ill, and as having no reason for being ashamed of his illness. Therefore, he should always be called a "patient," and not a "boarder," as is the custom in some hospitals, and has been in this one from its earliest days. This latter term implies an evasion of the fact of illness, as if it were a disgrace, and by a euphemism fosters the very feeling of which we are trying to disabuse the patient. Dr. Kirkbride has pointed out the same effect as inherent in the use of the word "asylum" for "hospital."

For the same reason, the word "attendant" is unfortunate, although it is so much better than the older term, "keeper." It would be only the truth to call them "nurses." While everything should be done to make the place homelike and cheerful, with pleasant parlors, books, pictures, music, diversion, and occupation suited to the individual, the idea of the hospital is in it all, and no attempt should be made to ignore it. It should appear rather that active attention is being given to the business of curing the sick. "Attendants" may attend the infirm and incurable; but "nurses" attend the sick, and the experience of recovery from illness is so common that the very idea of the presence of a nurse logically carries with it the other idea, that something is being done to promote recovery, and that itself inspires hope and is curative. The key-note of all that is addressed to the patient on this subject should be, " You are ill, you may get well."

In practically working out the general principle that has been stated, it is believed that successful results have also been gained in two other experiments during the past three years.

One of these is the employment of female nurses in men's wards, as described in my report of last year. For the majority of insane men, this-is practicable ; and every day's experience with it teaches me to prize more highly its value. To put a man accustomed to the comforts, or even if no more than to the habits, of domestic life, into a restricted association with men, would be to him an experience of which he probably has had no previous conception. Such a way of living would be unnatural and unattractive to most men, and to the sick man, whose mind is already disturbed, a cause of added discomfort. In such an association of men alone, the inevitable tendency is to degenerate in manner of speech and conduct; and this is true both of the patients, and, what is very important, of the men nurses also. There is something lacking after all efforts to make the wards homelike and agreeable.

The presence of female nurses in most of the wards, and of young women as ward-maids, is as easily managed as in the wards of a general hospital. Although some of the conditions differ, there is much to prove the practicability of this in ordinary hospitals, in the successful management of all the men's wards of the Mount Hope Retreat at Baltimore, by the Sisters of Charity. The insane man coming into such a ward is restrained and softened, and practises instinctively a degree of self-control that he would not have thought of trying to exercise in the presence of men alone. His first impressions upon entering the asylum are far more agreeable than in the former case, and continue so. The special qualifications of women for the care of the wards and the sick are of great value, and the moral and curative influence of their habitual presence in our wards for men is positive, and would not be willingly given up. The good results that have followed this practice flow directly from its influence in stimulating the exercise of the remaining sound elements of the mind, and of healthy and decent habits of thought and conduct.

The other experiment, which is believed to have given some special and good results, is in regard to the freedom of communication between patients and their relatives or friends, by visiting or correspondence. It is now two and a half years since my former liberal practice grew into the adoption of the present rule for the following reasons. Few of the insane have their understandings so confused and clouded as not to leave enough of normal mental function to conceive of the reasonableness of removing a sick person to a hospital. There is often, on the part of persons so removed, a consciousness of the propriety of this action, even in those who will not confess it. Even in cases of maniacal excitement and melancholia with stupor, we may rely upon being able to instil into the mind some degree of consciousness of the true nature of the act of removal to a hospital. When, however, we come to abruptly separate the insane person from all communication with relatives and friends, we institute a condition of things which is the more difficult to understand as the patient is more insane. The patient probably knows the usual fact, that the distance is not great from home and friends. Enforced separation and interdiction of communication beget suspicion of those friends, if it has not been entertained before, or of the physicians of the hospital. It is of the first importance not to increase or arouse this suspicion, and to convince the patient of the desire to treat him with generous fairness and indulgence. Therefore, the rule is that, from the outset, the relatives or friends shall be allowed to visit the patient. Care is taken to have it understood by all concerned that the physician will see no objection to such visiting *until the patient shall give cause for it.*

This is the *rule;* but, like all rules, it has its exceptions. The patient who has an antipathy and delusion regarding relatives might not be allowed to receive visits for some time after the first one, or even the first might be denied; but it is remarkable how few patients there are who require this restriction. In this asylum, of one hundred and sixty-seven patients present, there are only three who do not receive visits from relatives quite regularly. One man with chronic mania refuses to see them because of a violent antipathy; and the relatives of two other men with mania have to refrain from visiting on their own account, but visits are made by friends. It has been observed that, if excitement attends the first visit, which should be made early, it is as a rule no greater than attended contact with friends at the home recently left; and, in fact, this visit is regarded as a necessary part of the process of accommodating the patient to the new situation, and aids it. The first visits often have a remarkable effect in disarming the patient of fast-forming suspicions as to the purposes of friends, and help to inspire him with a salutary confidence, which aids in leading him to accept sooner the rôle of an invalid. The friends, and this term is used to include relatives, learn by these visits to render valuable aid in the management of the case, and most readily accede to the proposition that they should refrain from visiting, if it has proved not to be good for the patient.

This practice stands the test of the continuance of the visits, even though, as is sometimes the case, the first ones are attended with some degree of excitement. The visits are almost invariably desired by the patient, who soon comes to understand, if need be, that they are allowed or denied according to his conduct, and thus a means is given for stimulating self-control. Sometimes, the desire to see friends can be aroused when it has been absent; and a curative result is gained by the exercise of a normal function of the mind in the gratification of the desire.

In other exceptional cases, as of acute mania, or others with mental confusion or stupor, the seeing of friends may seem to give negative results, and little notice may be taken of the visitors; but, in these conditions, it is well known that impressions may still go in upon the obscured perceptions, when no outward sign is given, and are remembered.

As far as moral treatment goes, in these cases of mental confusion as well as in others, efforts calculated to arouse into activity the normal elements of the mind are often of inestimable value, though no evidence of the good impressions thus made appears till long afterward. What more potent means of arousing healthy mental action than is found in the exercise of the natural affections and emotions, and the consciousness of the occasional presence of friends whom the patient has been accustomed to love and trust?

The fact that patients who have been studiously separated from friends for a long time may have had relapses from convalescence almost established, following wearily longed-for visits from relatives, is not a conclusive argument to prove that the visits were made too soon. It is a fair question whether the excess of emotion, naturally aroused by a meeting after long separation, may not produce in such cases a disaster which might be averted under the opposite plan of training the patient from the outset to receive calmly the visits, by the deprivation of which he has not been allowed to become distressed.

Another important consideration is that, when the relatives also are wearied by long separation, they are apt to remove too soon a half-convalescent patient, at first sight of the improved condition, whereas by the other plan they act more understandingly and with calmer judgment. As a matter of fact, it rarely happens under this practice that too early removal of convalescents is urged.

In regard to correspondence, the rule is also a most liberal one, as far as the asylum is concerned. The patient and friends are carefully informed at the outset that no writings of the former, sealed or unsealed, will be intercepted by the asylum authorities, who prefer to be relieved of that responsibility. The patient is told that whatever he writes will be sent to the persons who are to be regarded as the natural or legal guardians, or to other proper persons agreed upon. Most patients readily join in this compact, if made at the outset; and the attitude thus taken by the Superintendent increases greatly his influence over the patient in advising or checking him in regard to writing. It often happens that what one is free to do he does not care to do, or, if he becomes dissatisfied sometimes with the action of friends in arresting letters,—as of course must be done for the protection of the patient from consequences he would afterward regret,—there is, as a rule, a good reason to be given. At all events, it is found that dissatisfaction is reduced to a minimum; and it is made clear that there is no reason known, as far as the asylum is concerned, why all letters should not freely go from it. It is easy to gain through friends the valuable information concerning the state of the patient's mind afforded by his letters; and the friends, being taken into the management of the case throughout, have a better understanding of their duty to the patient when his home relations are resumed.

One more important point is that every well-behaved visitor, if it is desired, is allowed to go to the room of any patient it is proper for him to visit, with due regard to the comfort of others. The nurses are trained to expect this at any time, and it is demonstrated to all concerned that there are no dark places in the asylum to be concealed.

In thus setting forth the working of what is, theoretically and virtually, a removal of restrictions that have been regarded as peculiar to hospitals for the insane, the aim is to show that this is justifiable as the logical sequence of the carrying out of the principles recited in the beginning of this discussion. As a practical demonstration of the results of the effort being made to put this asylum on the basis of a general hospital, particularly as to its being an open and accessible institution, it is shown by this report that the twenty-six recoveries of the last year were possible under the liberal rule which permitted, from the beginning of the treatment of these cases including various types of acute mania, melancholia, etc., regular communication with relatives and friends, guarded by a careful study of its effects and its occasional limitation.

It was the influence of the growth of the principles cited that wrought the improvement in asylum management from the days of Pinel and Tuke to the present time. It is not so many years since it was believed that there was a special curative influence in entire separation of the majority of the insane from friends for long periods, and in their strict seclusion in asylums. Not only was rest in bed enforced by mechanical restraint to prevent exhaustion in maniacal cases, but many appliances were employed to keep quiet the restless sufferers from nervous irritability. It has gradually come to pass that, at the present time, large freedom is accorded to the insane; and the former practice of seclusion from friends and interdiction of communication is greatly modified, and in some instances reduced to small proportions. The practice is not uniform in this regard, however; and there is reason to believe that the views held by many alienists are but a modification of the former ones as to the curative effect of strict seclusion in hospitals, although some have gone so far in this direction as to practically abandon it.

The truth lies somewhere between the older view and a modern one, in regard to the treatment of the insane at their homes. It is believed that the line may be drawn at the point of the removal of the patient to hospital and his separation from home and the former "moral and physical surroundings," and that, beyond this point, the accepted rule of practice should be that liberal communication with friends is to be used as a therapeutic means.

Some evidence of a negative character is available in support of this proposition. It appears not only that the growing liberality of modern times in this regard is doing no harm to the insane, but that there is some special evidence to show that in the treatment of melancholia, which includes so large a class of cases, the methodical employment of seclusion and rest outside of hospitals for the insane has actually failed to be of benefit. While the older views of seclusion and rest have been undergoing modification leading to practical abandonment by some of those who have treated the insane, one of the most important contributions to the healing art in modern times is that made by Dr. Weir Mitchell in the well-known doctrine of "Rest Treatment" by means of "seclusion, rest, massage, electricity, and overfeeding," so successfully employed in the treatment of nervous exhaustion.

If, then, "seclusion" and "rest" are of such essential value in the treatment of nervous exhaustion in persons not insane, why are they not also of value in insanity, which often is simply a greater degree of the same disorder of the nervous system? The answer is, possibly, that, in the former case, the functions of the reasoning faculties are so nearly in a normal state as to permit "seclusion" to be regarded and accepted by the patient as a reasonable necessity, and the path upward toward health is from a point where the mind is not controlled by delusions or given up to despair. After the mental functions are unbalanced, we have to deal with a new set of conditions; and our efforts must be more largely addressed to the moral treatment of the disordered and weakened mind.

In experiments with the rest treatment here, during the past three years, it has been found necessary to modify it. Cases of mental depression are apt to have this increased by rest in bed; and, to those in which melancholia is accompanied by a state of nervous irritability and constant uneasiness or anguish, enforced rest is intolerable, and positively harmful. While rest is useful in some conditions of melancholia and other cases, and benefit has been derived from massage, by producing tissue waste and improving nutrition, and from the other means· of treatment, " seclusion " has been almost entirely abandoned, as not useful and as depriving the patient of what is beneficial. Interesting and valuable evidence on this point is generously afforded me by Dr. Mitchell, who has given me permission to quote from a recent letter some statements which he has never published. He says that in the treatment of " not a small number of cases of melancholia, with bad nutritive break-down, ·in which I attempted to relieve by rest, etc., I made some successes, but more failures,— made in fact so many, that I gave up at last the effort to treat in this way distinct cases of melancholy." "· I may use massage or electricity in melancholy, but I do not seclude or rest these cases."

The rest treatment has been for some years extensively and most successfully employed by Dr. W. S. Playfair, in England. He says in the London *Lancet*, December, 1881, of the cases that are likely to lead to disappointment, that one class is of those in which there is some definite mental disease, and, after a short trial in melancholia, he felt bound to relinquish the treatment.

· What is true of " seclusion " in the treatment of melancholia has also been observed here to be true of other forms of insanity, and concurrent testimony is not lacking from those who treat the insane in hospitals.

While there is unquestionably a growing liberality in the matter of freedom of communication with the insane in hospitals, it is to be recognized that. more will be accomplished in this direction by acting upon a correct theory and with a clear purpose. Instead of a modification of the old rule, its reversal is advocated, and the making of limitations of communication the exception to the rule.

The point now desired to be made is that there is a scientific reason for putting the insane sick person upon the same basis, both as to medical and moral treatment, as the general hospital patient; and, in regarding him simply as the subject of a disease in which normal function is acting under abnormal conditions, it is therefore good practice to unhesitatingly foster, encourage, and, if need be, stimulate the exercise of all normal mental functions, being guided by symptoms as they appear as to all modifications of the general principle in regard to change of residence, restriction of liberty and seclusion, as well as medical treatment proper.

The appointment of a Superintendent of Nurses has already been mentioned. Miss Mary F. Palmer, who was appointed to that office in November, had been twelve years at the Vermont Asylum as attendant and matron, and is a graduate of the Massachusetts General Hospital Training School for Nurses.

A good beginning has been made in collecting a library upon the special subject of nervous and mental diseases. Contributions of any works, though not recently published, on this subject,— books, pamphlets, or journals,— would be gratefully received.

The usual attention has been given to the means of occupying the patients and for their recreation and entertainment. There have been the customary concerts, exhibitions, dancing parties, daily drives, and visits to places of amusement, concerts, etc., in Boston. A rowing machine, several sets of chest weights, etc., put into the building used by the gentlemen for billiards and bowling, have been diligently used and with benefit by some who have taken interest in this form of exercise.

The continued interest in the asylum manifested by its friends, is gratefully appreciated.

Very respectfully,

EDWARD COWLES,
Superintendent.

TABLE No. 2.

MONTHLY ADMISSIONS, DISCHARGES, AND AVERAGES.

Months.	Admissions.			Discharges (including Deaths).			Daily Average of Patients in the House.		
	Ma.	Fe.	Tot.	Ma.	Fe.	Tot.	Ma.	Fe.	Tot.
January, .	3	3	6	1	..	1	62.58	92.65	155 23
February, .	3	4	7	..	3	3	65.07	92.72	157.79
March, . .	4	4	8	3	2	5	66 58	91.48	158.06
April, . .	3	4	7	2	5	7	64.83	90 70	155 53
May, . .	6	4	10	5	1	6	64 39	90 80	155.19
June, . .	5	1	6	6	8	14	65.53	89 27	154 80
July, . . .	5	2	7	3	1	4	66 09	86.97	153 06
August, . .	2	3	5	4	4	8	66.32	88.58	154.90
September,	..	2	2	..	5	5	65 57	85.33	150.90
October, .	2	2	4	..	1	1	66.78	86.16	152.94
November, .	4	5	9	3	1	4	70.63	88 20	158.83
December, .	5	6	11	4	8	12	72 58	91.16	163.74
Total *persons,*	42	40	82	31	39	70	66.41	89 50	155.91

TABLE No. 3.

RECEIVED ON FIRST AND SUBSEQUENT ADMISSIONS.

Number of Admissions.	Cases admitted.			Times previously recovered.		
	Males.	Females.	Total.	Males.	Females.	Total.
First, ...	28	34	62	. .	. .	. .
Second, ...	9	1	10	2	1	3
Third, ...	4	2	6	5	4	9
Fourth, ...	. .	2	2	. .	2	2
Eleventh, ...	. .	1	1	. .	1	1
Eighteenth, ...	1	. .	1	17	. .	17
Total of *cases*, . . .	42	40	82	24	8	32
Total of *persons*, . .	42	40	82	. .	. .	. .

These 32 recoveries represent 11 persons, 5 having recovered 2 and one 17 times.

TABLE No. 4.

AGES OF PERSONS ADMITTED FOR THE FIRST TIME.

Ages.	At first attack of Insanity.			When admitted.		
	Males.	Females.	Total.	Males.	Females.	Total.
Fifteen years and less,	. .	1	1	. .	. .	. .
From 15 to 20 years,	3	2	5	2	1	3
" 20 to 25 "	2	6	8	. .	5	5
" 25 to 30 "	1	6	7	1	5	6
" 30 to 35 "	1	6	7	3	6	9
" 35 to 40 "	5	3	8	6	4	10
" 40 to 50 "	7	6	13	6	8	14
" 50 to 60 "	5	2	7	4	3	7
" 60 to 70 "	2	2	4	1	2	3
" 70 to 80 "	2	. .	2	5	. . 1	5
Total of *persons*, .	28	34	62	28	34	62

TABLE No. 5.

PARENTAGE OF PERSONS ADMITTED.

Places of Nativity.	Males.		Females.		Total.	
	Father.	Mother.	Father.	Mother.	Father.	Mother.
Maine, ...	3	3	5	8	8	11
New Hampshire, . .	5	5	2	1	7	6
Vermont, ...	2	2	..	.	2	2
Massachusetts, . . .	22	23	21	17	43	40
Rhode Island, . . .	..	..	1	2	1	2
Connecticut, ...	..	..	..	1	..	1
New York, ...	..	..	2	2	2	2
Pennsylvania, . . .	1	1	1	..	2	1
Virginia, ...	1	1	..	..	1	1
Georgia, ...	..	..	1	1	1	1
Canada, ...	1	1	..	..	1	1
England, ...	2	1	2	2	4	3
Germany, ...	1	1	1	1	2	2
Ireland, ...	3	3	3	3	6	6
New Brunswick, . .	..	..	..	1	..	1
Nova Scotia, . . .	..	..	1	1	1	1
Norway, ...	1	1	..	..	1	1
Total of *persons*, .	42	42	40	40	82	82

TABLE No. 6.

RESIDENCE OF PERSONS ADMITTED.

Places.	Males.	Females.	Total.
Massachusetts : —			
Suffolk County, ...	14	13	27
Middlesex County, ...	11	14	25
Bristol County, ...	..	1	1
Norfolk County, ...	3	3	6
Essex County, ...	2	2	4
Plymouth County, ...	2	..	2
Maine, ...	1	2	3
New Hampshire, ...	4	..	4
Vermont, ...	..	1	1
Rhode Island, ...	..	2	2
New York, ...	1	..	1
Georgia, ...	..	1	1
South Carolina, ...	1	..	1
Ohio, ...	1	..	1
Illinois, ...	1	..	1
Nova Scotia, ...	..	1	1
England, ...	1	..	1
Total of *persons*, ...	42	40	82

TABLE No. 7.

CIVIL CONDITIONS OF PERSONS ADMITTED.

Number of the Admission.	Unmarried.			Married.			Widowed.		
	Males.	Females.	Total.	Males.	Females	Total.	Males.	Females.	Total.
First, . .	7	15	22	14	16	30	7	3	10
Second, .	3	1	4	4	..	4	2	..	2
Third, . .	1	1	2	2	1	3	1	..	1
Fourth, .	..	1	1	..	..	..	..	1	1
Eleventh, .	..	..	..	..	..	..	..	1	1
Eighteenth,	1	..	1	..	..	..	..	..	..
Total *persons*,	12	18	30	20	17	37	10	5	15

TABLE No. 8.

OCCUPATIONS OF PERSONS ADMITTED.

Occupations.	Males.	Females.	Total.
Housewife, ...	..	14	14
Clerk, ...	4	..	4
Manufacturer, ...	2	..	2
Merchant, ...	12	..	12
Farmer, ...	3	..	3
Student, ...	1	1	2
Lawyer, ...	2	..	2
Physician, ...	1	..	1
Musician, ...	1	..	1
U.S. Consul, ...	1	..	1
Mechanic, ...	4	..	4
Laborer, ...	1	..	1
Servant, ...	..	1	1
Mason, ...	2	..	2
Civil engineer, ...	2	..	2
No occupation, ...	6	24	30
Total of *Persons*, ...	42	40	82

TABLE No. 9.

REPORTED DURATION OF INSANITY BEFORE LAST ADMISSION.

Previous Duration.	First Admission to any Hospital.			All other Admissions.			Total.		
	Ma.	Fe.	Tot.	Ma.	Fe.	Tot.	Ma.	Fe.	Tot.
Congenital,	..	..	..	..	..	..	..	..	..
Under 1 mo.,	5	8	13	3	3	6	8	11	19
Fr. 1 to 3 mo.,	7	10	17	1	1	2	8	11	19
" 3 " 6 "	3	4	7	3	1	4	6	5	11
" 6 " 12 "	5	6	11	..	..	..	5	6	11
" 1 " 2 yrs ,	5	..	5	2	..	2	7	..	7
" 2 " 5 "	1	5	6	3	1	4	4 -	6	10
" 5 " 10 "	2	1	3	1	..	1	3	1	4
" 20 " 30 "	..	..	..	1	..	1	1	..	1
Total *cases*,	28	34	62	14	6	20 ·	42	40	82
Total *persons*,	..	..	..	..	..	..	42	40	82
Average of known persons (in years).	1.11	1.01	1.06	3.03	.86	1.94			

TABLE No. 10.

FORM OF DISEASE IN THE CASES ADMITTED.

Form of Disease.	Males.	Females.	Total.
Mania, acute,	12	11	23
Mania, chronic,	7	3	10
Mania, hysterical,	..	2	2
Mania, puerperal,	..	3	3
Mania, recurrent,	1	..	1
Melancholia, acute,	9	14	23
Melancholia, chronic,	3	4	7
Dementia, chronic,	1	1	2
General paralysis,	5	..	5
Epilepsy,	4	..	4
Not insane,	..	2	2
Total of *cases*,	42	40	82
Total of *persons*,	42	40	82

TABLE No. 11.

ALLEGED CAUSES OF INSANITY IN PERSONS ADMITTED.

Causes	Males.	Females.	Total.
Mental.			
Grief, ...	3	3	6
Anxiety, ...	3	3	6
Physical.			
Ill-health, ...	5	7	12
Overwork, ...	7	4	11
Constitutional, ...	7	5	12
Change of life, ...	..	4	4
Child-birth, ...	..	4	4
Uterine disease, ...	..	3	3
Epilepsy, ...	4	..	4
Sunstroke, ...	1	1	2
Dissipation, ...	5	1	6
Unknown, ...	7	3	10
Not insane, ...	..	2	2
Total of *persons*, ...	42	40	82

TABLE No. 12.

RELATION TO HOSPITALS OF THE PERSONS ADMITTED.

	Males.	Females.	Total.
Never before in any Hospital, ...	28	34	62
Former inmates of this Hospital, ...	6	1	7
Former inmates of other Hospitals in this State : —			
Danvers, ...	1	..	1
South Boston, ...	1	..	1
Worcester, ...	2	..	2
Former inmates of Hospitals in other States, . .	3	3	6
Former inmates of this Hospital and of other Hospitals in this State : —			
Danvers, ...	1	..	1
Former inmates of this Hospital and of Hospitals in other States, ...	..	2	2
Total of *cases*, ...	42	40	82
Total of *persons*, ...	42	40	82

TABLE No. 13.

DISCHARGES CLASSIFIED BY ADMISSION AND RESULT.

Admission	Recovered			Much Improved			Improved			Unimproved			Died			Total		
	Ma.	Fe.	Tot.	Ma.	Fe.	Tot.	Ma.	Fe.	Tot.	Ma.	Fe.	Tot.	Ma.	Fe.	Tot.	Ma.	Fe.	Tot.
First,	6	12	18	1	3	4	4	5	9	5	7	12	6	2	8	22	29	51
Second,	2	..	2	..	1	1	2	1	3	..	1	1	..	..	..	4	3	7
Third,	1	2	3	..	1	1	1	..	1	1	1	2	..	..	..	3	4	7
Fourth,	..	1	1	..	..	..	..	..	..	..	..	..	..	..	..	..	1	1
Sixth,	1	..	1	..	..	..	..	..	..	..	..	..	..	..	..	1	..	1
Seventh,	..	..	..	..	..	..	..	1	1	..	..	..	..	..	..	..	1	1
Tenth,	..	..	..	..	..	..	..	1	1	..	..	..	..	..	..	..	1	1
Eleventh,	..	..	..	..	1	1	..	..	..	..	..	..	..	..	..	..	1	1
Eighteenth,	1	..	1	..	..	..	..	..	..	..	..	..	..	..	..	1	..	1
Total of *cases*,	11	15	26	1	6	7	7	7	14	6	9	15	6	2	8	31	39	70
Total of *persons*,	..	..	..	..	..	..	..	..	..	..	..	..	..	..	..	31	39	70

TABLE No. 14.

CASES DISCHARGED RECOVERED.— DURATION.

Period.	Duration before Admission.			Hospital Residence.			Whole Duration from the Attack.		
	Ma.	Fe.	Tot.	Ma	Fe.	Tot.	Ma.	Fe.	Tot.
Under 1 mo.,	5	6	11	1	..	1	1	..	1
Fr. 1 to 3 mo.,	3	7	10	5	2	7	1	1	2
" 3 " 6 "	1	2	3	3	4	7	3	5	8
" 6 " 12 "	..	..	..	1	6	7	3	5	8
" 1 " 2 yrs ,	1	..	1	1	2	3	2	3	5
" 2 " 5 "	1	..	1	..	1	1	1	1	2
Total *persons,*	11	15	26	11	15	26	11	15	26
Average of known cases (in months).	5 72	1.85	3.49	4.74	8.86	7.12	10 46	10.6	10 54

TABLE No. 15.

CASES RESULTING IN DEATH.— DURATION

Period.	Duration before Admission.			Hospital Residence.			Whole Duration from the Attack.		
	Ma.	Fe.	Tot.	Ma	Fe.	Tot.	Ma.	Fe.	Tot.
Under 1 mo.,	1	..	1	1	1	2	1	..	1
Fr. 1 to 3 mo.,	3	1	4	..	..	.	..	..	..
" 3 " 6 "	..	.	..	..	1	1	..	1	1
" 6 " 12 "	..	1	1	..	..	.	..	1	1
" 1 " 2 yrs.,	1	..	1	2	..	2	1	..	1
" 2 " 5 "	1	..	1	2	..	2	3	..	3
" 25 " 30 "	..	..	..	1	..	1	1	..	1
Total, . .	6	2	8	6	2	8	6	2	2
Average of known cases (in months).	8.04	6	7.53	75.6	2 23	57.26	66 87	8	52.16

TABLE No. 16.

CASES DISCHARGED BY RECOVERY OR DEATH.

Form of Insanity.	Recoveries.			Deaths.		
	Males.	Females.	Total.	Males.	Females.	Total.
Mania, acute, ...	9	8	17	1	1	2
Mania, chronic, ...	..	..	..	1	..	1
Mania, puerperal, ...	..	1	1	..	..	..
Melancholia, acute, ...	2	6	8	..	..	..
Melancholia, chronic, . . .	..	..	..	..	1	1
Dementia, chronic, ...	..	..	..	1	..	1
General Paralysis, ...	..	..	..	3	..	3
Total of *cases*, ...	11	15	26	6	2	8
Total of *persons*, ...	11	15	26	..	..	..

TABLE No. 17.

CAUSES OF DEATH.

Causes.	Males.	Females.	Total.
Cerebral Disease.			
General Paralysis, ...	3	..	3
Exhaustion from Mania, ...	1	1	2
Exhaustion from Melancholia, ...	..	1	1
Hemiplegia, ...	1	..	1
Other Causes.			
Bright's Disease, ...	1-	..	1
Totals, ...	6	2	8

TABLE No. 18.

RECOVERIES, CLASSIFIED BY RESULTS OF PREVIOUS ADMISSIONS.*

Number of the Admission.	Recovered.			Much Improved.			Improved.			Total.		
	Ma.	Fe.	Tot.	Ma.	Fe.	Tot.	Ma	Fe.	Tot.	Ma.	Fe.	Tot.
Second, ...	2	..	2	..	..	..	..	..	..	2	..	2
Third, ...	1	1	2	..	..	..	.	..	..	1	1	2
Fourth, ...	..	1	1	..	..	..	..	..	..	..	1	1
Eighteenth, ...	1	..	1	..	..	..	..	..	..	1	..	1
Total of *persons*, .	4	2	6	..	..	..	..	..	..	4	2	6

* This classification is based upon the result of the admission next preceding the last, in each case respectively.

TABLE No. 19.

DEATHS, CLASSIFIED BY DURATION OF INSANITY AND OF TREATMENT.

Period.	Duration of Insanity.			Whole known period of Hospital Residence.		
	Males.	Females.	Total.	Males.	Females.	Total.
Congenital, ...	..	..	..	..	..	..
Under 1 month, . .	1	..	1	1	1 .	2
From 3 to 6 months,	..	..	..	..	1	1
" 6 to 12 " .	..	1	1	..	..	..
" 1 to 2 years, .	1	1	2	2	..	2
" 2 to 5 " . .	3	..	3	2	..	2
" 20 to 30 " . .	1	..	1	1	..	1
Total, ...	6	2	8	6	2	8
Average of known *cases* (in months).	83.54	14	66.16	75.6	2.23	57.26

TABLE No. 20.

AGES OF THOSE WHO DIED.

Ages.	At time of the first attack.			At time of death.		
	Males.	Females.	Total.	Males.	Females.	Total.
From 20 to 25 years, .	..	1	1	..	..	..
" 30 to 35 " ..	..	1	1	..	1	1
" 35 to 40 " ..	3	..	3	1	..	1
" 40 to 50 " ..	1	..	1	2	1	3
" 50 to 60 " ..	2	..	2	2	..	2
" 60 to 70 " ..	..	..	..	1	..	1
Total, ...	6	2	8	6	2	8

TABLE SHOWING THE COST OF PRINCIPAL STORES AT THE McLEAN
ASYLUM. 1882.

Articles.		Quantity.	Cost.	Average.
Beef, ...	lbs.	57,936½	$7,869.37	.1358
Mutton and Lamb, ...	"	20,340	2,104.57	.1034
Veal, ...	"	13,367	1,445.17	.108
Hams, etc., ...	"	9,724¼	1,234.90	.126
Poultry, ...	"	18,946	3,815.64	.201
Eggs, ...	doz.	11,153½	3,143.77	.277
Lard, ...	lbs.	1,041	133.08	.1278
Flour, ...	bbls.	455	3,767.15	8.279
Butter, ...	lbs.	20,780	6,276.21	.3020
Coffee, ...	"	3,955	944.80	.2388
Tea, ...	"	1,522	501.31	.3294
Sugar, ...	"	26,489½ $\frac{5}{5}$	2,462.13	.0929
Lights, gas, etc., ...	feet.		3,858.49	
Coal, ...	tons.	1,200$\frac{2}{2000}$	7,284.95	6.07
Wood, ...	cords.	14¼	103.31	7.25
Ice, ...	tons.	423$\frac{1800}{3000}$	759.46	1.79

TABLE OF ADMISSIONS, DISCHARGES, AND RESULTS AT THE McLEAN ASYLUM.

FROM ITS OPENING, OCTOBER 6, 1818, TO DECEMBER 31, 1882, INCLUSIVE.

Years.	Admitted.	Discharged.	Whole No. under care.	Died.	Much improved, etc.	Recovered.	Remaining at end of year.	Average No. of Patients.
1818–25	398	344	623	29	205	110	279	..
1826	47	46	101	5	21	20	55	..
1827	58	56	113	5	17	34	57	..
1828	77	65	134	5	37	23	69	..
1829	73	77	142	9	42	26	65	..
1830	82	78	147	10	34	34	69	..
1831	83	84	152	8	46	30	68	..
1832	94	98	162	10	45	43	64	..
1833	103	100	167	8	50	42	67	..
1834	108	95	174	7	47	41	80	..
1835	83	84	163	11	28	45	77	..
1836	106	112	183	10	38	64	71	..
1837	120	105	191	8	25	72	86	80
1838	138	131	224	12	45	74	93	95
1839	132	117	225	10	38	69	108	112
1840	155	138	263	13	50	75	125	128
1841	157	141	283	11	55	75	142	135
1842	129	138	271	15	43	80	133	143
1843	126	126	260	18	45	63	134	131
1844	158	140	292	20	52	68	152	146
1845	119	120	271	13	33	74	151	149
1846	148	126	299	9	52	65	173	164
1847	170	170	343	33	50	87	173	172
1848	143	155	316	23	50	82	155	171
1849	160	137	321	15	58	64	184	177
1850	173	157	357	28	51	78	200	201
1851	164	173	364	29	69	75	191	195
1852	145	135	336	15	48	72	201	200
1853	114	120	315	17	45	58	195	194
1854	120	120	315	16	45	59	195	195
1855	123	126	318	24	46	56	192	192
1856	149	145	341	19	58	68	196	195
1857	141	159	337	28	60	71	178	191
1858	155	147	333	25	50	72	186	187
1859	131	142	317	28	53	61	175	185
1860	121	109	296	24	46	39	187	185
1861	111	110	298	23	33	54	188	193
1862	82	94	270	18	37	39	176	190
1863	94	69	270	13	20	36	201	191
1864	101	107	302	27	38	42	195	200
1865	82	85	277	17	33	35	192	186
1866	103	98	295	29	23	46	197	197
1867	89	108	286	27	36	45	178	186
1868	92	94	270	23	37	34	176	166
1869	108	100	284	18	31	51	184	187
1870	79	85	263	12	40	33	178	187
1871	75	81	253	13	47	21	172	178
1872	93	101	265	23	63	15	164	173
1873	92	95	256	13	63	19	161	165
1874	75	88	236	10	58	20	148	159
1875	85	83	233	16	51	16	150	156
1876	92	74	242	20	36	18	168	160
1877	110	103	278	20	68	15	175	175
1878	63	84	238	12	66 .	6	154	168
1879	76	79	230	12	48	19	151	157
1880	51	48	202	6	30	12	154	152
1881	66	65	220	14	37	14	155	150
1882	82	70	237	8	36	26	167	156
	6,604	6,437.		944	2,708	2,785		

TABLE OF APPLICATIONS, ADMISSIONS, ETC., FOR NINETEEN YEARS,—1864-1882.

Years	Applications, Hospital	Admissions, Hospital	Admissions, Asylum	American, Hospital	American, Asylum	Foreign, Hospital	Foreign, Asylum	Not admitted, Hospital	Discharged cured, relieved, or improved, Hospital	Discharged, Asylum	Percentage of same on Admissions, Hospital	Percentage, Asylum	Died, Hospital	Died, Asylum	Accidents	Whole number under care in the year, Hospital	Whole number, Asylum	Number of free patients, Hospital	Paying all the time, Hospital	Paying part of the time, Hospital	Greatest total number at any time, Hospital	Greatest total, Asylum	Least total at any one time, Hospital	Least total, Asylum	Average, Hospital	Average, Asylum	Greatest number at any one time of Free, Hospital	Greatest number Paying, Hospital	Average time in weeks Paying, Hospital	Average time Free, Hospital	Out-Patients, Hospital
1864	1932	1599	101	654	99	945	2	333	1306	80	81.68	79.1	130	27	242	1749	302	1388	350	11	157	208	110	192	138	200	139	33	3.2	4.4	5619
1865	1430	1199	82	571	80	628	2	231	997	68	83.15	82.9	104	17	140	1347	277	687	592	68	164	195	88	181	113	186	137	72	3.7	4.8	5356
1866	1328	1120	103	542	100	587	3	208	909	69	81.17	66.9	96	20	132	1224	295	556	623	45	109	203	78	192	9A	197	62	58	3.4	5.1	5508
1867	1419	1206	89	558	88	648	1	213	968	81	79.43	91.0	94	27	113	1301	286	676	601	24	126	200	72	172	104	186	77	63	3.4	4.3	4553
1868	1474	1265	92	604	92	661	0	209	1015	71	80.03	77.1	85	23	98	1373	218	840	602	31	132	181	69	109	102	166	97	62	3.0	3.5	5264
1869	1633	1390	108	681	108	709	0	243	1123	82	80.03	75.9	107	18	93	1217	284	930	563	24	139	196	90	177	118	187	98	56	3.4	4.3	6963
1870	1706	1302	79	584	76	718	3	404	1083	73	83.20	92.4	85	13	127	1427	342	958	439	30	137	195	98	181	120	187	106	55	3.4	4.8	8767
1871	1781	1427	75	649	75	778	0	354	1143	52	80.09	69.3	109	13	178	1537	253	1056	456	25	154	187	91	167	122	167	126	45	3.1	3.9	9792
1872	1815	1547	93	665	78	882	5	268	1271	52	82.15	55.9	120	23	259	1701	265	1289	396	16	160	179	97	163	135	173	133	43	3.1	4.3	11878
1873	1958	1550	92	640	85	910	7	408	1201	64	77.48	69.5	186	10	291	1700	236	1195	441	64	183	171	129	158	156	165	156	42	3.3	6.0	13517
1874	2153	1639	75	713	68	926	7	514	1342	54	81.88	72	127	16	234	1800	233	1251	394	120	183	167	111	144	149	159	146	44	2.7	5.6	15612
1875	2357	1841	85	799	82	1022	13	516	1412	57	76.70	67	189	20	285	1989	242	1565	336	88	199	165	132	145	166	156	176	41	2.8	5.2	16993
1876	2560	1906	92	900	103	1006	10	654	1621	45	85.04	48.9	150	20	245	1847	233	1696	308	92	210	173	163	168	185	160	182	31	3.2	5.7	17292
1877	2131	1657	110	863	58	794	1	474	1339	57	80.80	51.8	130	20	147	1950	278	1270	339	48	194	184	135	154	164	175	178	36	2.8	5.5	18004
1878	2275	1794	63	946	46	848	5	481	1461	46	80.63	71.4	134	12	200	1971	230	1578	334	38	187	182	132	150	165	157	170	33	2.8	5.2	18744
1879	2310	1813	76	979	63	834	13	497	1462	32	81.53	60.5	143	12	222	2284	202	1577	352	42	188	164	131	146	163	157	165	34	2.8	5.1	18960
1880	2701	2123	51	1117	57	1006	5	578	1731	37	82.19	62.7	151	6	351	2270	220	1864	371	45	188	159	156	147	170	152	165	30	2.5	4.5	20566
1881	2786	2106	66	1074	57	1032	9	680	1853	37	82.19	56	189	14	391	2270	220	1835	419	26	195	161	139	147	166	150	168	35	2.79	4.41	18443
1882	2587	2147	82	1127	73	1020	9	440	1775	47	87.83	57.3	177	8	348	2302	237	1876	399	12	195	166	143	149	168	156	167	35	2.84	4.41	16304

1821 to 1843	8743	390	327	34	..	..	..	3991	..	2902	913	105	624	..	..	..	123	54	..	..	..	..	..			
1843	365	183	167	15	..	..	.	136	37	115	55	17	41	11	..	..	56	33	47*	..	..	4	6			
1844	435	250	174	11	..	..	..	183	43	137	41	23	47	11	..	30	71	40	53	55	12*	3 6-7	7 1-7			
1845	453	265	176	12	..	..	..	205	45	130	37	28	54	12	44	34	72	37	56	62	14	5 4-7	6 6-7			
1846	459	250	182	27	..	..	..	211	46	137	30	33	36	8	44	28	72	37	55	59	13	3 1-2	4 3-4			
1847	674	354	279	41	..	..	..	340	50	145	54	30	57	8	82	41	123	54	81	74	11	3 1-2	4 1-2	..	..	328
1848	804	460	283	61	..	..	..	400	50	219	52	39	103	13	86	38	124	94	108	103	12*	3 1-7	5	..	..	378
1849	870	543	273	54	..	.	..	436	50	218	75	58	84	9	89	38	127	90	112	97	11	2 4-7	5 5-7	..	..	272
1850	746	427	242	77	..	..	..	363	48	200	56	49	76	10	103	33	136	83	108	98	13	2 6-7	6	..	..	294
1851	839	477	298	64	..	..	..	387	46	235	47	63	98	11	93	48	141	77	112	123	15	3	6	..	..	237
1852	826	472	271	83	..	..	..	410	50	234	52	47	82	10	105	41	133	104	119	132	16	3 1-4	5	..	..	248
1853	925	505	335	85	..	..	..	431	46	287	70	66	82	9	108	39	142	108	120	159	17	3 1-6	7	..	..	358
1854	922	490	321	111	..	..	..	423	46	257	73	41	115	12	112	45	145	125	133	212	23	4	10	..	..	477
1855	915	414	352	147	..	..	..	456	50	238	59	51	102	11	107	59	152	114	134	157	17 3-10	3 3-7	11 4-7	..	..	645
1856	976	545	335	96	..	..	..	478	49	230	77	71	117	12	114	48	153	120	140	189	19	3	5	..	..	887
1857	920	549	280	91	..	..	..	510	55	195	57	66	130	14	119	40	157	103	128	163	17 7-10	2 2-3	5	..	..	1574
1858	1015	718	251	46	..	..	..	514	50	229	65	50	127	13	120	31	144	91	123	186	18*	4	7*	..	..	2223
1859	1240	934	257	49	287	49	1040	653	53	280	54	94	141	11	145	37	165	92	131	212	17	4	4 2-3	14	140	3523
1860	1240	997	201	42	215	42	1137	698	56	305	73	58	121	9¾	149	33	175	80	128	233	18 7-10	4	6	15	121	4433
1861	1416	1131	253	32	268	32	1252	831	59	318	79	57	99	7	135	37	162	120	140	297	21	4	5 3-4	16	124	4676
1862	1611	1175	425	11	441	11	1299	843	52	431	77	154	101	6¼	133	45	166	102	134	271	16 3-4	2 1-10	4 1-10	25	120	4800
1863	1648	1348	283	17	308	17	1468	856	52	459	96	70	162	9¾	135	29	158	116	137	292	17 7-10	3 4-10	4	24	126	4987
1864	1199	1262	326	11	350	11	1388	916	57	390	84	61	130	8	139	33	157	110	138	242	15 2-10	3.18	4.37	25	123	5619
1865	1199	564	567	68	592	68	687	702	59	295	68	74	104	8⅓	137	72	164	88	113	140	11 7-10	3.67	4.85	45	59	5356
1866	1120	497	578	45	693	45	556	677	60	82	50	74	96	8½	62	58	109	78	95	132	11 7-10	3.40	5.10	45	50	5608
1867	1206	626	556	24	601	24	676	676	56	282	62	141	94	7.8	77	62	126	72	104	113	9.36	3.37	4.26	39	69	4553
1868	1265	771	463	31	302	31	840	757	60	258	64	82	85	7	97	56	132	69	102	98	7.74	3.00	3.50	31	96	5264
1869	1390	834	532	24	563	24	930	771	55½	352	78	84	107	7.7	98	55	139	90	118	93	6.69	3.40	4.30	25	100	6953
1870	1302	858	414	30	439	30	958	780	60	303	65	68	85	6.45	106	45	137	98	120	140		3.37	4.82	24	86	8767
1871	1427	970	432	25	456	25	1056	821	57½	322	58	73	109	7.64	126	43	154	91	122	178		3.12	3.92	28	126	9792
1872	1547	1163	368	16	396	16	1289	958	62	313	76	84	120	7.75	133	42	160	97	135	259		3.15	4.35	30	120	11878
1873	1550	1075	411	64	441	64	1195	880	57	321	66	86	186	12	156	44	187	129	156	291		3.28	6.09	35	126	13517
1874	1639	1125	394	120	429	120	1251	946	57½	396	81	102	127	7.69	146	41	183	111	149	234		2.73	5.64	28	120	15612
1875	1841	1445	308	88	336	88	1565	1032	56	380	78	120	189	10.27	176	31	199	132	166	285		2.82	5.18	26	164	16993
1876	1906	1532	282	92	308	92	1696	1019	53½	502	91	144	150	7.86	182	36	210	163	185	245		3.22	5.73	19	171	17292
1877	1657	1270	339	48	358	42	1441	930	50	409	92	130	130	7.68	178	33	194	135	164	147		2.84	5.54	11	145	18004
1878	1794	1433	323	38	334	38	1578	956	50	505	59	138	134	7.46	170	34	187	132	165	200		2.80	5.27	17	141	18744
1879	1813	1436	335	42	352	42	1577	1040	57	422	84	125	143	7.94	165	30	188	131	163	222		2.84	5.16	17	140	18960
1880	2123	1724	354	45	371	45	1864	1186	54	545	74	150	151	7.16	165	35	188	156	170	351		2.58	4.53	17	157	20566
1881	2106	1678	402	26	419	26	1835	1324	62	429	70	103	189	8.96	168	39	195	139	166	391		2.79	4.41	15	140	18443
1882	2147	1736	399	12	414	12	1876	1312	61	463	59	13	177	8.13	167	35	195	143	168	348		2.84	4.41	24	141	16304
	68673							21438		14870	3551	3217	5105													270565

OFFICERS OF THE HOSPITAL.

Resident Physician.
JAMES H. WHITTEMORE, M.D.

Visiting Physicians.

GEORGE C. SHATTUCK, M.D.
FRANCIS MINOT, M.D.
CALVIN ELLIS, M.D.

SAMUEL L. ABBOT, M.D.
BENJAMIN S. SHAW, M.D.
GEORGE G. TARBELL, M.D.

Visiting Surgeons.

HENRY J. BIGELOW, M.D.
RICHARD M. HODGES, M.D.
CHARLES B. PORTER, M.D.

JOHN COLLINS WARREN, M.D.
HENRY H. A. BEACH, M.D.
JOHN HOMANS, M.D.

Physicians to Out-Patients.

DAVID H. HAYDEN, M.D.
WILLIAM L. RICHARDSON, M.D.
EDWARD N. WHITTIER, M.D.

ELBRIDGE G. CUTLER, M.D.
F. GORDON MORRILL, M.D.
FREDERICK C. SHATTUCK, M.D.

Surgeons to Out-Patients.

MAURICE H. RICHARDSON, M.D.   ARTHUR T. CABOT, M.D.
GEORGE W. WEST, M.D.

Physician to Out-Patients with diseases of the Skin.
JAMES C. WHITE, M.D.

Physician to Out-Patients with diseases of the Nervous System.
JAMES J. PUTNAM, M.D.

Physicians to Out-Patients with diseases of the Throat.
FREDERICK I. KNIGHT, M.D.   S. W. LANGMAID, M.D.

Ophthalmic Surgeon to Out-Patients.
OLIVER F. WADSWORTH, M.D.

Dental Surgeon.
VIRGIL C. POND, D.M.D.

Microscopist, and Curator of the Pathological Cabinet.
REGINALD H. FITZ, M.D.

Chemist.
EDWARD S. WOOD, M.D.

Artist.
HENRY P. QUINCY, M.D.

Medical House Officers, 1882–1883.
FRANKLIN A. DUNBAR.   ANDREW H. HODGDON.

Surgical House Officers, 1882–1883.
CLARENCE M. GODDING.   FRED. M. BRIGGS.
CHARLES S. HOLDEN.   CHARLES W. GALLOUPE.

Matron.
Miss G. L. STURTEVANT.

Apothecary.
JOHN W. PRATT.

OFFICERS OF THE McLEAN ASYLUM.

Superintendent.
EDWARD COWLES, M.D.

1st Assistant Physician.
GEORGE T. TUTTLE, M.D.

2d Assistant Physician.
FREDERICK M. TURNBULL, M.D.

Medical House Officers.
G. E. THOMPSON.   A. G. SMITH.

Purveyor.
JOHN P. BRADBURY.

Superintendent of Nurses.
Miss M. F. PALMER.

Clerk.
Miss F. E. GILBERT.

Supervisors.
E. W. BOARDMAN.   Miss L. E. WOODWARD.

Apothecary.
J. H. POTTS.

VISITING COMMITTEE.

January and July.

Messrs. MORRILL and ENDICOTT.

February and August.

Messrs. LOTHROP and BOWDITCH.

March and September.

Messrs. ELIOT and THAYER.

April and October.

Messrs. HALE and WARREN.

May and November.

Messrs. BEMIS and PROCTOR.

June and December.

Messrs. KIDDER and WALCOTT.

LADIES' VISITING COMMITTEE.

January.

Miss E. GRAY.   Miss H. THAYER.

Miss M. CURTIS.

February.

Miss GRAY.   Miss E. GOODWIN.

Miss S. LORING.

March.

Miss GOODWIN.   Miss L. LORING.

Miss S. LORING.   Miss H. THAYER.

April.

Miss L. LORING.   Miss CURTIS.

Miss THAYER.   Miss ELIOT.

May.

Miss CURTIS.   Miss ELIOT.

June and October.

Mrs. S. ELIOT.   Mrs. W. W. VAUGHAN.

November and December.

Mrs. H. W. HAYNES.   Miss A. W. MORRILL.

STANDING COMMITTEES.

On admitting Asylum Patients.

Messrs. WARREN and ENDICOTT.

On Finance.

Messrs. KIDDER and MORRILL.

On Accounts and Expenditures.

Messrs. WOLCOTT and THAYER.

On Buildings and Repairs.

Messrs. ENDICOTT, WARREN, and ELIOT.

On Free Beds.

Messrs. BOWDITCH and PROCTOR.

On the General Library and Warren Fund.

Messrs. ELIOT and HALE.

On the Book of Donations.

Dr. BEMIS.

SEVENTIETH ANNUAL REPORT

OF THE

TRUSTEES

OF THE

MASSACHUSETTS GENERAL HOSPITAL

AND

McLEAN ASYLUM,

1883.

Printed at the Expense of the Bowditch History Fund.

BOSTON:

GEO. H. ELLIS, PRINTER, 141 FRANKLIN STREET.

1884.

SEVENTIETH ANNUAL REPORT

OF THE

TRUSTEES

OF THE

MASSACHUSETTS GENERAL HOSPITAL

AND

McLEAN ASYLUM,

1883.

Printed at the Expense of the Bowditch History Fund.

BOSTON:
GEO. H. ELLIS, PRINTER, 141 FRANKLIN STREET.
1884.

REPORT OF THE TRUSTEES

OF THE

MASSACHUSETTS GENERAL HOSPITAL

For the Year 1883.

———

THE Committee of the Trustees appointed to prepare the annual report of the Board to the Corporation, to whom the accounts of the Treasurer and the reports of the other officials have been referred, respectfully submit the

SEVENTIETH ANNUAL REPORT.

To those who are accustomed to read each annual report of this and other similar institutions, there is little to be said that is novel in reference to their daily routine work. The tables prepared by Dr. Cowles and Dr. Whittemore, and presented herewith, will best explain and illustrate the work that is being done in the Hospital, the Asylum, and the Convalescent Home. We shall only allude to a few prominent features in their past year's history, and note some changes and improvements which have been made.

We desire to express our general satisfaction with the results, while we feel also compelled to call attention to what is still needed to make these Institutions what they should be.

The average number of patients in the Hospital during the past year was 172. In the previous year, the average number was 168.

In the Asylum, the average number of patients the past year was 164. In the previous year, the average number was 156.

The Treasurer's account shows that the excess of expense over income of the three establishments — namely, the Hospital, the Asylum, and the Convalescents' Home — has been $10,085.46, which has been charged to the General Fund; but, as the average deficiency for the past three years has been $29,860.72 annually, the result this year must be deemed highly satisfactory.

The legacies and donations received the past year have been large, and the Trustees gratefully acknowledge the receipt of the following: —

Donation, W. S. Adams, Free Bed Fund, ...	$2,000.00
Donation, children of Mrs. Henry Windsor, for a permanent free bed, ...	1,000.00
Bequest, J. W. Estabrooks, income for free beds, ...	1,000.00
Bequest, Nathaniel Thayer, income for free beds, ...	30,000.00
Bequest, Charlotte Harris, General Fund (as valued by the corporation), ...	132,976.80
Bequest, J. G. Kidder, General Fund, ...	25,000.00
Bequest, J. G. Kidder, income for Convalescent Home, .	15.000.00
Bequest, M. P. Sawyer, in part, income for free beds, . .	20,743.20
Total, ...	$227,720.00

The annual subscriptions for free beds have amounted to $10,600.

During the past year, important changes have occurred in the Corporation and in the Board of Trustees as well as in the Board of Visiting Physicians. We, in common with many other charitable organizations, have to lament the death of Nathaniel Thayer, Esq., who had been Vice-President of the Corporation for the past fourteen years. His last bequest to the Hospital for free beds has already been noted.

Early in the year, the new building for the Nurses of the Hospital was occupied. It had been named the "Thayer Building," previous to Mr. Thayer's death, in recognition of his valuable services and generous donations. At our request, a portrait of Mr. Thayer has been given to the Hospital by Mrs. Thayer, which has been hung in the Thayer Building.

We have also to lament the death of Dr. Calvin Ellis of the Board of Visiting Physicians, who had for nineteen years been a most faithful and efficient member of that body.

A valuable member of the Board of Trustees, Mr. Thornton K. Lothrop, resigned in the month of April, having been a member of the Board for five years.

Dr. Benjamin S. Shaw has recently resigned as Visiting Physician, after a connection with the Hospital, in different capacities, of twenty-five years, in reference to which the Trustees passed the following vote : " That the Secretary be requested to express to Dr. Shaw the high appreciation in which his long services have been held by the Trustees, and their regret that his connection with the Institution must be terminated."

We regret to announce also that Mr. David R. Whitney, who has been the efficient Treasurer of the Corporation for the past three years (except during a temporary absence in Europe), has resigned. During Mr. Whitney's absence, Mr. Edmund Dwight kindly consented to take the office of Treasurer.

During the year, the " George H. Gay Ward " for the Out-Patient Department has been erected. This building for the relief of suffering humanity was the gift of a benevolent gentleman, whose name is withheld at his own request, in memory of his deceased friend, Dr. Gay. It is justly regarded as being a model building for the purposes for which it is designed.

The Dental Department has been removed to the building formerly occupied by the Harvard Medical School, where it will find much more capacious and desirable quarters than it was possible to provide in the Hospital Buildings ; but its connection with the Hospital remains the same as before.

During the past year, we have sold to the city of Boston, for the sum of $62,000, the Dock, Wharf, and Flats on Charles Street for the purposes of a Public Park.

We desire to call attention to the fact that our Convalescent Home at Belmont is designed not only for Convalescents from our own, but also from other hospitals, private families, boarding-houses, etc. We desire to have it availed of to its fullest capacity.

It is now ten years since the Training School for Nurses was organized, and it seems proper that the Trustees should express to the officers of the school, more fully than has heretofore been done, their high appreciation of the services rendered the Hospital.

The Hospital has, from the beginning, had the advantage of many excellent and skilful nurses; but, since the nursing has been wholly in the charge of the Training School, there is no doubt that the average quality of the service has been higher than ever before.

This Institution began in 1873 with six pupils, who were allowed to take charge of two wards as an experiment. It increased steadily till 1877, when the nursing of the whole Hospital was placed in its charge. At the present time, the Training School consists of forty-two pupils, twelve head nurses, a night Superintendent, and the Superintendent of the whole school,— all these being under the supervision of a Board of

Directors, several of whom are physicians connected with the Hospital.

The general management of the health, discipline, and education of the nurses rests with this Board, though the school is in fact a part of the active staff of the Hospital, and acts under the direction of the Resident Physician. As a result of this organization, the character of the nursing in the Hospital has materially improved; and the public has benefited by the yearly graduation of fifteen or twenty well-trained nurses.

A somewhat similar system of training female nurses for their work has been introduced at the Asylum, and we look for like beneficial results there.

We desire to express to the Ladies' Visiting Committee of the Hospital the thanks of the Trustees for their constant and careful attention.

We have in several former reports called attention to the favorable results to both children and adults arising from their being occupants of the same wards in the Hospital, and we hope in future, even more than in the past, that sick children will be sent to the Hospital to be cared for in connection with adults.

We note with satisfaction that about one-third of the patients admitted to the Asylum the past year have been voluntary, and that beneficial results to the patients have followed the adoption of the plan of allowing them to make short visits to their homes and families.

We tried the experiment the past year of a cottage on the sea-shore at Lynn for some of the patients from the McLean Asylum during the summer months, and the results were so satisfactory that it will be repeated the coming summer on a somewhat larger scale.

We note also that the employment of female nurses

in the men's wards of the Asylum works satisfactorily and with beneficial results to the patients.

In our last report, we said: "Your Trustees cannot express too strongly the hope that they will soon be able to move the Asylum from Somerville to Belmont. This they consider their most pressing need, and it is to be hoped that this object will be especially borne in mind by the generous public." Another year's consideration and experience have confirmed this opinion. We have secured a large estate at Belmont admirably adapted by nature and by its surroundings for the purposes of an Asylum, and it is of the utmost importance that we should shortly commence to erect the necessary buildings; but, up to the present time, we have not had sufficient encouragement to induce us to attempt to raise the large sum of money which would be needed for the purpose.

THOMAS E. PROCTOR, } *Committee.*
EDMUND DWIGHT, }

REPORT OF THE TREASURER

OF THE

MASSACHUSETTS GENERAL HOSPITAL.

To the Board of Trustees:

Gentlemen,— In accordance with the Fifth Article of the By-Laws the report of the accounts of the Massachusetts General Hospital, made up to the last day of December, 1883, is respectfully submitted, to be laid before the Corporation at its annual meeting.

Dr.   D. R. WHITNEY, *Treasurer, in account with the* MASSACHUSETTS GENERAL HOSPITAL.   *Cr.*

Jan. 1, 1883.		By Cash paid J. H. Whittemore, Resident Physician, balance in		
To Balance on hand,	$8,847.50	" " Edw. ..., balance in account,		$2,980.70
" Railroad Bonds sold,	105,000.00	" " ...		4,018.84
" Real Estate sold,	71,000.00	" " ...		4,738.49
" City of Boston Bonds collected,	2,000.00	" " ...		1,406.00
" Union League Club Bonds called,	3,000.00	" " Annual Report, 1882,		247.76
" Bills Receivable,	43,900.00	" " Improvements at Belmont,		7,871.40
" Donations,	3,000.00	" " ... Building,		9,031.19
" Legacies,	98,679.40	" " ... Building,		15,800.23
" One-third profits Mass. Hospital Life Ins. Co.,	5,000.00	" " Expenses Hospital,		109,054.98
" Income from investments,	92,609.14	" " Expenses Asylum,		137,801.56
" Board of paying patients at Asylum,	134,334.50	" " Expenses ...,		6,204.15
" Board of paying patients at Hospital,	20,150.07	" " ...		226,400.00
" Board of paying patients at Convalescent Home,	344.00	" " Library,		241.77
" Subscribers for Free Beds ($3,050 additional received for this purpose in 1882),	7,550.00	" " ... Legs,		130.00
" Subscribers for Free Beds for 1884 in advance,	900.00	" " Premiums,		11,460.24
		" " ... at Waltham,		152.32
		" " Taxes and ... on land in Chicago,		498.13
		" " C. C. Darling, ... account,		33.70
		" Balance Cash on hand,		57,343.15
	$596,314.61			$596,314.61

MASSACHUSETTS GENERAL HOSPITAL, BOSTON, Dec. 31, 1883.

E. & O. Ex.   D. R. WHITNEY, *Treasurer.*

The expense of carrying on the business of the Corporation for the year 1883 has been $257,279.18, namely: —

On account of Hospital Department,	$111,363.64
" " " McLean Asylum,	139,711.39
" " " Convalescent Home,	6,204.15
	$257,279.18

This expense has been met from: —

Amount charged to patients,	$154,828.57
Income from various funds applicable,	92,365.15
Deficit drawn from the General Fund,	10,085.46
	$257,279.18

The receipts at the McLean Asylum have exceeded the expenses by $4,341.18, which amount has been credited to the General Fund; while the expenses at the Hospital have exceeded the receipts by $13,296.47, and at the Convalescent Home by $1,130.17, which amounts have been charged to the General Fund, making the net balance drawn from the General Fund $10,085.46, as above.

TABLE No. 1.

EXPENSES AND RECEIPTS OF THE HOSPITAL DEPARTMENT.

Disbursements for the year 1883: —

Expenses at Hospital (see Table 4).	$109,054.98
Insurance,	2,308.66
	$111,363.64

Receipts.

Income from Redman Fund (see Table 7),	$26,169.01
" " Free Bed Funds (see Table 7),	30,757.50
" " Funds with income unrestricted (see Table 7),	2,300.00
" " General Fund (see Table 7),	8,090.59
Free Bed Subscriptions (see Table 8),	10,600.00
Amount charged to patients,	20,150.07
Deficit from General Fund,	13,296.47
	$111,363.64

TABLE No. 2.

EXPENSES AND RECEIPTS AT THE McLEAN ASYLUM.

Disbursements for year 1883 : —

Expenses at Asylum (see Table 5), ...	$137,801.56
Insurance, ...	1,909.83
	$139,711.39

Receipts.

Income from Fund for Beneficiaries (see Table 7), . . .	$4,255 57
Income from Fund for Female Beneficiaries (see Table 7),	4,887.50
Income from Amusement Fund (see Table 7), ...	575.00
Amount charged to Patients, ...	134,334.50
	$144,052.57
Balance of Receipts over Expenses, ...	
Credited to General Fund, ...	$4,341.18

TABLE No. 3.

EXPENSES AND RECEIPTS AT CONVALESCENT HOME.

Disbursements for year 1883 : —

Expenses at Convalescent Home (see Table 6), ...	$6,204.15

Receipts.

Income from Convalescent Home Fund, ...	$4,729.98
Amount charged to patients, ...	344.00
Deficit from General Fund, ...	1,130.17
	$6,204.15

TABLE No. 4.

EXPENSES OF THE HOSPITAL DEPARTMENT.

For Stores, ...	$39,426.20
Gas and Oil, ...	2,074.17
Water, ...	1,805.30
Wages, ...	26,283.50
Medicine, ...	2,725.21
Furniture, ...	9,507.92
Surgical Instruments, ...	1,211.98
Stationery, ...	714.23
Wines and Liquors, ...	2,698.65
Salaries, ...	5,274.00
One-half General Expenses, ...	1,084.86
Fuel, ...	9,514.51
Contingencies, ...	845.51
Repairs, ...	5,888.94
	$109,054.98

These expenditures have been for account of: —

1,492 Free Patients for 7,176 weeks, ...	$90,665.70
528 Paying Patients for 1,456 weeks, ...	18,389.28
	$109,054.98

The average number of patients was, in 1882, ...	168
The average number of patients has been, in 1883, ...	166
The average cost per week was, in 1882, 8,736 weeks, ...	$12.43
The average cost per week has been, in 1883, 8,632 weeks, ...	12.63
The total expenses were, in 1882, ...	108,590.43
The total expenses have been, in 1883, . . .	109,054.98
The amount paid for account of free patients has been, ...	$90,665.70
The amount received for them has been: —	
From Income Free Bed Funds, ...	30.757.50
From 88 Subscribers for this object (see Table 8), ...	10,600.00
	41,357.50
	$49,308.20

The deficiency has been drawn in part from the income of the various funds applicable to the purpose, and the remainder from the General Fund.

TABLE No. 5.

EXPENSES OF THE ASYLUM DEPARTMENT.

For Stores, ...	$44,150.51
Laundry, ...	8,510.48
Fuel, ...	6,569.89
Stationery, ...	468.50
Medicines and Liquors, ...	2,529.82
Contingencies, ...	1,570.98
Furniture, ...	8,788.03
Repairs, ...	13,347.32
Diversions, ...	1,086.59
Water and Ice, ...	2,765.91
Lights, ...	3,379.25
Wages, ...	29,779.87
Salaries, ...	6,873.53
One-half General Expenses, ...	1,084.87
Library, ...	400.00
Stables, ...	3,689.99
Garden, ...	2,726.65
Lynn Cottage, ...	1,525.77
	$139,247.96
Less Cr. Clothing, $383.79, and Farm, $1,062.61, ...	1,446.40
	$137,801.56

14

These expenditures have been for account of: —

Patients paying cost and more, ...	$39,994.42
" " less than cost, ...	97,807.14
	$137,801.56
The average number of patients was, in 1882, . . 156	
The average number of patients has been, in 1883, 164	
The average cost per week was, in 1882, ... $17.02	
The average cost per week has been, in 1883, . . 16.16	
The total expenses were, in 1882, ...	138,518.36
The total expenses have been, in 1883, ...	137,801.56

The amount expended at the Asylum for patients who have paid less than cost has been, ...	97.807.14
The amount received has been: —	
From patients, 6,033 1-7 weeks' board, at less than cost, ... $56,546.92	
From Income of Funds for Beneficiaries, . . 4,255.57	
Income of Funds for Female Beneficiaries, 4,887.50	
Income of Amusement Fund, ... 575.00	
	66,264.99
	$31,542.15

The deficiency has been drawn in part from patients paying more than cost, and the remainder from Funds applicable to the purpose.

TABLE No. 6.

EXPENSES OF THE CONVALESCENT HOME.

For Stores, ...	$2,982.22
Gas and Oil, ...	38.22
Medicine, ...	15.93
Furniture, ...	159.40
Wages, ...	1,871.30
Fuel, ...	610.84
Stationery, ...	16.70
Ice, ...	100.93
Wines, Spirits, and Malt Liquors, ...	13.39
Repairs, ...	143.26
Contingencies, ...	251.96
	$6,204.15

Whole number of patients admitted during the year, males, ... 92	
Whole number of patients admitted during the year, females, ... 93	
	185
Whole number discharged during same time, . . .	195
Remaining, Jan. 1, 1884, males, ... 3	
" " " females, ... 4	

TABLE No. 7.

The Income from Investments has been: —

From Annuities Receivable,	$6,400.00
City of Boston Bonds,	1,175.00
Mass. Hospital Life Ins. Co. Stock,	4,000.00
Railroad Bonds,	32,269.67
Manufacturing Stocks,	3,309.00
Bank Stocks,	4,729.70
Real Estate, Productive,	23,090.93
Notes Receivable,	15,772.10
Union League Club Bonds,	600.00
Interest,	1,121.29
Delaware Mutual Ins. Co.'s Scrip Interest,	27.00
Railroad Stocks,	114.45
	$92,609.14

Which has been distributed as follows: —

To G. H. Gay Fund,		$862.50
Redman Fund,		26,169.01
Warren Prize Fund,		172.50
Bowditch History Fund,		115.00
Wooden Leg Fund,		287.50
Redman Annuities,		936.00
Clara Barton Annuity,		186.35
Surgical Instrument Fund,		77.67
Amusement Fund,		575.00
Free Bed Funds, { for use,	$30,757.50	31,457.50
{ for Joy Annuities,	700.00	
Beneficiaries at Asylum Funds,		4,255.57
Warren Library Fund,		57.50
Treadwell Library Fund,		287.50
One-half Lincoln Fund,— Female Beneficiaries,		4,887.50
Funds with Income Unrestricted,		2,300.00
General Fund,		8,090.59
Convalescent Home Fund,		4,729.98
Asylum Building Fund,		7,161.47
		$92,609.14

The Income for 1881 was	$94,199.47
The Income for 1882 was	82,698.22
The Income for 1883 has been	92,609.14

16

TABLE No. 8.

SUBSCRIBERS FOR FREE BEDS.

Hoosac Tunnel Dock and Elevator Co.,	$100	*Amount brought up,* John Foster,	$5,700 100
F. L. Higginson,	100	Mrs. Jas. McGregor,	100
H. S. Shaw,	100	Webster & Co.,	100
M. Brimmer,	300	Eastern Railroad Co.,	100
F. R. Sears,	100	W. O. Grover,	100
Mrs. Susan O. Brooks,	100	Henry B. Rogers,	100
J. R. Coolidge,	100	Samuel Eliot,	100
Mrs. L. M. Case,	100	C. J. Morrill,	100
J. P. Bradlee,	100	Geo. D. Howe,	100
Chas. P. Curtis,	100	W. D. Pickman,	100
Sidney Bartlett,	100	Jos. S. Fay,	100
Theodore Lyman,	100	Mrs. G. H. Shaw,	100
William Amory,	100	A. A. Lawrence,	100
Fitchburg Railroad Co.,	100	R. C. Winthrop, Jr.,	100
J. L. Bremer,	100	A L. Rotch,	100
Miss Anne Wigglesworth,	200	Charles Merriam,	100
Union Railway Co.,	100	C. H. Dalton,	100
Boston & Providence R.R. Co.,	100	Ida M. Mason,	100
George Higginson,	100	Nathaniel Thayer,	500
T. Jefferson Coolidge,	100	Henry Saltonstall,	100
H. P. Kidder,	200	H. H. Fay,	100
F. H. Peabody,	100	Otis E. Weld,	100
Boston & Maine R.R. Co.,	100	F. Gordon Dexter,	100
S. D. Warren,	100	W. Powell Mason,	100
Shepherd Brooks,	100	Greely S. Curtis,	100
Miss C. A. Brewer,	100	R. C. Greenleaf,	100
W. W. Tucker,	100	Henry Woods,	100
Mrs. J. G. Cushing,	100	J. F. Anderson,	100
Mrs. Anna C. Lodge,	100	Sarah S. Fay,	200
S. R. Payson,	100	R. W. Hooper,	100
J. B. Glover,	100	J. H. Wolcott,	100
P. C. Brooks,	100	Mrs. Ozias Goodwin,	100
J. L. Gardner, Jr.,	100	Miss Eliza Goodwin,	100
Mrs. Peter C. Brooks,	100	Mrs. Caroline Merriam,	100
Miss Eunice Hooper,	100	Miss Madeline C. Mixter, Miss Helen K. Mixter,	100
Mass. Humane Society,	600	J. M. Sears,	100
Mrs. E. B. Bowditch,	200	J. T. Coolidge, Jr.,	100
Samuel Johnson,	100	Pacific Mills Board of Relief,	200
William Endicott, Jr.,	100	J. P. Squire & Co.,	100
Mrs. Charlotte A. Johnson,	100	J. L. Little,	100
George A. Gardner,	100	Mrs. James Lawrence,	100
Miss A. W. Davis,	100	Boston Gaslight Co.,	100
Geo. W. Wales,	100	C. W. Amory,	100
Dr. C. E. Ware,	100		$10,600
George Dexter,	300		
Amount carried up,	$5,700		

Total Free Bed Subscriptions (80) in 1882, ... $10,215.00
Total Free Bed Subscriptions (88) in 1883, ... 10,600.00

TABLE No. 9.

LIBRARY ACCOUNT.

Paid for Books, ...	$241.77
Income Treadwell Library Fund, ...	287.50
The surplus is credited to the Fund, ...	$45.73

TABLE No. 10.

WOODEN LEG ACCOUNT.

The amount received for this purpose has been Income of the Wooden Leg Fund, ...	$287.50
The amount expended for Artificial Limbs has been, . . .	130.00
The surplus is credited to the fund, ...	$157.50

TABLE No. 11.

THE BOWDITCH HISTORY FUND.

Balance, December 31, 1882 : —		
Principal, ...	$2,000.00	
Income, ...	1,786.31	
		$3,786.31
Amount of Income received, ...	$115.00	
Amount of Income expended, ...	247.76	
		132.76
		$3,653.55
Balance, December 31, 1883 : —		
Principal, ...	$2,000.00	
Income, ...	1,653.55	
		$3,653.55

TABLE No. 12.

GENERAL FUND.

Balance, December 31, 1882, ...	$978,397.20	
Add one-third profits Mass. Hospital Life Ins. Co., ...	5,000.00	
Add donations and legacies, ...	157,976.80	
		$1,141,374.00
Less balance of premiums paid for Railroad Bonds, Bank Stocks, and Railroad Stocks,	$11,460.24	
Balance of Expenses over Income, ...	10,085.46	
		21,545.70
Balance, December 31, 1883, ...		$1,119,828.30

Income devoted to Free Beds: —

The Joy Fund, being a bequest from Miss Nabby Joy, ...	$20,000.00
Belknap Fund, being a bequest from Jeremiah Belknap, ...	10,000.00
Wm. Phillips Fund, being a bequest from Wm. Phillips, ...	5,000.00
Williams Fund, being a bequest from John D. Williams, of estate No. 17 Blackstone Street, ...	19,600.00
Bromfield Fund, being half of a bequest from John Bromfield, ...	20,000.00
Miss Townsend Fund, being a donation from the Executors of the will of Miss Mary P. Townsend, ...	11,486.50
Brimmer Fund, being a bequest from Miss Mary Ann Brimmer, ...	5,000.00
Wilder Fund, being a bequest from Charles W. Wilder, ...	12,000.00
Sever Fund, being a bequest from Miss Martha Sever, ...	500.00
Thompson Fund, being a bequest from S. B. Thompson, ...	500.00
Tucker Fund, being a bequest from Miss Margaret Tucker, ...	3,312.37
Davis Fund, being a bequest from Mrs. Eleanor Davis, ...	900.00
Loring Fund, being a bequest from Abigail Loring, ...	5,000 00
Nichols Fund, being a bequest from B. R. Nichols, ...	6,000.00
Gray Fund, being a donation from John C. Gray, ...	1,000.00
Dowse Fund, being a bequest from Thomas Dowse, ...	5,000.00
Todd Fund, being a bequest from Henry Todd, ...	5,000.00
J. Phillips Fund, being a bequest from Jonathan Phillips, ...	10,000.00
Greene Fund, being a bequest from Benj. D. Greene, ...	5,000.00
Percival Fund, being a bequest from John Percival, ...	950.00
Amount carried forward, . . .	$146,248.87

Amount brought forward, ...	$146,248.87
Pickens Fund, being a bequest from John Pickens, ...	1,676.75
Treadwell Fund, being part of a bequest from J. G. Treadwell, ...	38,703.91
Raymond Fund, being a bequest from E. A. Raymond, ...	2,820.00
Harris Fund, being part of a bequest from Charles Harris, ...	1,000.00
Mason Fund, being a bequest from Wm. P. Mason, ...	9,400.00
Sawyer Fund, being part of a bequest from M. P. Sawyer, ...	7,000.00
J. L. Gardner Fund, being a donation from J. L. Gardner, ...	20,000.00
B. T. Reed Fund, being a donation from Benj. T. Reed, ...	1,000.00
Wm. Reed Fund, being a bequest from Wm. Reed, ...	5,233.92
McGregor Fund, being half of a donation and bequest from James McGregor, .	7,500.00
Miss Rice Fund, being a bequest from Miss Arabella Rice, ...	5,000.00
Templeton Fund, being half of a bequest from John Templeton, ...	5,000.00
Mrs. J. H. Rogers Fund, being a donation from J. H. Rogers, ...	1,177.50
Beebe Fund, being a bequest from J. M. Beebe, ...	50,000.00
Lincoln Fund, being half of a bequest from Mrs. F. W. Lincoln, ...	85,000.00
Blanchard Fund, being a bequest from Mrs. M. B. Blanchard, ...	4,000.00
George Gardner Fund, being a donation from George Gardner, ...	1,000.00
Hemenway Fund, being a donation from the Executors of the will of Augustus Hemenway, ...	20,000.00
Jessup Fund, being part of a bequest from Dr. Chas. A. Jessup, ...	1,000.00
Tufts Fund, being a bequest from Quincy Tufts, ...	10,000.00
Read Fund, being half of a bequest from Jas. Read, ...	1,000.00
Parker Fund, being a bequest from Jno. Parker, Jr., ...	10,000.00
Amount carried forward, . .	$433,760.95

Amount brought forward, ...	$433,760.95	
Miss Shaw Fund, being a donation and bequest from Miss M. Louisa Shaw, .	5,500.00	
Eliza Perkins Fund, being a donation from Mrs. H. B. Rogers, ...	1,000.00	
Dwight Fund, being a donation from Mrs. T. Bradford Dwight, ...	1,000.00	
Hunnewell Fund, being a donation from H. H. Hunnewell, ...	10,000.00	
R. M. Mason Fund, being a bequest from R. M. Mason, ...	5,000.00	
Anna Lowell Cabot Fund, being a donation from Dr. Samuel Cabot, ...	1,000.00	
Welles Fund, being a donation from Miss Jane Welles, ...	5,000.00	
Black Fund, being a bequest from Miss Marianna Black, ...	2,000.00	
Eben Wright Fund, being an assignment of legacies by the children of T. Jefferson Coolidge, ...	14,000.00	
Paraclete Holmes Fund, being a donation from W. S. Adams, ...	2,000.00	
Estabrooks Fund, being a bequest from J. W. Estabrooks, ...	1,000.00	
Thayer Fund, being a bequest from Nathaniel Thayer, ...	30,000.00	
Sawyer Fund, being part of a bequest from M. P. Sawyer, ...	20,743.20	
		$532,004.15

Income devoted to Beneficiaries at Asylum : —

The Bromfield Fund, being half of a bequest from John Bromfield, ...	$20,000.00	
Read Fund, being half of a bequest from Jas. Read, ...	1,000.00	
Appleton Fund, $10,010 being a bequest from Samuel Appleton, $20,000 being a donation from Wm. Appleton, . .	30,010.00	
McGregor Fund, being half of a donation and bequest from James McGregor, .	7,500.00	
Austin Fund, being part of a bequest from Mrs. Agnes Austin, ...	5,000.00	
Kittredge Fund, being a bequest from Rufus Kittredge, ...	5,500.00	
Templeton Fund, being half of a bequest from John Templeton, ...	5,000.00	
		74,010.00
Amount carried forward, . . .		$606,014.15

Amount brought forward, . . $606,014.15

Income devoted to Female Beneficiaries at Asylum: —

The Lincoln Fund, being half of a bequest from Mrs. F. W. Lincoln, ... 85,000.00

Income unrestricted: —

The Waldo Fund, being a bequest from Daniel Waldo, ... 40,000.00

Income devoted to any purpose except buildings: —

The Redman Fund, being a bequest from John Redman, ... 455,113.34

Income devoted to a Triennial Prize: —

The Warren Prize Fund, being a bequest from Dr. J. M. Warren, ... 2,299.61

Income devoted to the Library: —

The Treadwell Library Fund, being part of a bequest from J. G. Treadwell, . . . 5,000.00

Income devoted to Books for Patients: —

The Warren Library Fund, being a donation from Dr. J. C. Warren, ... ˙1,000.00

Income and Principal devoted to the publication of a History of the Hospital: —

The Bowditch History Fund, being a bequest ˙from N. I. Bowditch, ... 2,000.00

Income devoted to Amusements at the Asylum: —

The Amusement Fund, $5,000 being a bequest from Miss Mary Louisa Shaw, $5,000 being a donation from Mrs. Quincy A. Shaw and other Ladies, ... 10,000.00

Amount carried forward, . . . $1,206,427.10

Amount brought forward, . . .	$1,206,427.10

Income devoted to Special Surgical Instruments : —

The Surgical Instrument Fund, being a donation from Dr. H. J. Bigelow, $1,250 ; donation of Mr. R. M. Moore, $100,	1,350.00

The Wooden Leg Fund : —

Being a bequest from N. I. Bowditch, . . .	5,000.00

The Convalescent Home Fund, .

	82,260.66

Permanent Free Beds : —

Miss Marian Hovey, ...	$1,000.00	
Mrs. Fanny H. Morse, ...	1,000.00	
Henry S. Hovey, ...	1,000.00	
Edward Woodman, ...	1,000.00	
Children of Mrs. Henry Windsor, ...	1,000.00	5,000.00

Redman Annuities, ...

	15,600.00

Clara Barton Annuity, ...

	3,241.00

Asylum Building Fund, ...

	124,547.31

G. H. Gay Fund, ...

	25,000.00

Add unused income at credit of

The Warren Prize Fund, ...	$296.65	
Warren Library Fund, ...	409.62	
Bowditch History Fund, ...	1,653.55	
Surgical Instrument Fund, ...	1,164.69	
Wooden Leg Fund, ...	762.19	
G. H. Gay Fund, ...	1,137.50	
Treadwell Library Fund, ...	107.85	
Asylum Building Fund, ...	25,312.84	
Clara Barton Annuity, ...	32.09	
		30,876.98
Total of Restricted Funds, ...		$1,499,303.05

TRIAL BALANCE, Dec. 31, 1883.

Dr.			*Cr.*
abd und Buildings for Asylum,	$320,794.75	Redman Fnd, ...	$455,113.34	
Land und Buildings for Hospital,	520,008.53	Warren Prize uRd, . . .	3,000.00	$296.65
abd and Impro vents, Belmont,	60,651.99	...h History Fund, . .	2,000.00	1,653.55
Gay i Bldg, ...	15,800.23	W..n Leg Fnd, . . .	5,000.00	762.19
abd at Waltham, . . .	2,352.32	Redman ...is, . . .	15,600.00	
...tes Receivable, . . .	160,000.00	Ezra Barton ...ity, . .	3,241.00	32.09
City of Boston Loan, . . .	22,000.00	Surgical Instrument Fnd, .	1,350.00	1,164.69
...dance Stocks, . . .	50,000.00	...nt Fund, ...	10,000.00	
Delaware Mutual Insurance Company's Scrip,	885.00	Free Bed Fds, ...	532,004.15	
Railroad Bonds, ...	405,600.00	Warren ...bry Fnd, . . .	1,000.00	409.62
Union ...ge ...lb Bonds, . .	9,000.00	Beneficiaries at ...em Funds, .	74,010.00	
Manufacturing Stocks, . .	41,400.00	Treadwell ...bry Fnd, . .	5,000.00	107.85
Bank Stocks, ...	74,500.00	...ln Fund, ...	85,000.00	
Real Estate Productive, . .	397,391.64	Fnds with ...me Unrestricted,	40,000.00	
Railroad S...ks, . . .	25,000.00	...an Building Fnd, . .	124,547.31	25,312.84
Notes Receivable, . . .	420,600.00	Convalescent ...le Fund, .	82,260.66	
Cash, ...	57,343.15	G. H. Gay Fund, . . .	25,000.00	1,137.50
Reversions (see item "Suspense" on Cr. side),	10.00	General Fund, ...	1,119,828.30	
C. C. Darling, Balance in ...unt,	33.70	Permanent Free Beds, . .	5,000.00	
Edward ...ds, ...unt, . .	36,553.28	Suspense (see item "Reversions" on Dr. side),	10.00	
J. H. ...le, Resident Physician,	4,737.15	N...es Payable, ...	3,500.00	
		Subscribers for Free Beds, 1884,	900.00	
		Redman Annuitants, . .	420.00	
			$2,593,784.76	$30,876.98
			30,876.98	
	$2,624,661.74		$2,624,661.74	

Trial Balance at Close of Busi ness, Dec. 31, 1883.

Property on hand belonging to the Corporation invested as follows: —

INVESTMENTS PRODUCING NO INCOME.

Asylum.— Land and Buildings occupied for
Asylum,	$320,794.75	
Superintendent's balance,	36,553.28	
		$357,348.03

Hospital.— Land and Buildings occupied for
Hospital,	$520,008.53	
Resident Physician's balance,	4,737.15	
Gay Building,	15,800.23	
		540,545.91

Convalescent Home.— Land and Buildings occupied for Convalescent Home,		60,651.99
Sundries.— Land in Waltham,	$2,352.32	
C. C. Darling, balance in account,	33.70	
Memorandum of expectancies,	10.00	
		2,396.02
		$960,941.95

INVESTMENTS PRODUCING INCOME.

Policies Mass. Hospital Life Ins. Co.,	$160,000.00
500 shares Mass. Hospital Life Ins. Co.,	50,000.00
$22,000 City of Boston Bonds,	22,000.00
$28,000 Eastern Railroad Co.'s Bonds,	21,700.00
$1,000 Kansas City & Cameron Railroad Bonds,	1,000.00
$5,000 Boston & Lowell Railroad 7 per cent. Bonds,	5,000.00
$5,000 Boston & Albany Railroad 7 per cent. Bonds,	5,000.00
$100,000 Chicago, Bur. & Quincy R.R. 7 per cent. Bonds,	100,000.00
$15,000 Chicago, Bur. & Quincy R.R. 5 per cent. Bonds,	13,900.00
$9,000 Union League Club Bonds,	9,000.00
$100,000 Atchison, Topeka & Santa Fé 7s.,	100,000.00
$100,000 Atchison, Topeka & Santa Fé 4 1-2s.,	100,000.00
$29,000 Bur. & Mo. River in Neb., Non-Ex. 6s.,	29,000.00
$10,000 Bur. & Mo. River in Neb., Exempt 6s.,	10,000.00
$10,000 Atchison Land Grant 7s.,	10,000.00
$10,000 Kansas City, Topeka & Western R.R. 1st M. 7s.,	10,000.00
100 Shares Old Colony Railroad Co.,	10,000.00
150 " Boston & Albany Railroad Co ,	15,000.00
14 " Merrimack Manufacturing Co.,	14,000.00
1 " Appleton " "	1,000.00
9 " Amory " "	900.00
9 " Amoskeag " ..	9,000.00
25 " Great Falls " "	2,500.00
Amount carried forward,	$699,000.00

	Amount brought forward, ...	$699,000.00
5 Shares	Boston Manufacturing Co., ...	5,000.00
9 "	Stark Mills, ...	9,000.00
100 "	National Union Bank, ...	10,000.00
70 "	Tremont National Bank, ...	7,000.00
50 "	Old Boston " "	2,500.00
100 "	Suffolk " "	10,000.00
50 "	State	5,000.00
100 "	Columbian " "	10,000.00
100 "	Merchants' " "	10,000.00
50 "	New England National Bank, ... · . .	5,000.00
40 "	Massachusetts " "	10,000.00
50 "	Eagle " "	5,000.00

Land and Store, 17 Blackstone Street, ... 19,600.00
" " " 168 Washington Street, ... 45,000.00
" " House, 61 Dartmouth Street, · 10,000.00
Redman Mansion Estate, Washington Street, ... 106,000.00
Land and Houses on Warrenton Street, ... 17,700.00
" " Store, 496 Washington Street, ... 55,500.00
" " Houses on Chambers Street, ... 23,900.00
" " " 42–50 Cross Street, ... 12,691.64
Union Block, Union and Marshall Streets, ... 66,875.00
Robertson House, Hanover Street, ... 40,125.00
Notes secured by Mortgage, ... 260,600.00
$20,000 Notes Phila., Wilmington & Baltimore R.R. Co. . 20,000.00
Notes Receivable, with Personal and Collateral Securities, 140,000.00
$885 Scrip. Delaware Mutual Ins. Co., ... 885.00
Cash deposited in bank at interest, ... 57,343.15

Investments producing Income, ... $1,663,719.79
Investments producing no Income, ... 960,941.95
The exact foot of Trial Balance, ... $2,624,661.74

D. R. WHITNEY, *Treasurer.*

26

TABLE OF THE EXPENSES OF THE HOSPITAL AND ASYLUM FOR TWENTY-TWO YEARS, — 1862 TO 1883.

ORDINARY EXPENSES.

Year.	Cost of Paying Patients. Hospital.	Cost of Free Patients. Hospital.	Other Charities. Hospital.	Total Expenses of Hospital.	Total Expenses of Asylum.	Avg cost per week Hospital	Avg cost per week Asylum	Cost over Board. Hospital.	Cost over Board. Asylum.
1862	$6,628.65	$35,072.01	$414.15	$42,114.81	$71,823.46	$6.04	$7.27	$36,260.92	$6,640.81
1863	6,151.27	40,575.14	695.30	47,421.71	69,300.63	6.66	6.98	41,109.46	2,170.56
1864	10,224.81	49,286.53	648.21	60,159.55	101,484.38	8.38	9.76	52,445.01	4,523.85
1865	23,119.62	34,131.83	717.35	57,968.80	120,885.84	9.86	12.49	43,121.53	9,507.86
1866	30,086.08	37,538.12	1,162.60	68,786.80	126,015.83	13.88	12.30	53,809.36	558.19
1867	26,086.67	33,758.02	1,164.53	61,009.22	133,844.14	11.28	13.84	44,291.54	::::::
1868	23,663.50	42,481.71	1,419.26	67,564.47	142,535.36	12.74	16.51	52,893.02	14,642.07
1869	20,128.86	40,736.44	1,373.30	62,238.60	138,132.02	10.14	14.21	48,811.90	::::::
1870	15,844.35	46,087.42	883.05	62,814.82	134,339.63	10.05	13.83	50,811.01	::::::
1871	15,266.51	47,126.12	1,133.74	63,526.37	146,191.23	9.96	15.80	52,447.68	9,996.88
1872	12,664.70	56,537.74	1,497.86	70,700.30	153,327.60	10.10	16.93	59,547.91	14,917.57
1873	16,681.66	69,109.97	2,135.29	87,926.92	165,023.79	10.29	19.23	72,435.94	26,404.27
1874	14,198.41	64,266.27	2,634.60	81,099.28	161,934.11	10.13	19.59	67,548.81	2,750.66
1875	10,677.72	71,447.23	1,761.59	83,886.54	165,660.47	9.72	21.07	71,989.93	11,872.47
1876	11,344.58	82,033.60	1,312.94	94,691.12	164,973.80	9.41	19.72	82,027.86	13,019.51
1877	10,833.10	72,678.63	279.16	83,790.89	143,148.94	9.47	15.66	72,957.79	::::::
1878	11,252.42	85,102.61	588.98	96,944.01	136,394.36	9.87	15.55	83,516.61	::::::
1879	11,564.44	77,216.88	514.25	89,295.57	117,250.02	10.54	14.30	73,440.58	10,078.33
1880	10,529.35	81,085.73	462.82	92,077.90	131,172.69	10.39	16.48	79,280.61	20,719.30
1881	13,462.12	88,241.17	450.51	102,153.80	134,561.14	11.87	16.92	88,268.68	18,172.21
1882	12,947.98	95,642.45	8,928.82*	117,519.25	138,518.26	12.43	17.02	95,684.95	5,376.89
1883	18,389.28	90,665.70	6,575.92†	115,630.90	139,711.39	12.63	16.16	91,213.57	
22 years,								$1,413,914.67	$171,351.43

*Including Convalescent Home, $8,365.94. † Including Convalescent Home, $6,204.15.

OF THE

MASSACHUSETTS GENERAL HOSPITAL

For the Year 1883.

Number of Patients in the Hospital, January 1, 1883.

Paying, ... 24
Free, ... 141

Total, ... 165

Admitted from January 1, 1883, to January 1, 1884.

	Males.	Females.	Total.
Patients paying board, ...	271	178	449
Patients paying board part of the time, . . .	49	30	79
Patients entirely free, ...	947	545	1,492
	1,267	753	2,020

	Medical.	Surgical.
Males (Boys, 97), ...	351	905
Females (Girls, 63), ...	350	414
	701	1,319

Of these, 2 paid $50 per week; 1 paid $49; 29 paid $35; 1 paid $28; 4 paid $25; 42 paid $21; 1 paid $18; 6 paid $15; 74 paid $14; 4 paid $12; 75 paid $10.50; 9 paid $10; 243 paid $7; 2 paid $6; 18 paid $5; 2 paid $4.50; 2 paid $4; 1 paid $3.50; 8 paid $3; 2 paid $2.

Whole number of patients treated during the year: paying, 473; paying a part of the time, 79; free, 1,633; total, 2,185.

Discharged during the Year.

	Medical.	Surgical.	Male.	Female.	Total
Well, ...	366	920	809	477	1,286
Much relieved, ...	112	87	101	98	199
Relieved, ...	94	95	94	85	179
Not relieved, ...	40	22	28	33	61
Not treated, ...	32	80	55	53	108
Dead, ...	53	113	128	53	181
Insane and eloped, ...	4	7	7	4	11
	701	1,324	1,222	803	2,025

Number of Patients remaining December 31, 1883.

Males, ...	97
Females, ...	63
Total, ...	160

Paying, ...	32
Free, ...	128
Total, ...	160

Medical, ...	60
Surgical, ...	100
Total, ...	160

Proportion of deaths to whole number of results, 8.93 per cent.

Number of patients received on account of accidents, 432.

The greatest number of paying patients at any one time was 49; in private rooms, 8; the greatest number of free patients, 168; the greatest total, 189. The least number of paying patients at any one time was 15; in private rooms, 3; the least free, 118; the least total, 143. The proportion of ward beds occupied by free patients was 77 per cent.; by paying patients, 23 per cent. About 13.7 of the paying patients occupied private rooms. The average number of patients was 168: males, 105.5; females, 62.5.

The average number of paying patients was 28: Americans, 20; foreigners, 8.

The average number in private rooms was 6.

The average number of free patients was 138: Americans, 70; foreigners, 68.

The average time of paying patients was 2.75 weeks; and that of free patients, 4.80.

Residences.

Boston,	945
Massachusetts (excepting Boston),	953
Maine,	27
New Hampshire and Vermont,	45
Rhode Island and Connecticut,	14
Other States,	10
British Provinces,	26
	2,020

Birthplaces.

Boston,	104
Massachusetts (excepting Boston),	555
Maine,	123
New Hampshire,	83
Vermont,	42
Rhode Island and Connecticut,	34
New York,	37
Southern and Western States,	57
Total Americans,	1,035

British Provinces,	196
Great Britain,	132
Ireland,	562
Germany,	26
Norway and Sweden,	31
France,	7
Western Islands,	
Belgium and Holland,	
Italy,	8
Switzerland,	
Other places,	23
Total Foreigners,	985

Occupations.

Males.	Paying.	Free.	Partial Payment.
Mechanics, ...	65	233	14
Laborers, ...	51	430	16
Farmers, ...	21	22	4
Minors, ...	22	89	3
Seamen, ...	17	29	6
Clerks, ...	18	32	2
Teamsters, ...	2	32	1
Traders, ...	10	10	1
Servants, ...	3	19	1
Lawyers, ...		1	
Clergymen, ...	2	2	
Physicians, ...	4	·5	
Merchants, ...	7	6	
Students, ...	4	4	
Other professions, ...	45	33	1
	271	947	49

Total males, 1,267. Of these, 31 were in private rooms.

Females.	Paying.	Free.	Partial Payment.
Domestics, ...	16	236	8
Minors, ...	19	46	4
Wives, ...	98	149	10
Widows, ...	5	20	
Seamstresses, ...	13	24	2
Spinsters, ...	21	17	
Operatives, ...	3	19	4
Teachers, ...	2	2	1
Clerks, ...		3	
Nurses, ...	1	29	1
	178	545	30

Total females, 753. Of these, 43 were in private rooms.

Sixteen per cent. of the free patients were female domestics; twenty-nine per cent. were laborers; fifteen per cent. were mechanics; and nine per cent. were minors.

Admissions Refused.

Phthisis (Consumption),	56
Syphilis,	21
Chronic Ulcers,	20
Scrofula and Abscesses,	18
Insanity and Delirium Tremens,	9
Hip and Spine,	48
Debility and Senility,	19
Chronic Rheumatism,	22
Paralysis,	19
Epilepsy,	7
Cancer,	13
Uterine,	23
Injuries,	13
Of Skin,	15
Contagious,	17
Other diseases,	210
Total,	440

Males,	331
Females,	199
Americans,	443
Foreigners,	187
Residents of Boston,	176
Residents of Massachusetts,	262
Residents of other places,	92

Out-Patients.

Number of new patients,	7,102
Men,	2,596
Women,	3,174
Children,	1,332
Americans,	4,145
Foreigners,	2,957
Residents of Boston,	4,747
Of other places,	2,355
Medical department for women,	1,630
Medical department for men and children,	1,386
Surgical department,	5,285
Ophthalmic department,	980
Dental department,	3,075
Department for diseases of the skin,	1,731
Department for diseases of the nervous system,	1,169
Department for diseases of the throat,	1,175
Total attendance,	16,431

Average daily attendance, ... 130
Fractures and dislocations, ... 142
Wounds, ... 216
Sprains and injuries, ... 121
Abscesses, ... 95
Ulcers, ... 30
Felons, ... 41
Tumors, ... 84
Diseases of hip, ... 17
Diseases of spine, ... 21
Genito-urinary, ... 117
Club-foot, ... 6
Specific, ... 18
Hernia, ... 31
Necrosis, ... 10
Fistula in ano, ... 5
Diseases of joints, ... 99
Referred, ... 75
Miscellaneous, ... 453

Of the dental patients, 848 had 1,089 teeth filled, 1,459 had 2,299 teeth extracted.

Whole number of new patients in the Out-Patient Department
  in 1880, ... 20,566
Whole number of new patients in 1881, ... 18,443
Whole number of new patients in 1882, ... 16,304
Whole number of new patients in 1883, ... 7,102
Whole number refused admission in 1883, ... 387
Whole number of visits of investigation, ... 503
Whole number found deserving of charity, ... 349
Whole number found undeserving of charity, ... 154

Out-Patient Department open only five months.

Convalescent Home : —

	Males.	Females.	Total.
Remaining January 1, 1883,	9	6	15
Admitted,	94	93	187
Total,	103	99	202
Discharged,	100	95	191
Remaining January 1, 1884,	3	4	7

Respectfully submitted,

JAMES H. WHITTEMORE,
Resident Physician.

Jan. 1, 1884.

Articles.	1877. Quantity	1877. Cost	1877. Average	1878. Quantity	1878. Cost	1878. Average	1879. Quantity	1879. Cost	1879. Average	1880. Quantity	1880. Cost	1880. Average	1881. Quantity	1881. Cost	1881. Average	1882. Quantity	1882. Cost	1882. Average	1883. Quantity	1883. Cost	1883. Average
Beef, Sirloin, lbs.	9,100	$1,927.38	.2118	7,729	$1,610.72	.2084	8,375	$1,716.87	.205	8,815	$1,692.09	.1941	8,658	$1,792.20	.207	7,856	$1,931.95	.245	8,793	$1,975.38	.224
" for Soup, "	500	23.80	.0425	132	5.28	.04	…	…	…	…	…	…	…	…	…	…	…	…	…	…	…
" Corned, "	5,889	479.54	.0816	4,378	324.72	.07415	123	288.61	.07	4,952	346.64	.07	5,183	367.99	.07	6,622	673.76	.103	6,925½	670.88	.095
" Round, "	9,327	805.85	.0864	11,944	1,016.43	.0851	12,973	1,054.70	.0813	16,414	1,148.98	.084	19,477	1,636.06	.084	19,705	1,976.68	.103	22,327	2,120.83	.095
" Rump, "	6,882	1,163.05	.169	4,158	635.34	.1528	…	…	…	…	…	…	…	…	…	…	…	…	…	…	…
" Roasting, "	11,584	1,274.24	.11	14,998	1,349.82	.09	14,141	1,341.98	.0949	16,439	1,643.90	.10	16,438	1,758.86	.107	16,221	2,159.07	.133	16,962	2,047.78	.120
Mutton,	18,416	2,509.04	.13624	15,808	1,903.28	.1204	12,592	1,385.12	.11	15,522	1,876.60	.1208	21,093	2,720.99	.129	16,365	2,216.01	.135	21,075	2,999.89	.142
Poultry,	13,509	2,475.65	.184	14,079	2,276.57	.1617	14,488	2,433.98	.168	13,682	2,123.44	.1552	13,562	2,278.41	.168	12,082	2,348.41	.195	10,263	2,318.56	.225
Butter,	10,056	2,644.72	.263	10,156	2,500.40	.2462	10,536	2,589.39	.246	11,011	3,366.06	.3057	11,129	3,505.63	.315	16,843	3,770.97	.221	10,468	3,329.97	.317
Eggs, doz.	4,608	967.68	.21	5,495	967.12	.176	4,392	843.26	.192	4,214	866.39	.2056	4,401	1,188.27	.26	5,234	1,470.59	.281	5,479	1,491.60	.272
Flour, bbls.	40	362.48	9.062	42	323.82	7.71	37	266.80	7.49	51	440.15	8.65	49	468.73	9.565	49	459.25	9.937	52	406.00	7.80
Bread, . lbs.	34,343	1,717.15	.05	35,800	1,790.00	.05	36,556	1,827.80	.05	40,536	2,036.80	.05	34,892	1,744.60	.05	35,340	1,943.70	.055	34,971	1,923.42	.055
Ice, . tons.	180¾	627.54	3.48	238½	808.25	3.333	271¼	714.70	2.63	280¼	1,297.56	4.63	305	887.55	2.91	352¼	737.72	2.209	380 1/16	679.27	1.78
Sugar, . lbs.	10,592	982.88	.0928	12,979	1,023.65	.0781	15,462	1,189.32	.0769	21,005	2,003.87	.0954	20,552	1,901.06	.09	22,192	2,021.57	.091	20,980	1,801.38	.086
Tea, . lbs.	503	222.96	.376	738	254.61	.345	848	337.82	.398	1,134½	471.95	.416	555	244.22	.44	1,114	446.85	.401	1,074	432.60	.402
Milk, . qts.	97,554	4,879.70	.05	107,618	5,380.90	.05	96,186	4,934.34	.0513	89,904½	4,495.22½	.05	92,350	4,617.50	.05	95,358	5,007.70	.052	106,032	5,637.78	.053
Potatoes, . bush.	909	915.36	1.007	973	964.61	.77	942	1,010.76	1.073	1,039½	902.58	.808	981	1,101.66	1.125	1,005	1,374.72	1.368	1,062½	1,129.15	1.063

The Ambulance

OF THE

MASSACHUSETTS GENERAL HOSPITAL,

Accompanied by a medical officer, will be despatched to any point within the city proper for the conveyance of cases of *accident* or *urgent sudden sickness, not contagious*, to this Hospital, or elsewhere, upon notice from a physician, the police, or other responsible source, subject to the approval of the undersigned.

In cases requiring gratuitous treatment, no charge will be made.

By order of the Board of Trustees.

JAMES H. WHITTEMORE,
Resident Physician,
Mass. Gen. Hospital, Blossom St.

SIXTY-SIXTH ANNUAL REPORT

OF THE

SUPERINTENDENT OF THE MCLEAN ASYLUM FOR THE INSANE,

TO THE

TRUSTEES OF THE MASS. GENERAL HOSPITAL,

For the Year 1883.

TO THE TRUSTEES OF THE MASSACHUSETTS GENERAL HOSPITAL:

Gentlemen,— The following report, with tabular statements relating to the number and condition of the patients treated in the Asylum during the year 1883, is respectfully presented:—

TABLE No. 1.

GENERAL STATISTICS OF THE YEAR.

	Males.	Females.	Total.
Patients in the Asylum, Jan. 1, 1883, . . .	74	93	167
Admissions within the year, ...	48	61	109
Whole number of *cases* within the year, . .	122	154	276
Discharged within the year, ...	52	59	111
Namely,— as Recovered, ...	18	19	37
Much improved, ...	5	11	16
Improved, ...	7	4	11
Unimproved, ...	12	18	30
Deaths, ...	10	7	17
Patients remaining Dec. 31, 1883, } supported as private patients, }	70	95	165
Number of different *persons* within the year,	119	151	270
" " " " admitted, . . .	48	59	107
" " " " recovered, . .	18	19	37
Daily average number of patients, ...	69.20	94.65	163.85

During the year, two women were twice admitted, one of whom, once discharged recovered, and once much improved, was a voluntary patient on both occasions, and is still under treatment; and the other, also a voluntary patient, was discharged not improved, and afterward committed in the regular way.

Two men, after being discharged improved and much improved, were admitted and again discharged, not improved and improved respectively. Another man was admitted having been previously discharged not improved. Thus there were two hundred and seventy-six cases treated, representing two hundred and seventy persons.

Of the one hundred and seven persons admitted, sixty-seven were regarded as recent cases and forty as chronic, or as incurable at the time of admission.

Seventy-five persons, thirty-four men and forty-one women, had never been in any hospital. Of the remaining thirty-two persons, eighteen, seven men and eleven women, were admitted for the second time; seven, five men and two women, for the third time; three, two men and one woman, for the fourth time.

Thirty-four cases, representing thirty-three persons, ten men and twenty-three women, were admitted as voluntary patients upon their written applications. Two of the men were not insane: one, a case of the opium habit, was discharged recovered; and the other, of alcoholism, was discharged improved. Of the remaining thirty-one persons, twenty-five, five men and twenty women, were cases of melancholia; four, one man and three women, were cases of mania; and two men were cases of general paralysis. Of these voluntary patients, three, one man and two women, were committed while still resident at the Asylum; and one woman, already referred to, was

discharged, and afterwards returned under a commitment. Eleven of the thirty-four voluntary cases, two
men and nine women, were discharged within the
year recovered; four more, two men and two women,
as improved or much improved; and two men and
one woman as not improved.

There are remaining in the Asylum, under the
voluntary relation, fifteen persons, three men and
twelve women, who entered during the year. Eleven
of these voluntary patients had formerly been inmates
of the Asylum.

There were twenty-seven more admissions, forty-
one more discharges, and thirty-nine more cases under
treatment than during the year 1882; and the number present was two less at the end than at the
beginning of the year.

Of the one hundred and eight persons discharged,
including deaths, nineteen were transferred to other
hospitals, five men and thirteen women to those in
this State, and one woman to a State hospital in
Virginia.

Of the thirty-seven persons discharged recovered,
twenty-six had never before been inmates of any
hospital; and, of the remaining eleven persons, nine
had been in this Asylum. These eleven persons had
previously made twenty recoveries, three of which
were at other hospitals.

The average duration of illness, from the beginning
of attack, of all cases recovered, was 13.39 months;
and the average duration of their hospital residence
was 8.32 months.

The percentage of recoveries on admissions was
33.94. The number of recoveries was larger by
eleven than in the previous year.

Of the seventeen deaths during the year, three
were of elderly persons who had been many years in

the Asylum, and died of senility and senile gangrene. Five persons died of general paralysis, six of exhaustion from mania and melancholia, two of pneumonia, and one of hystero-epilepsy and syncope. Two of the deaths were of persons between seventy and eighty years old and two between eighty and ninety years.

The results of the year and those just preceding show that the Asylum, in common with the State hospitals, has felt the 'demand for increased accommodations for the insane. During the last three years, the increase has been constant in the numbers admitted, treated, recovered, and discharged. The average number present at any one time has not been much increased, and the results have been gained by a more rapid movement of the population. This has no doubt been promoted by the practice of free visiting of friends to patients and of the latter to their homes. The home visits, begun early in suitable cases, at first brief, and then gradually prolonged, have undoubtedly a positive curative influence. It being the general understanding among the patients that such visits can be made, they are thereby strongly encouraged to make such efforts in the direction of self-control and good conduct as will render the visits possible.

In connection with this practice, and contributing with it in a curative way to the common result, by promoting a feeling of mutual confidence among all concerned, the marked success of the voluntary system becomes a noteworthy feature of the operations of the year. According to the report of the Board of Health, Lunacy, and Charity for the year 1882, there were admitted in that year twenty-three voluntary cases to all the hospitals and asylums in the State. Eleven of them were at this Asylum; and this number was increased to thirty-four admissions of such cases as before stated during the past year, equal to nearly one-third of all the admissions for the year. Omitting those not insane, the remaining thirty-one persons, only four of whom were afterwards committed in the regular way, afforded eleven recoveries; and others are doing well.

These voluntary cases not having been pronounced insane by a formal examination and commitment, a question arises as to their diagnoses and classification. Cases of nervous disease with mild or impending mental disturbance might be included with those designated as "not insane"; but to report them in that way might imply the presence in a hospital for the insane of persons discovered to be not properly there, and thus deprive the hospital of credit due for the most satisfactory of all its work, — the saving of the patient from worse illness or his early cure.

For purposes of classification, the thirty-one cases under consideration are treated as insane. Some of them had been in hospital before,— eleven in this Asylum. Of these readmissions, some were saved from the impending attacks; and others became worse after admission, as was to have been expected. The same was true of others for whom it was their first admission. Others were subjects of suicidal impulse without delusions, who understandingly sought self-protection in the Asylum. The comparatively mild melancholia that also characterized some of these cases was all the disturbance that appeared in a few remaining ones. Some of the cases would have been good ones for home treatment, had circumstances permitted it; but still there were those who were undoubtedly benefited by removal from home to new surroundings and by the influences of the Asylum.

The presence in the house of voluntary cases in

increasing numbers has a good effect, particularly upon new comers, who, influenced by example, become sooner wonted to their residence here. It is to be said, however, that sometimes the indecision of patients as to whether to remain or go away is not beneficial; but, on the other hand, it is not the least of the advantages of the system that it makes hospital people careful and attentive to such patients in endeavoring to make them contented, and not only are their mutual relations modified, but those of the friends of patients to the hospital are more satisfactory. It has been suggested that "it is a question how far these admissions will be strictly voluntary, if the number become large; for the will of an insane person is often but the will of some stronger person for the time being." While this is undoubtedly true of some cases, it is probable that seeking hospital care was as purely voluntary in most of these cases as voluntary acts usually are that are products of unfortunate necessity, under the persuasion or advice of friends upon whom the invalid leans under such circumstances. But, of the cases of which the above statement is true, it is only according to the natural order of things that it should be so; for most persons who are seriously ill do submit, as it is reasonable they should, to such guidance by friends, who also have rights that should be considered in this matter. It is a valuable consideration, also, that, when a sick insane person is persuaded to go to a hospital, it involves at least the necessity of giving the patient an understanding of the purposes of his friends and the reasons for them. As the number of these admissions becomes larger here, they do not appear to be less strictly voluntary; but the fact that there is a number of such cases in the Asylum has an influence in persuading others who need hospital care to more willingly follow the example.

Much benefit was derived from the occupation of a cottage at the seashore in Lynn during four months, from June to October. Six ladies spent all or a part of the season there; and, communication by railroad being easy, nearly every week parties of ladies were sent to spend the afternoon there, and to dine or take tea. This usually included some pleasant hours spent in strolling on the beach or sitting on the rocks, and was altogether a source of much pleasure and benefit.

Some repairs and alterations have been made during the year, of the kind noticed in previous reports, for the purpose of improving and making more.pleasant some of the wards and rooms. All the windows of the first and second stories of the two principal buildings of the department for women have had the bars removed, and their removal from those of the third story is in progress. Similar changes have been begun in one of the men's wards.

In the matter of improving the nursing service by introducing a Training School system, progress has been made; and the employment of women as nurses in the men's wards continues to meet with unqualified success.

The usual means have been employed for the occupation and entertainment of the patients. There have been the usual concerts, exhibitions, and dancing parties; and the daily drives and visits to places of interest have formed an important part of the outdoor recreation.

Special thanks are due to Mr. S. D. Warren for the gift of a Steinway piano, and the interest manifested in the Asylum by other friends is gratefully remembered.   Very respectfully,

EDWARD COWLES,
Superintendent.

TABLE No. 2.

MONTHLY ADMISSIONS, DISCHARGES, AND AVERAGES.

Months.	Admissions.			Discharges (including Deaths).			Daily Average of Patients in the House.		
	Ma.	Fe.	Tot.	Ma.	Fe.	Tot.	Ma.	Fe.	Tot.
January, . .	2	3	5	..	1	1	71.97	93.32	165.29
February, .	4	3	7	3	4	7	75.11	90.68	165.79
March, . .	5	4	9	4	..	4	71.87	93.13	165.
April, . . .	4	5	9	6	4	10	71.56	94.47	166.03
May, . . .	3	7	10	4	8	12	73.41	94.69	168.10
June, . . .	4	7	11	6	3	9	70.70	98.67	169.37
July, . . .	1	7	8	6	2	8	64.51	98.88	163.39
August. . .	5	3	8	4	7	11	59.32	95.39	154.71
September, .	6	8	14	4	8	12	65.50	93.20	158.70
October, . .	2	7	9	2	7	9	66.87	94.71	161.58
November, .	7	5	12	4	6	10	70.13	95.97	166.10
December, .	5	2	7	9	9	18	69.52	92.67	162.19
Total cases, .	48	61	109	52	59	111	69.20	94.65	163.85
" persons,	48	59	107	50	58	108	..	..	..

TABLE No. 3.

RECEIVED ON FIRST AND SUBSEQUENT ADMISSIONS.

Number of Admissions.	Cases admitted.			Times previously recovered.		
	Males.	Females.	Total.	Males.	Females.	Total.
First, ...	34	41	75	2	6	8
Second, ...	7	12	19	1	7	8
Third, ...	5	2·	7	2	5	7
Fourth, ...	2	1	3	..	3	3
Fifth, ...	..	2	2	..	4	4
Seventh, ...	..	1	1	..	6	6
Twelfth, . . .	..	1	1	..	2	2
Thirteenth, . . .	..	1	1	..	..	..
Total of cases, . .	48	61	109	5	33	38
Total of persons, .	48	59	107	..	..	..

These 38 recoveries represent 22 persons, 14 having recovered one, 4 two, 2 three, 1 four, and 1 s x times.

TABLE No. 4.

AGES OF PERSONS ADMITTED FOR THE FIRST TIME.

Ages.	At first attack of Insanity.			When admitted.		
	Males	Females.	Total.	Males.	Females.	Total.
15 years and less,	..	..	..	..	..	..
From 15 to 20 yrs.,	..	1	1	..	..	..
" 20 to 25 "	4	8	12	3	5	8
" 25 to 30 "	1	7	8	1	9	10
" 30 to 35 "	4	6	10	4	6	10
" 35 to 40 "	8	4	12	6	5	11
" 40 to 50 "	3	10	13	4	10	14
" 50 to 60 "	7	5	12	9	6	15
" 60 to 70 "	6	..	6	5	..	5
" 70 to 80 "	1	..	1	2	..	2
Total of *persons*,	34	41	75	34	41	75

TABLE No. 5.

PARENTAGE OF PERSONS ADMITTED.

Places of Nativity.	Males.		Females.		Total.	
	Father.	Mother.	Father.	Mother.	Father.	Mother.
Maine, ...	5	7	6	6	11	13
New Hampshire, .	4	3	8	5	12	8
Vermont, ...	3	4	2	..	5	4
Massachusetts, . .	20	18	28	35	48	53
Rhode Island, . .	..	..	1	..	1	..
Connecticut, . . .	1	1	..	..	1	1
New York, . . .	1	1	2	1	3	2
Pennsylvania, . .	2	2	..	..	2	2
Virginia, ...	1	1	..	..	1	1
Minnesota, . . .	1	1	..	..	1	1
Washington, D.C.,	..	..	1	1	1	1
England, ...	2	2	3	3	5	5
Germany, ...	1	1	1	1	2	2
Ireland, ...	6	6	3	3	9	9
New Brunswick, .	..	..	1	1	1	1
Nova Scotia, . . .	..	..	2	2	2	2
Poland, ...	..	..	1	1	1	1
Surinam, ...	1	1	..	..	1	1
Total of *persons*, .	48	48	59	59	107	107

TABLE No. 6.

RESIDENCE OF PERSONS ADMITTED.

Places.	Males.	Females.	Total.
Massachusetts : —			
Suffolk County, ...	17	24	41
Middlesex County, ...	10	19	29
Essex County, ...	7	7	14
Norfolk County, ...	2	. .	2
Barnstable County, ...	1	2	3
Plymouth County, ...	1	2	3
Bristol County, ...	. .	2	2
Hampden County, ...	. .	1	1
Hampshire County, ...	. .	1	1
New Hampshire, ...	1	. .	1
Vermont, ...	2	. .	2
New York, ...	4	1	5
Pennsylvania, ...	1	2	3
Minnesota, ...	1	. .	1
Colorado, ...	1	. .	1
Total of *cases*, ...	48	61	109
Total of *persons*, ...	48	59	107

TABLE No. 7.

CIVIL CONDITIONS OF PERSONS ADMITTED.

Number of the Admission.	Unmarried.			Married.			Widowed.		
	Ma.	Fe.	Tot.	Ma.	Fe.	Tot.	Ma.	Fe.	Tot.
First, . . .	11	22	33	19	15	34	4	4	8
Second, . .	3	5	8	3	6	9	1	1	2
Third, . . .	2	2	4	3	. .	3	. .	. .	. .
Fourth, . .	. .	. .	. .	1	1	2	1	. .	1
Fifth, . . .	. .	2	2	. .	. .	. .	. .	. .	. .
Seventh, . .	. .	1	1	. .	. .	. .	. .	. .	. .
Twelfth, . .	. .	. .	. .	. .	. .	. .	. .	1	1
Thirteenth, .	. .	. .	. .	. .	. .	. .	. .	1	1
Total *cases*, .	16	32	48	26	22	48	6	7	13
Total *persons*,	16	32	48	26	21	47	6	6	12

TABLE No. 8.

OCCUPATIONS OF PERSONS ADMITTED.

Occupations.	Males.	Females.	Total.
Housewife, ...	. .	23	23
Clerk, ...	5	2	7
Manufacturer, ...	1	. .	1
Merchant, ...	15	. .	15
Farmer, ...	2	. .	2
Student, ...	. .	1	1
Teacher, ...	1	6	7
Lawyer, ...	4	. .	4
Physician, ...	3	. .	3
Clergyman, ...	2	. .	2
Musician, ...	. .	1	1
U.S. Consul, ...	1	. .	1
Mechanic, ...	9	. .	9
Seamstress, ...	. .	1	1
Servant, ...	. .	2	2
No occupation, ...	5	23	28
Total of *persons*, ...	48	59	107

TABLE No. 9.

REPORTED DURATION OF INSANITY BEFORE LAST ADMISSION.

Previous Duration.	First Admission to any Hospital.			All other Admissions.			Total.		
	Ma.	Fe.	Tot.	Ma.	Fe.	Tot.	Ma.	Fe.	Tot.
Congenital, .	. .	. .	. .	. .	. .	. .	. .	. .	. .
Under 1 mo., .	13	7	20	1	6	7	14	13	27
Fr. 1 to 3 mo.,	5	13	18	1	5	6	6	18	24
" 3 " 6 "	1	10	11	. .	1	1	1	11	12
" 6 " 12 "	6	5	11	2	1	3	8	6	14
" 1 " 2 yrs.,	6	4	10	3	1	4	9	5	14
" 2 " 5 "	1	1	2	4	5	9	5	6	11
" 5 " 10 "	1	. .	1	3	1	4	4	1	5
"10 " 20 "	1	. .	1	. .	. .	. .	1	. .	1
"20 " 30 "	. .	1	1	. .	. .	. .	. .	1	1
Total *cases*, .	34	41	75	14	20	34	48	61	109
Total *persons*,*	. .	. .	. .	14	18	32	48	59	107
Average of known persons (in years),	1.23	.58	.87	2.74	1.57	2.09			

* Two persons not insane.

TABLE No. 10.

FORM OF DISEASE IN THE CASES ADMITTED.

Form of Disease.	Males.	Females.	Total.
Mania, acute, ...	9	16	25
Mania, chronic, ...	6	4	10
Mania, puerperal, ...	. .	1	1
Mania, recurrent, ...	1	2	3
Melancholia, acute, ...	16	28	44
Melancholia, chronic, ...	2	3	5
Dementia, chronic, ...	2	6	8
Dementia, senile, ...	2	. .	2
General paralysis, ...	8	. .	8
Opium habit, ...	1	. .	1
Alcohol habit, ...	1	. .	1
Hystero-epilepsy, ...	. .	1	1
Total of *cases*, ...	48	61	109
Total of *persons*, ...	48	59	107

TABLE No. 11.

ALLEGED CAUSES OF INSANITY IN PERSONS ADMITTED.

Causes.	Males.	Females.	Total.
Mental.			
Grief, ...		3	3
Anxiety, ...	12	9	21
Physical.			
Ill-health, ...	7	15	22
Overwork, ...	6	4	10
Constitutional, ...	2	7	9
Change of life, ...	. .	4	4
Child-birth, ...	. .	1	1
Lactation, ...	. .	1	1
Uterine disease, ...	. .	1	1
Epilepsy, ...	2	. .	2
Sunstroke, ...	1	. .	1
Alcohol,*	3	. .	3
Opium,*	1	1	2
Apoplexy, ...	. .	1	1
Senility, ...	2	. .	2
Unknown, ...	12	14	26
Total of *cases*, ...	48	61	109
Total of *persons*, ...	48	59	107

* Two of these persons not insane.

TABLE No. 12.

RELATION TO HOSPITALS OF THE PERSONS ADMITTED.

	Males.	Females.	Total.
Never before in any Hospital, ...	34	41	75
Former inmates of this Hospital, ...	7	10	17
Former inmates of other Hospitals in this State : —			
Danvers, ...	1	. .	1
South Boston, ...	1	. .	1
Worcester, ...	1	. .	1
Private Asylum, ...	. .	2	2
Former inmates of Hospitals in other States,	1	3	4
Former inmates of this Hospital and of other Hospitals in this State : —			
Danvers, ...	1	. .	1
Private Asylum, ...	1	. .	1
Former inmates of this Hospital and of Hospitals in other States, ...	1	5	6
Total of *cases*, ...	48	61	109
Total of *persons*, ...	48	59	107

TABLE No. 13.

DISCHARGES CLASSIFIED BY ADMISSION AND RESULT.

Admission.	Recovered.			Much Improved.			Improved.			Unimproved.			Died.			Total.		
	Ma.	Fe.	Tot.	Ma.	Fe.	Tot.	Ma.	Fe.	Tot.	Ma.	Fe.	Tot.	Ma.	Fe.	Tot.	Ma.	Fe.	Tot.
First,*	15	10	25	4	7	11	4	1	5	8	16	24	8	5	13	39	39	78
Second,	2	5	7	1	2	3	2	.	2	2	2	4	.	1	1	7	10	17
Third,	1	1	2	.	.	.	.	.	.	1	.	1	2	.	2	4	1	5
Fourth,	.	.	.	.	1	1	1	1	2	1	.	1	.	1	1	2	3	5
Fifth,	.	1	1	.	.	.	.	1	1	.	1	1	.	.	.	.	3	3
Seventh,	.	1	1	.	.	.	.	.	.	.	.	.	.	.	.	.	1	1
Eleventh,	.	1	1	.	.	.	.	.	.	.	.	.	.	.	.	.	1	1
Twelfth,	.	.	.	.	1	1	.	.	.	.	.	.	.	.	.	.	1	1
Total of *cases*,	18	19	37	5	11	16	7	3	10	12	19	31	10	7	17	52	59	111
Total of *persons*,	.	.	.	.	.	.	.	.	.	.	.	.	.	.	.	50	58	108

*Two of these persons not insane.

TABLE No. 14.

CASES DISCHARGED RECOVERED.—DURATION.

Period.	Duration before Admission.			Hospital Residence.			Whole Duration from the Attack.		
	Ma.	Fe.	Tot.	Ma.	Fe.	Tot.	Ma.	Fe.	Tot.
Under 1 mo.,	8	8	16	..	..	..	..	..	..
Fr. 1 to 3 mo.,	2	5	7	8	3	11	3	1	4
" 3 " 6 "	4	4	8	4	5	9	6	3	9
" 6 " 12 "	1	1	2	4	7	11	2	8	10
" 1 " 2 yrs.,	2	1	3	2	3	5	5	6	11
" 2 " 5 "	1	..	1	..	..	..	2	..	2
" 5 " 10 "	..	..	..	..	1	1	..	1	1
Total *persons,**	18	19	37	18	19	37	18	19	37
Average of known cases (in months),	6.48	3.75	5.08	5.41	11.06	8.32	12.79	13.96	13.39

* One of these persons not insane.

TABLE No. 15.

CASES RESULTING IN DEATH.—DURATION.

Period.	Duration before Admission.			Hospital Residence.			Whole Duration from the Attack.		
	Ma.	Fe.	Tot.	Ma.	Fe.	Tot.	Ma.	Fe.	Tot.
Under 1 mo.,	3	3	6	3	3	6	1	3	4
Fr. 1 to 3 mo.,	1	..	1	2	1	3	2	..	2
" 3 " 6 "	1	1	2	1	..	1	..	..	..
" 6 " 12 "	2	2	4	1	..	1	..	..	..
" 1 " 2 yrs.,	3	..	3	1	..	1	3	..	3
" 2 " 5 "	..	1	1	1	1	2	3	2	5
" 5 " 10 "	..	..	..	..	1	1	..	1	1
" 10 " 15 "	..	..	..	1	..	1	1	..	1
" 20 " 25 "	..	..	..	..	1	1	..	1	1
Total, ..	10	7	17	10	7	17	10	7	17
Average of known cases (in months),	8.37	10.07	9.07	21.37	58.91	36.75	30.03	68.68	45.94

TABLE No. 16.

CASES DISCHARGED BY RECOVERY OR DEATH.

Form of Insanity.	Recoveries.			Deaths.		
	Males.	Females.	Total.	Males.	Females	Total.
Mania, acute, ...	8	7	15	2	1	3
Mania, chronic, . . .	..	..	..	1	1	2
Melancholia, acute, .	9	12	21	..	2	2
Melancholia, chronic, .	..	..	..	1	..	1
Dementia, chronic, . .	..	..	..	1	1	2
Dementia, senile, . .	..	..	..	1	..	1
General Paralysis, . .	..	..	..	4	1	5
Hystero-epilepsy, . .	..	..	..	..	1	1
Opium habit,* . . .	1	..	1	..	..	..
Total of *cases*, . . .	18	19	37.	10	7	17
Total of *persons*, . .	18	19	37	10	7	17

* Not insane.

TABLE No. 17.

CAUSES OF DEATH:

Causes.	Males.	Females	Total.
Cerebral Disease.			
General Paralysis, ...	4	1	5
Exhaustion from Mania, ...	3	..	3
Exhaustion from Melancholia, ...	1	2	3
Hystero-epilepsy, ...	..	1	1
Other Causes.			
Pneumonia, ...	1	1	2
Senile Gangrene, ...	..	1	1
Senility, ...	1	1	2
Totals, ...	10	7	17

TABLE No. 18.

RECOVERIES, CLASSIFIED BY RESULTS OF PREVIOUS ADMISSIONS.*

Number of the Admission.	Recovered.			Much Improved.			Improved.			Total.		
	Ma.	Fe.	Tot.	Ma.	Fe.	Tot.	Ma.	Fe.	Tot.	Ma.	Fe.	Tot.
Second, ...	..	4	4	2	..	2	..	..	..	2	4	6
Third, ...	1	1	2	..	..	..	..	..	..	1	1	2
Fifth, ...	..	1	1	..	..	..	..	..	..	..	1	1
Seventh, ...	..	1	1	..	..	..	..	..	..	..	1	1
Eleventh, ...	..	1	1	..	..	..	..	..	..	..	1	1
Total of *persons*, .	1	8	9	2	..	2	..	..	..	3	8	11

*This classification is based upon the result of the admission next preceding the last, in each case respectively.

TABLE No. 19.

DEATHS, CLASSIFIED BY DURATION OF INSANITY AND OF TREATMENT

Period.	Duration of Insanity.			Whole known period of Hospital Residence.		
	Males.	Females.	Total.	Males.	Females.	Total.
Congenital, ...	..	..	..	..	..	..
Under 1 month, .	1	3	4	2	3	5
From 1 to 3 months,	2	..	2	2	..	2
" 3 " 6 "	..	..	..	1	..	1
" 6 " 12 "	..	..	..	1	1	2
" 1 " 2 years,	3	..	3	2	..	2
" 2 " 5 "	3	2	5	1	1	2
" 5 " 10 "	..	1	1	..	1	1
" 10 " 15 "	1	..	1	1	..	1
" 25 " 30 "	..	..	..	..	1	1
" 50 " 55 "	..	1	1	..	..	..
Total, ...	10	7	17	10	7	17
Average of known *cases* (in months),	31.15	117.18	66.57	23.42	62.28	39.42

TABLE No. 20.

AGES OF THOSE WHO DIED.

Ages.	At time of the first attack.			At time of death.		
	Males.	Females.	Total.	Males.	Females.	Total.
From 20 to 25 yrs.,	. .	1	1	. .	. .	. .
" 35 " 40 "	4	3	7	3	2	5
" 40 " 50 "	1	1	2	2	2	4
" 50 " 60 "	3	1	4	1	1	2
" 60 " 70 "	1	. .	1	2	. .	2
" 70 " 80 "	1	1	2	2	. .	2
" 80 " 90 "	. .	. .	. .	. .	2	2
Total, ...	10	7	17	10	7	17

TABLE No. 21.

TABLE OF ADMISSIONS, DISCHARGES, AND RESULTS AT THE McLEAN ASYLUM.

FROM ITS OPENING, OCTOBER 6, 1818, TO DECEMBER 31, 1883, INCLUSIVE.

Years.	Admitted.	Dis-charged.	Whole No. under care.	Died.	Much improved, etc.	Re-covered.	Remaining at end of year.	Average No. of Patients.
1818–25	398	344	623	29	205	110	279	..
1826	47	46	101	5	21	20	55	..
1827	58	56	113	5	17	34	57	..
1828	77	65	134	5	37	23	69	..
1829	73	77	142	9	42	26	65	..
1830	82	78	147	10	34	34	69	..
1831	83	84	152	8	46	30	68	..
1832	94	98	162	10	45	43	64	..
1833	103	100	167	8	50	42	67	..
1834	108	95	174	7	47	41	80	..
1835	83	84	163	11	28	45	77	..
1836	106	112	183	10	38	64	71	..
1837	120	105	191	8	25	72	86	80
1838	138	131	224	12	45	74	93	95
1839	132	117	225	10	38	69	108	112
1840	155	138	263	13	50	75	125	128
1841	157	141	283	11	55	75	142	135
1842	129	138	271	15	43	80	133	143
1843	126	126	260	18	45	63	134	131
1844	158	140	292	20	52	68	152	146
1845	119	120	271	13	33	74	151	149
1846	148	126	299	9	52	65	173	164
1847	170	170	343	33	50	87	173	172
1848	143	155	316	23	50	82	155	171
1849	160	137	321	15	58	64	184	177
1850	173	157	357	28	51	78	200	201
1851	164	173	364	29	69	75	191	195
1852	145	135	336	15	48	72	201	200
1853	114	120	315	17	45	58	195	194
1854	120	120	315	16	45	59	195	195
1855	123	126	318	24	46	56	192	192
1856	149	145	341	19	58	68	196	195
1857	141	159	337	28	60	71	178	191
1858	155	147	333	25	50	72	186	187
1859	131	142	317	28	53	61	175	185
1860	121	109	296	24	46	39	187	185
1861	111	110	298	23	33	54	188	193
1862	82	94	270	18	37	39	176	190
1863	94	69	270	13	20	36	201	191
1864	101	107	302	27	38	42	195	200
1865	82	85	277	17	33	35	192	186
1866	103	98	295	29	23	46	197	197
1867	89	108	286	27	36	45	178	186
1868	92	94	270	23	37	34	176	166
1869	108	100	284	18	31	51	184	187
1870	79	85	263	12	40	33	178	187
1871	75	81	253	13	47	21	172	178
1872	93	101	265	23	63	15	164	173
1873	92	95	256	13	63	19	161	165
1874	75	88	236	10	58	20	148	159
1875	85	83	233	16	51	16	150	156
1876	92	74	242	20	36	18	168	160
1877	110	103	278	20	68	15	175	175
1878	63	84	238	12	66	6	154	168
1879	76	79	230	12	48	19	151	157
1880	51	48	202	6	30	12	154	152
1881	66	65	220	14	37	14	155	150
1882	82	70	237	8	36	26	167	156
1883	109	111	276	17	57	37	165	164
	6,713	6,548		961	2,765	2,822		

TABLE No. 22.

TABLE OF APPLICATIONS, ADMISSIONS, ETC., FOR TWENTY YEARS,—1864-1883.

Years	Applications Hospital	Admissions Hospital	Admissions Asylum	American Hospital	American Asylum	Foreign Hospital	Foreign Asylum	Not admitted Hospital	Discharged, cured, relieved, or improved Hospital	Discharged, cured, relieved, or improved Asylum	Percentage of same on Admissions Hospital	Percentage of same on Admissions Asylum	Died Hospital	Died Asylum	Accidents	Whole number under care in the year Hospital	Whole number under care in the year Asylum	Number of free patients Hospital	Paying all the time Hospital	Paying part of the time Hospital	Greatest total number at any time Hospital	Greatest total number at any time Asylum	Least total at any one time Hospital	Least total at any one time Asylum	Average Hospital	Average Asylum	Greatest number at any one time Free	Greatest number at any one time Paying	Avg. time in weeks Paying	Avg. time Free	Out-Patients Hospital
1864	1932	1599	101	654	99	945	2	333	1306	80	81.68	79.1	130	27	242	1749	302	1388	350	11	157	208	110	192	138	200	139	33	3.2	4.4	5619
1865	1430	1199	82	571	80	628	2	281	997	68	83.15	79.1	104	17	140	1347	277	687	592	68	164	195	88	181	113	186	137	72	3.7	4.8	5356
1866	1328	1120	103	542	100	587	3	208	909	69	81.17	82.9	104	17	132	1301	295	556	623	45	109	203	78	192	95	197	62	58	3.4	5.1	5608
1867	1419	1206	89	558	88	648	1	213	958	81	79.43	66.9	96	29	113	1217	286	676	601	24	126	200	72	172	104	186	77	62	3.4	4.3	4563
1868	1474	1265	92	604	92	661	0	209	1015	71	80.03	91	94	27	98	1301	218	840	502	31	124	181	69	160	102	166	97	56	3.0	3.5	5264
1869	1633	1390	108	681	108	709	0	243	1123	82	80.03	75.9	85	23	93	1217	284	930	563	24	139	196	90	177	118	187	98	45	3.4	4.3	6953
1870	1706	1302	79	584	79	718	3	404	1083	73	83.20	92.4	107	18	140	1427	342	958	439	30	137	195	98	181	120	187	106	45	3.4	3.9	8767
1871	1781	1427	75	649	75	778	0	354	1143	62	82.15	69.3	85	12	178	1701	253	1056	456	25	154	187	91	167	122	178	126	43	3.1	4.8	9792
1872	1815	1647	93	665	88	882	5	268	1271	52	82.15	55.9	109	12	259	1701	253	1289	396	16	160	187	97	163	135	173	133	42	3.3	4.3	11878
1873	1958	1550	92	640	88	910	7	268	1201	64	77.48	69.5	120	23	291	1800	265	1195	441	64	187	179	129	158	156	165	156	44	2.7	6.0	13517
1874	2153	1639	75	713	68	926	7	514	1342	54	81.88	72	127	13	234	1800	236	1251	394	120	183	171	111	144	149	159	146	41	3.3	5.6	15612
1875	2560	1841	85	799	72	1022	13	516	1412	57	76.70	67	186	10	285	1989	242	1565	336	88	199	165	132	148	166	160	176	31	2.8	5.2	16993
1876	2131	1906	92	900	92	1006	10	516	1621	45	80.80	51.8	189	16	245	1989	256	1696	339	92	210	167	163	145	185	166	182	36	2.8	5.7	17292
1877	2275	1657	110	863	103	794	7	474	1339	57	80.80	71.4	150	20	147	1847	278	1270	334	48	194	184	135	168	164	175	178	33	2.8	5.5	18004
1878	2310	1794	58	946	58	848	5	481	1461	45	81.43	60.5	130	20	200	1850	238	1578	352	38	187	182	132	154	165	168	170	34	2.8	5.5	18744
1879	2701	1813	76	979	63	834	13	497	1462	46	80.63	62.7	134	12	222	1971	230	1577	352	42	188	164	131	150	163	157	165	30	2.8	5.2	18960
1880	2701	2123	76	1117	46	1006	5	578	1731	32	81.53	62.7	143	6	351	2284	202	1864	371	45	188	159	156	146	170	152	165	35	2.5	4.5	20566
1881	2786	2106	57	1074	57	1032	9	680	1853	37	82.19	56	151	14	391	2270	220	1835	419	26	188	161	139	147	166	150	168	39	2.79	4.41	18443
1882	2587	2147	82	1127	73	1020	9	440	1775	47	87.83	57.3	189	8	348	2302	237	1876	399	12	195	166	143	149	168	156	167	35	2.84	4.41	16304
1883	2460	2020	109	1035	93	985	16	440	1664	63	82.33	57.8	181	17	432	2185	276	1633	473	79	189	171	143	151	168	164	168	35	2.75	4.80	*7102

*Out-Patient Department open only five months.

TABLE No. 23.

TABLE SHOWING THE COST OF PRINCIPAL S[illegible]ES AT [illegible]N ASYLUM.

Articles.		1880. Quantity.	1880. Cost.	1880. Average.	1881. Quantity.	1881. Cost.	1881. Average.	1882. Quantity.	1882. Cost.	1882. Average.	1883. Quantity.	1883. Cost.	1883. Average.
Beef, ...	lbs.,	57,462	$6,625.64	.115	56,835½	$6,467.14	.1137	57,936½	$7,869.37	.1358	67,534	$8,604.15	.1274
Mutton and Lamb,	"	19,794½	2,107.14	.106	23,583	2,308.16	.0978	20,340	2,104.57	.1034	23,280	2,406.70	.1033
Veal, ...	"	12,288	1,372.34	.111	19,707	1,846.00	.094	13,367	1,445.17	.108	10,401	1,173.42	.1128
Poultry, ...	"	23,714½	3,726.80	.157	20,052¾	3,517.55	.175	18,946	3,815.64	.201	11,324	2,422.44	.213
Ham, etc., ...		8,932½	899.85	.1007	10,148¼	1,087.55	.107	9,724¼	1,234.90	.126	7,970	1,043.39	.13
Eggs, ...	doz.,	11,295	2,337.09	.2069	11,523	3,084.19	.269	11,153½	3,143.77	.277	10,758	3,009.04	.279
Lard, ...	lbs.,	1,849	159.24	.086	2,093	244.44	.1167	1,041	133.08	.127	1,680	186.75	.111
Flour, ...	bls.,	418	3,296.63	7.886	413	3,219.16	7.794	455	3,767.15	8.279	507	3,690.67	7.279
Butter, ...	lbs.,	19,511¾	5,405.80	.277	21,979¾	6,163.79	.2804	20,780	6,276.21	.302	21,612	5,939.32	.274
Coffee, ...	"	4,124	1,212.62	.294	3,841	945.95	.246	3,955	944.80	.2388	3,530	862.57	.244
Tea, ...	"	1,492½	486.41	.325	1,609	513.58	.319	1,522	501.31	.3294	1,406	460.54	.327
Sugar, ...	"	24,330	2,290.05	.094	24,932	2,338.88	.0938	26,489½	2,462.13	.0929	27,672	2,421.10	.874
[illegible]ts, Gas, etc.,	feet,	....	2,515.78	....	....	2,771.42	....	....	3,858.49	....	....	3,379.25	....
Coal, ...	tons,	1,158 $\frac{1020}{2000}$	5,972.06	5.15	1,099 $\frac{350}{2000}$	6,635.44	6.036	1,200 $\frac{252}{2000}$	7,284.95	6.07	1,022 $\frac{1050}{2000}$	6,303.39	6.164
Wood, ...	cords,	25⅛	219.84	8.75	15	140.70	9.38	14¼	103.31	7.25	8½	55.25	6.50
Ice, ...	tons,	462 $\frac{1500}{2000}$	2,069.31	4.47	366 $\frac{300}{2000}$	849.88	2.33	423 $\frac{1800}{2000}$	759.46	1.79	481 $\frac{100}{2000}$	841.79	1.75

Year.						Out-Patients treated
21to						
1843						
1844						
1845						
1846	62					
1847	59					328
1848	74					378
1849	103					272
1850	97					294
1851	98					237
1852	123					248
1853	132					358
1854	159					477
1855	212					645
1856	157					887
1857	189					1574
1858	163					2223
1859	186		50	65	229	3523
1860	212		94	54	280	4433
1861	233	28	58	73	305	4676
1862	271	40	57	77	318	4800
1863	292	34	54	96	431	4987
1864	242	37	70	84	459	5619
1865	140	38	61	68	390	5356
1866	132	13	74	50	295	5608
1867	113	95	74	62	82	4553
1868	98	04	41	64	282	5264
1869	93	02	82	78	258	6953
1870	140	18	84	65	352	8767
1871	178	20	68	58	303	9792
1872	259	22	73	76	322	11878
1873	291	35	84	66	313	13517
1874	234	56	86	81	321	15612
1875	285	49	02	78	396	16093
1876	245	66	20	91	380	17292
1877	147	85	44	92	502	18004
1878	200	64	30	59	409	18744
1879	222	65	38	84	505	18060
1880	351	63	25	74	422	20566
1881	391	70	50	70	545	18443
1882	348	66	13	59	429	16304
1883	432	68	08	61	463	7102*

58

OFFICERS OF THE HOSPITAL.

Resident Physician.
JAMES H. WHITTEMORE, M.D.

Visiting Physicians.

GEORGE C. SHATTUCK, M.D. GEORGE G. TARBELL, M.D.
FRANCIS MINOT, M.D. WM. L. RICHARDSON, M.D.
SAMUEL L. ABBOT, M.D. EDWARD N. WHITTIER, M.D.

Visiting Surgeons.

HENRY J. BIGELOW, M.D. JOHN COLLINS WARREN, M.D.
RICHARD M. HODGES, M.D. HENRY H. A. BEACH, M.D.
CHARLES B. PORTER, M.D. JOHN HOMANS, M.D.

Physicians to Out-Patients.

DAVID H. HAYDEN, M.D. FREDERICK C. SHATTUCK, M.D.
ELBRIDGE G. CUTLER, M.D.
F. GORDON MORRILL, M.D.

Surgeons to Out-Patients.

ARTHUR T. CABOT, M.D. MAURICE H. RICHARDSON, M.D.
GEORGE W. WEST, M.D.

Physician to Out-Patients with diseases of the Skin.
JAMES C. WHITE, M.D.

Physician to Out-Patients with diseases of the Nervous System.
JAMES J. PUTNAM, M.D.

Physicians to Out-Patients with diseases of the Throat.
FREDERICK I. KNIGHT, M.D. S. W. LANGMAID, M.D.

Ophthalmic Surgeon to Out-Patients.
OLIVER F. WADSWORTH, M.D.

Dental Surgeon.
VIRGIL C. POND, D.M.D.

59

Microscopist, and Curator of the Pathological Cabinet.
REGINALD H. FITZ, M.D.

Chemist.
EDWARD S. WOOD, M.D.

Artist.
HENRY P. QUINCY, M.D.

Medical House Pupils, 1883–84.
HERBERT W. NEWHALL.   JOHN T. BOWEN.

Surgical House Pupils, 1883–84.
FRED. M. BRIGGS.   WILLIAM M. CONANT.
CHARLES W. GALLOUPE.   OSCAR J. PFIEFFER.

Matron.
Miss G. L. STURTEVANT.

Apothecary.
JOHN W. PRATT.

OFFICERS OF THE McLEAN ASYLUM.

Superintendent.
EDWARD COWLES, M.D.

1st Assistant Physician.
GEORGE T. TUTTLE, M.D.

2d Assistant Physician.
FREDERICK M. TURNBULL, M.D.

Medical House Pupils.
I. P. DANA.   J. H. POTTS.

Purveyor.
JOHN P. BRADBURY.

Superintendent of Nurses.
Miss M. F. PALMER.

Clerk.
Miss F. E. GILBERT.

Supervisors.
E. W. BOARDMAN.   Miss L. E. WOODWARD.

Apothecary.
D. W. SPENCE.

VISITING COMMITTEE.

January and July.
Messrs. DWIGHT and BOWDITCH.

February and August.
Messrs. ELIOT and THAYER.

March and September.
Messrs. HALE and WARREN.

April and October.
Messrs. BEMIS and PROCTOR.

May and November.
Messrs. KIDDER and WOLCOTT.

June and December.
Messrs. MORRILL and ENDICOTT.

LADIES' VISITING COMMITTEE.

January and February.
Miss E. GRAY.   Miss E. GOODWIN.

March.
Mrs. J. F. ANDREW.   Miss T. DODGE.

April.
Mrs. ANDREW.   Miss M. CURTIS.
Miss DODGE.   Miss E. M. ELIOT.

May.
Miss CURTIS.   MISS ELIOT.

June and October.
Mrs. S. ELIOT.   Miss J. G. BEAL.

November and December.
Mrs. H. W. HAYNES.   Miss A. W. MORRILL.

STANDING COMMITTEES.

On admitting Asylum Patients.
Messrs. WARREN and DWIGHT.

On Finance.
Messrs. KIDDER and MORRILL.

On Accounts and Expenditures.
Messrs. WOLCOTT, THAYER, and DWIGHT.

On Buildings and Repairs.
Messrs. DWIGHT, WARREN, and ELIOT.

On Free Beds.
Messrs. BOWDITCH and PROCTOR.

On the General Library and Warren Fund.
Messrs. ELIOT and HALE.

On the Book of Donations.
Dr. BEMIS.

Committee on New Asylum and Grounds.
Messrs. DWIGHT, ELIOT, WARREN, ENDICOTT, and BOWDITCH.

CPSIA information can be obtained
at www.ICGtesting.com
Printed in the USA
BVHW041421220219
540923BV00007B/120/P